Truffles and Trash

KELLY ALEXANDER

Truffles and Trash

Recirculating Food in a Social Welfare State

The University of North Carolina Press *Chapel Hill*

This book was published with the assistance of the H. Eugene and Lillian Lehman Fund of the University of North Carolina Press.

© 2024 The University of North Carolina Press
All rights reserved
Set in Arno Pro by Westchester Publishing Services
Manufactured in the United States of America

Library of Congress Cataloging-in-Publication Data
Names: Alexander, Kelly, author.
Title: Truffles and trash : recirculating food in a social welfare state / Kelly Alexander.
Description: Chapel Hill : The University of North Carolina Press, [2024] | Includes bibliographical references and index.
Identifiers: LCCN 2024034311 | ISBN 9781469678580 (cloth ; alk. paper) | ISBN 9781469678597 (pbk. ; alk. paper) | ISBN 9781469678603 (epub) | ISBN 9781469681207 (pdf)
Subjects: LCSH: Food waste—Social aspects—Belgium—Brussels. | Food supply—Social aspects—Belgium—Brussels. | Food waste—Belgium—Brussels—Prevention. | Waste minimization—Belgium—Brussels. | Food security—Belgium—Brussels. | Food industry and trade—Belgium—Brussels. | BISAC: SOCIAL SCIENCE / Anthropology / Cultural & Social | POLITICAL SCIENCE / NGOS (Non-Governmental Organizations)
Classification: LCC HD9015.B43 B77 2024 | DDC 338.1/949332—dc23/eng/20240821
LC record available at https://lccn.loc.gov/2024034311

Cover art: Photo from the series *Waste Not*, 2016, courtesy of Aliza Eliazarov.

This book is dedicated to the people of Brussels who welcomed me into their kitchens, lives, and hearts. You will forever have a place in mine . . . especially Luigi Ciciriello, Eva De Baerdemaeker, Filip DeBoeck, Tom Dedeurwaerder, François Huet and Odile Repolt, Tony Michiels, and Rob Renaerts. It is also for Andrew Davidson.

Contents

List of Illustrations, Maps, and Table ix

INTRODUCTION
La Truffe et la Poubelle, or the Truffle and the Trash 1

CHAPTER ONE
A World-Class Problem—Everybody Says So 13

CHAPTER TWO
Why Belgium? 55

CHAPTER THREE
Church, State, Food, Waste 87

CHAPTER FOUR
When Food Waste Goes to Work 129

CHAPTER FIVE
The Affective Abattoir 147

CONCLUSION
A Spectrum of Edibility 167

Acknowledgments 185

Appendix. Works Consulted on the History of the Occupations of Belgium 189

Notes 191

Bibliography 199

Index 217

Illustrations, Maps, and Table

ILLUSTRATIONS

How it started 2

How it's going 2

Truffle jar still life 10

Good Food Brussels 33

European Commissioner for Health and Food Safety and Brussels Food Bank administrators 38

Food Bank of Brussels 89

Food Bank sorting room 93

Weekly food distribution site 98

Le Magasin 108

Le Magasin interior 111

Bel Mundo's dining room 130

Tom Dedeurwaerder 140

Bel Mundo interns 141

Anderlecht Abattoir in Brussels 148

Parc Maximilien 158

The People's Kitchen 178

The People's Kitchen community fridge 179

MAPS

Europe 57

Brussels 79

TABLE

Social assistance growth in Brussels 82

Truffles and Trash

INTRODUCTION

La Truffe et la Poubelle, or the Truffle and the Trash

This book is not about a truffle restaurant, but it begins in one. If I were to show you one of those "how it started . . . how it's going" meme comparisons from 2020, the first image would be me standing in a crisply ironed black chef's jacket, my hair pulled back in a tight bun for sanitary reasons, my starched white apron snugly tied around my waist, reporting for kitchen duty in a Michelin-starred restaurant.[1] The second photo would show me in a sweaty pink t-shirt and jeans standing with other volunteers in a public park, with a messy ponytail and wearing an apron and jeans stained with vegetable soup. What these images show is that much like the flow of a lot of the food in wealthy nations, I, too, began my journey in a rarefied place where much is discarded, and concluded it in one where what had once been trash became food again. The hundreds of hours I spent in between—most often engaged in a combination of cooking, interviewing, and volunteering—constitute this book. The hundreds of hours in between also constitute a spectrum of edibility. On this spectrum, I situate various forms of food and food waste alongside the actions, ethics, and forms of social belonging produced when people and institutions work to recirculate food from the set of consumers who have overlooked it in the marketplace to another set who are willing, if not eager, to make good use of it.

The journey I've taken here goes far beyond the things that have drawn me to food, an admittedly personal passion, in the first place. What I have seen and the work I've done in Brussels forced me to think about food not only as a source for unity, communion, and commensality, not only as a special material that brings people together, but as a divisive and sometimes even destructive source of profound tensions that can threaten social belonging and even life itself. Yet this is not a book about sad, resourceless, voiceless people eating cruddy food. It is about finding new ways around old problems by revitalizing surplus food. It's about finding solutions to big problems in small ways, not because doing something is better than doing nothing but because sharing food from people and places where there is too much is much easier, more hopeful, and less dependent on charity than the way such activities are often cast. Thus, this book is not about food waste; it's about recirculating food

How it started... how it's going. In conducting this research, I went from hand-forming truffle raviolis in a Michelin-starred restaurant to pureeing vegetables for soup for refugees camping in a city park. Author photo.

before it can become so; it's about some people in Brussels who are interested in doing that, and some people whom such activities and efforts benefit. It outlines a spectrum of edibility that widens acceptable social norms of what gets to count as food and for whom, challenging charitable models that pair cast-off food with cast-out people in the process. Yes, it is about some of the failures of a social welfare state, but it is also about some of the successes, particularly the attempts to move food to people who need it before it becomes useless. This sense of discovery is what I aim to bring to the page here.

Beginning in a temple of haute cuisine might seem like I am going backward somehow—that both the quality of the food and the ambience of where I was cooking it went from high end to low instead of the other way around—but it reflects a perception that was part of what I hoped to learn more about, which is, which foods count as edible (only the ones consumers are willing to pay market value for, for example?), which count as necessary for maintaining human life, is there a difference between these categories, and if so, for whom?

This is a tremendously broad question about the role of food in human social life, one that one project could never answer. To address it in one case study, I chose to focus on food waste reduction policies in the European Union (EU), and the ways in which they are interpreted and enacted by local stakeholders including globally renowned restaurateurs, local soup kitchen volunteers, urban farmers, social workers, sustainability advocates, retired corporate executives, EU health and food safety ministers, charity administrators, and members of Brussels's relatively new—and quickly growing—class of the urban working poor (Cendrowicz, 2017). I chose Brussels because it is the capital of the European Union and because, since 2017, policymakers here have been redirecting the edible unsold food from supermarkets to organizations that specialize in feeding fragile populations.

In this book, you will follow me as I followed the flow of surplus food around Brussels. Where will we go? I'll take you all around—it's not particularly large as global cities go, as I will discuss in chapter 2—and especially to the following three sites where, over five years of fieldwork, I volunteered and observed food waste recirculation ethics and efforts, including those of the workers as well as the recipients:

1. *The Food Bank of Brussels* is the largest clearinghouse of edible but unsellable food in Belgium. Five days a week—the Food Bank of Brussels is open more days and hours than any other food bank in the nation—its trucks, donated to the bank by both corporate donors and

state funding, pick up surplus supermarket food and bring it back for sorting—anything that has been opened or whose packaging is compromised (about 1 percent of all food) is tossed; the rest is boxed. From here, the food is distributed to the bank's vast clientele of more than six hundred charities. The all-volunteer staff is composed almost entirely of white pensioners. Because more than 80 percent of the bank's six hundred recipients are church-sponsored or otherwise religious charities, it is easy to see the way in which food waste recuperation efforts here map onto an established network of care in the city, and onto an ethical framework of Catholic hospitality. Catholic doctrines of hospitality assert that sharing food builds communities, brings individuals closer to God, and reinforces a central belief that God has produced a world where there is always enough, where a stranger will always be cared for as if he or she were Christ himself (Day, 1963). Although most pensioners do not cite Catholicism as motivation, others, like the human resources director at the food bank, a retired social worker, do so quite explicitly: "This is how we've always fed the hungry here." Underlying this ethic of sharing is a tacit evaluation of worthiness; embedding the EU mandate to recuperate otherwise waste-bound food into models of Catholic charity brings with it a hierarchical structure of givers and receivers.

2. *Bel Mundo* is a "social restaurant," an eating establishment subsidized by the city and designed to serve those on social security, disability, and unemployment by selling low-cost meals that offer the experience of dining out to people who live on a fixed income. Bel Mundo is more than that, though: it is a chic café where people on social assistance can intern for the purposes of learning restaurant management skills, professional cooking techniques, and foreign language proficiencies necessary to be competitive in the Brussels bilingual job market. Full-time paid staff include social workers, chefs, and job placement coaches. The combined activities of all involved are designed to promote the capabilities of "needy people" who cannot otherwise access the local job market, in the hopes that one day, they, too, will become taxpayers instead of welfare recipients.

3. *Cultureghem* is a grassroots-style nongovernmental organization founded by a public-school teacher and an architect, funded by a combination of grants from governmental agencies and private foundations, and based on a model that recuperates and redistributes

one large outdoor market's unsold produce while simultaneously revitalizing the social interactions in a formerly abandoned urban space. By setting up mobile kitchens in the city's poorest areas and using surplus spoiling but still edible produce to make and sometimes even sell simple meals, the organization's goal is to inspire citizens and residents to "meet, eat, and feel like the city belongs to them, too" (De Baerdemaeker, 2017). In recuperating and redistributing spoiling produce, Cultureghem recuperates an abandoned urban center and produces a new form of waste-fueled sociality in the process. Ethically, we might think of this as "salvage hospitality," an updated version of the Catholic Worker Movement's soup kitchen model but with salvaged food and a more equitable and inclusive labor-volunteer structure.

So, How It Started...

There is arguably no better place to observe the people, conditions, and activities surrounding the foods that constitute expensive fine dining experiences than at La Truffe Noir. Since it opened in 1998 in the diplomatic quarter of Brussels, it has specialized in *la cuisine de la truffe*, or meals made from the peculiar woody spore that has become one of the world's most expensive ingredients. For example, in 2014 the dog of the fourth-generation son of an Italian truffle hunting family unearthed a two-pound, thirteen-ounce specimen that was subsequently sold to an anonymous buyer from Macau for $330,000 (Jacobs, 2014). This restaurant is the kind of place that people imagine food snobs and professional foodies—food magazine writers and editors, for example—frequent. That was, in fact, how I heard of it.

I had been a journalist for more than twenty years, on the staffs of food magazines including *Saveur* and *Food & Wine*, before I entered the doctoral program in Cultural Anthropology at Duke University. It was nothing short of a miracle that I had been able to find and convince an actual anthropologist that I could become one: that I understood participant-observation very well and had aspects of the social life of food that I wanted to learn more about that their expertise could only aid. Luckily, one could relate: Orin Starn's own books on culture range from explorations of the grassroots politics of the Marxist Revolution in Peru, to the intersection of race and professional golf through the career of Tiger Woods, to the historic cross-country search for the brain of Ishi, the so-called "last wild Indian" of the Yahi tribe. Starn's curiosity about a food-writing course I was teaching at Duke gave me a chance to tell him that I believed I was *already* in tune with anthropologists like him, that the work I did as a food journalist involved much more than interviewing people about their recipes. He believed me when I said my work involved questions of identity, culture, memory, and politics and that cooking with people in their kitchens and observing their habits and practices were excellent windows into the most important issues of human social life. Unfortunately, not many of his colleagues initially agreed, and my application did not meet a warm reception: who did this food magazine editor think she was, waltzing into their realm confident that she could produce social theory, that she understood ethnography? I believe that most of the department hoped I'd get bored and go back to baking pies, because that is what they imagined I did.

Starn did not give up on me. He put me through the paces before going back to his colleagues to argue my case: Did I know that this was going to be a lot of work? Would I be bored in intense seminars about Weber's theory of social stratification? Would a "descriptive" writer like me be able to write a grant for research funding? And could I handle epic amounts of mansplaining?

These are all real questions he asked me when we hunkered down to discuss how serious I was about the program. And I was not sure how to answer. I had accomplishments I was proud of: I had cowritten a *New York Times* best-selling cookbook with a barbecue pitmaster from Unadilla, Georgia; I had won a James Beard Journalism Award for an article about Clementine Paddleford, the fabled food editor of the *New York Herald Tribune* throughout the 1950s and 1960s who was the first person to coin the term "regional American food"; I had nursed and potty-trained two small children. Yet even I had to acknowledge that none of these skills had to do with managing the rigors of a doctoral program in anthropology.

Why I wanted to try in the first place was Starn's best question. The answer was twofold. One, the shape of food journalism was shifting under my feet: I started working for food magazines in 1994, and by the time ten years had passed, the same publications that had been stalwarts of the homelives of Americans, particularly American women, were losing subscribers to the internet, where you could find any recipe for any dish at any time. When the Condé Nast Publishing Company made the decision to fold *Gourmet* magazine in 2009, the news shocked its then-editor Ruth Reichl, former restaurant critic at the *New York Times* and best-selling memoirist. If a title that had been in print since 1941 with a devoted following, a coterie of luxury brands as advertisers, and perhaps the most well-known food writer in America at its helm was not a viable business any longer, where did that leave a person like me, who wanted to think and write seriously about food? Two, as food magazines were becoming scarce, so, too, was the amount of space in them devoted to research and knowledge. I was increasingly required to produce short charts and infographics about things like "best $10 wines," which, while not exactly useless, did not feed my longing to tell more involved stories not only about food trends in the marketplace (e.g., "Chipotle is the flavor of the year!"), but about the real people responsible for producing ingredients and the real stories behind how people in their wild array of economic and social circumstances in American life use them.

It was not only that I worried about shrinking job prospects, though. I had grown restless with the depth I could give to my subjects; I often walked away from stories with so much good additional material—from interviews I had done, observations I had made cooking and eating with the people I reported on, and stories about their lives in food that the magazine just didn't have the space or breadth to cover. What often ended up on the cutting room floor, after a story was illustrated with (admittedly very beautiful) photos and (admittedly very useful) recipes were the ideas about what the food meant to the communities where I traveled. Also, a reporter must move on to the next story, and I often finished assignments wishing I'd had not only more space to cover what I'd seen but more time "in the field" to research the backgrounds and histories of the people I'd met and what I'd learned from them. Mostly, I wanted to work toward furthering food studies as a viable academic discipline, as an area of study that I wish had existed when I was a college student. I had no idea how challenging it would be. I missed my son's fifth-grade graduation for a final exam. At forty-one, I gained the "freshman fifteen" all over again. I got acne. I stayed up until 2 A.M. studying on too many nights to count. And every day I had to figure out how to fit in as a student when I was the same age as, and sometimes older than, my professors. Would I do it again? In a heartbeat.

Why? Because there were tremendous upsides, too. When it came time to do my first summer of fieldwork, I was obsessed with questions about how ingredients acquire value, specifically a truffle, which, if you didn't already know what one was and saw it growing on the ground you could easily mistake for a little pile of dirt. This curiosity led me to offer my services as a kitchen apprentice at La Truffe Noire, where I sent an email plea along with my résumé as a food editor. I included assurances that I was qualified to chop, sweep, wash vegetables, and do anything else the chefs asked me to do without complaint. To my delight, they took me up on the offer. When I look back, I see now that I was not nearly as nervous as I should have been. I had worked in restaurants before, and I imagined this one would be like those, or like any number of other high-end restaurants I had visited as a food reporter. I was wrong.

"La Truffe is not a restaurant, it's an *emotion*," I said one night after a particularly grueling service to my supervisor Esteban, a twenty-five-year-old cook from Spain who had come to La Truffe after graduating at the top of his class at a local culinary school. This is mostly because La Truffe in 2015 was on the heels of its thirtieth anniversary (and before the COVID-19 pandemic's devastating effects on the restaurant business in big cities around the world), and it has always been the vision of one singular, exceptional person: founder and owner Luigi Ciciriello. "The Magician" is painted on Ciciriello's black office door in gold cursive, and when you meet him, it becomes clear why. While he is a diminutive presence (he may not be 5'4"), he seems to have an endless supply of charisma. He told me that he came from a rural town with the romantic name of Francavilla Fontanta, in Puglia, "in the heel of the boot," where he began waiting tables in restaurants at the age of nine for pocket money so that he could go to the tailor and have his own clothes made. He was wearing an electric blue silk suit when he said this. When I inquired about his current age, all he would say was, "I stopped counting my age when I turned fifty, but fifty was a bit of a long time ago."

Ciciriello knew how to run every aspect of a restaurant: he could converse on wines as authoritatively as a sommelier, he could cook every dish on the menu himself, and he could converse with guests in any one of the seven languages he spoke fluently (which comes in handy if you're hosting EU dignitaries). Yet Ciciriello's top talent was selling an experience of exquisite taste—measured out in shavings of truffles atop dishes served on plates made exclusively for the restaurant. For the three and a half hours or so that were required for a customer to dine here, she was treated like an empress.

It was not that Ciciriello was too good to be true; in fact, he had trained all his life for this, first by earning a scholarship to a Parisian hotel school straight out of high school, the tuition for which was met by his father's Italian war bonds, and then by landing an apprenticeship with the Parisian chef Abel Bernard at his Brussels restaurant La Cravache d'Or, "*the* place to go in Brussels in the eighties" according to Ciciriello and one of the first restaurants outside of France to earn three stars from the *Guide Michelin*. It was also that he had tremendous mentorship from Bernard and was introduced to the truffle: "It was in his kitchen at the age of thirty-three that I got illuminated, by which I mean when I got to know truffles. Because before I didn't even know they existed. I immediately fell in love with them; the preciousness and rareness of this intrigued me from the beginning," Ciciriello said. This love is on display in his self-published cookbook, a coffee table tome of more than two hundred pages containing handmade paintings and illustrations plus lavish full-color food photographs. In one chapter, he described the truffle as his one true object of desire, "the child-king of the underground world" (Ciciriello & Renoy, 1999).

With Bernard's blessing and investment, Ciciriello opened his own restaurant. It was a canny move to open one devoted to truffles, because in a city of French speakers in which French culture is much imitated and admired, an Italian person like him did not have to pretend to be something he was not. He was not serving cuisine that belonged to any nation; it was all about the truffle. Ciciriello also figured out that to market such an expensive ingredient, he, too, needed to look like one of his wealthy customers—and he does: His white Lamborghini, license plate "LC," is parked right in front of his restaurant. He reinvents the décor of the dining room every five years or so, and it's always flashy and stunning; when I worked there, it involved plush purple carpets, lavender-hued walls, and fine French table linens hand embroidered with purple truffles. There were floor-to-ceiling oil paintings of two great Italian beauties, Sophia Loren and Monica Bellucci. It had changed by the summer of 2022, when I last visited virtually by Zoom and noticed that now the walls were robin's egg blue, and there was a floor-to-ceiling oil painting of Princess Diana near a (much smaller) photograph of Prince Charles with Ciciriello, taken some time in the late '90s, when the prince, as he was then, dined with his entourage.

It is not difficult to imagine that in this restaurant, the presentation of the food is paramount. My favorite first course took more than a month to learn to compose. It involved layering very thin slices of rare tuna over equally thin slices of house-made pâté de foie gras and incorporating twenty-seven additional ingredients over and around this neatly arranged stack, including microgreens, tiny dollops of butternut squash puree, and truffle vinaigrette. To prepare to make a dish like this, cooks do an inordinate amount of sorting produce. I spent hundreds of hours going through wooden crates of fruits and vegetables, choosing the most beautiful and intact specimens, and throwing the rest away. For example, I was often in charge of the daily examination of a large bucket of fresh spinach leaves. I was required to hold each individual leaf up to the light to scan it for blemishes, and then to save the best ones and toss the rest. On one hand this activity seems absurd, wasteful on the scale of Nero. On the other hand, consider: the spinach was the foundation for the restaurant's signature "Salade Stéphanie." The name is not incidental: Princess Stéphanie Clotilde Louise Herminie Marie Charlotte of Belgium

Truffle jar still life. La Truffe Noire is one of the few "truffle restaurants" in the world, and a big part of my fieldwork there involved a daily routine of brushing dirt off the pricey truffles, airtight jars of which were painstakingly stored in the restaurant's kitchen. Author photo.

(1864–1945) was a beloved Belgian aristocrat who became Crown Princess of Austria. "Stéphanie" is also the name of one of Ciciriello's own daughters. The dish features a mélange of sauteed wild mushrooms, Jerusalem artichokes, and a hefty grating of imported aged Parmigiano-Reggiano. In 2017 it cost €32, but for €10 more diners could opt for a shaving of black truffles atop it, or, for €20, a shaving of the even rarer white ones. Perhaps if you were paying this much for a salad, you'd expect the leaves to be individually sorted, too.

At least that is what the French sociologist Pierre Bourdieu would argue. Based on the evidence of his observations of the daily habits and practices of the high-status upper class and the lower-status working class in Paris, Bourdieu argued strongly that an individual's position in society is the primary influence on his taste in food just like his taste in music, film, fine art, et cetera (1977, 1984). Bourdieu found that with food in particular, the lower class expressed preferences for traditional hearty meals that were heavy in starches and fats, and generous in portion size. The high-status classes, though, tended to value and pursue more exotic and trendy foods. Further, Bourdieu argued that a high-status group maintained its status by legitimizing some tastes and negating others, and then passing on these tastes to their children in the guise of cultural preferences. For him, taste is "first and foremost . . . negation . . . of the tastes of others" (1984, 49).[2]

The typical diners at La Truffe Noire are people who either could personally afford to spend €500 (approximately $533 USD) per person on dinner or had access to institutional privileges that allowed them to do so. Quite simply, this is the food that is the fantasy of what ambassadors eat. And it must look nothing if not stately.

I quickly learned that for the chefs to consider any dish worthy of being served guests at La Truffe Noire, it had to be nothing short of aesthetically perfect. The creation of such food necessitates producing a tremendous amount of waste. I came to La Truffe Noire to study how a food becomes valuable, to dive deep into the world of this mysterious and, to my mind, overvalued ingredient. And something in that kitchen absolutely commanded my attention in the way I had hoped it would. It just wasn't the truffle. In the process of working at La Truffe Noire, I became transfixed instead by *la poubelle*.

The kitchen's industrial-sized garbage bin contained all ingredients that fell short of flawless, but La Truffe Noire's discards could easily have been another restaurant's main event. Inarguably delicious stuff landed in there all the time: chocolate-dipped strawberries (the pastry chef dipped them fresh daily; day-old ones were immediately binned); shiitake mushrooms (deemed by a sous chef as "too bumpy" to be served in a dish where they were required to sit flat); imported French carrots (judged by another sous chef as too short); loaves of homemade baguettes (again, day old and thus not worth serving according to this establishment's rules of distinction). I confess that I *may* have, once or twice, snuck a chocolate-covered strawberry, still on top of its little paper doily, from that bin and popped it into my mouth.

To my eyes, the bin was filled with lost potential—potential to provide gustatory enjoyment, sure, but perhaps more significantly potential to sustain the conditions of a life—this was not only good food, but it was certainly viable and wholesome. I asked Ciciriello what he thought about all the food his chefs threw away. He is hardly a heartless person, but he is also a good businessman. "There's nothing I can do," he said. "If some organization wants to send someone to come get it and do something with it, fine, but I'm not going to pay my cooks and waiters to take it somewhere else when they should be in the restaurant."

I felt ill peering into that bin every day, seeing so much good-looking food go uneaten. Who could see all that good food in the trash and not wonder: where did all those edible but unsellable foods go, who transported them, and what happened to them after they left the restaurant? I began to consider the prospects of "following the food waste" around the city of Brussels. Not (just) the waste from La Truffle Noire, but the waste in a larger sense: the food that was still good to eat that was somehow ending up in bins all over the city. How much was there, and where did it go?

CHAPTER ONE

A World-Class Problem—Everybody Says So

When my son, who was eight years old when I began this project, asked me what my work was about, I read him the first paragraph of what would become my dissertation. It goes like this:

> This is an investigation about food and waste in the age of global capitalism. According to the latest data from the UN's World Food Programme, one-third of food produced for human consumption is lost or wasted globally, amounting to 1.3 billion tons per year, worth approximately US$1 trillion (Gustavsson et al., 2011). My work exploring what this data looks like on the ground for some consumers began in the kitchen of a fine dining restaurant in the capital of the European Union, proceeded to include making soup with rotting vegetables alongside refugees in a Brussels public park as they prayed for better futures, and will conclude with a call for new government policies around food waste throughout high-income nations, and new collaborations between people, institutions, and corporations. To conduct it, I began working in restaurants in Brussels in the summer of 2015, and by the summer of 2019 was also volunteering in a food bank, a state-funded training restaurant for immigrants and social welfare recipients that relied on surplus discarded supermarket food, and an ecofeminist zero-food waste pop-up restaurant in the city's historic Abattoir quarters.

His response: "Everybody says we should reduce food waste." Then he went outside to catch bugs.

I wondered how it was possible that an eight-year-old American child could hold this position—expressing that it was a topic "everyone" talked about and already knew what they were supposed to do to mitigate—especially since I could not recall ever having said the words "food waste" to him. I decided to try to see if he was right, to somehow determine if indeed "everybody" was saying that "we" should reduce food waste. Of course, to do that, I had to see who "everybody" might be, who "we" might be, and why this message.

I did what I bet any researcher would do next: typed "reduce food waste" into the Google search engine. On the evening of October 13, 2022, the number of results was 749 million. These are the top, accompanied by their publication sources:

1. "Here are 7 ways you can reduce food waste in your kitchen," the Mayo Clinic Healthcare Systems, a.k.a. the top-ranked hospital in the world (*Mayo Health System*, 2021)
2. "Food Waste: How to Stop Throwing Good Food Away," the British Broadcasting Corporation ("the BBC"), a.k.a. the world's leading public service broadcaster (Ortiz, BBC, June 2019)
3. "How to Reduce Food Waste at Home," the European Union Food Information Council (EUFIC), "a consumer-oriented non-profit organization, founded to make the science behind food and health more accessible and easier to understand among the public"
4. "15 Quick Tips for Reducing Food Waste and Becoming a Food Hero," the Food and Agriculture Commission of the United Nations
5. "Preventing Food Waste at Home," the United States Environmental Protection Agency
6. "Food: Toward Zero Waste," the National Environment Agency of Singapore
7. "Frozen Food Foundation Is Elevating Frozen Food's Role in Reducing Food Waste," the American Frozen Food Institute
8. "How Do I Get My Family to Reduce Their Food Waste?" the Sierra Club
9. "Reduce Your Food Waste Using Your Smartphone," the World Economic Forum
10. "11 Expert Tips to Reduce Food Waste," Yahoo! Environment

Subsequent pages showed a staggering array of institutions posting messages urging their web visitors to reduce food waste, from local municipalities such as the Montgomery County, Maryland, local government ("Tips to Reduce Food Waste"); to private family farms ("Feeling Scrappy: Reducing Food Waste," Weaver's Orchard in Berks County, Delaware, original breeders of the Star Gala apple); to corporations ("7 Ways to Reduce Food Waste in Your Restaurant") from Lavu, creators of a New Mexico–based iPad point-of-sale system custom built for food businesses.

So "everybody" is more than 749 million entities that publish information free to anyone with a Wi-Fi connection on why you—yes, you—should do your part to reduce food waste. In a world where so few people agree on so few things, it's rather amazing to see 749 million institutions of varying sizes, shapes, and locales agree on such a singular idea.

I could see where my son was coming from, so I continued to analyze the discourse. Why did all these various concerns urge us to reduce food waste? From the hundreds of millions of urgings, strategies, and tactics, just two main reasons emerged:

1. You should reduce food waste to reduce world hunger
   or
2. You should reduce food waste to improve the environment

This highlights an exceedingly difficult conundrum that an assortment of policymakers and farmers all over the world have struggled with since the dawn of agriculture, which is how it's possible for hunger to exist alongside food waste. It also shows that food waste is heavily entwined in the public imagination with environmental risk and damage. Indeed, data show that food waste can have a significant impact on global warming because when food waste is buried in landfills, it rots and emits greenhouse gases—an estimated three billion tons of greenhouse gases, to be exact. This gives rise to what in my experience is the second-most oft-repeated statistic about food waste: "If wasted food were a country it would be the third largest producer of carbon dioxide in the world after the U.S. and China" (UN World Food Program USA, 2021).

Most nations that don't bury their food waste in landfills incinerate it, which comes with its own set of environmental hazards, including releasing pollutants into the air such as particulate matter, which cause lung and heart diseases; releasing heavy metals such as lead and mercury into the air, which cause neurological diseases; and releasing toxic chemicals, such as PFAS and dioxins, which cause cancer and other health problems (Rosenberg et al., 2021). These concerns have been especially amplified since the dawn of the new geological age scientists refer to as the Anthropocene. How we have come to associate the foods we discard with the future health of the planet is worth understanding. To me, considering food waste as a constituent material of the Anthropocene broadens debates surrounding life in an age characterized by unrelenting population growth, dwindling natural resources, and climate change that together portend an uncertain future, mostly because it interweaves tensions between hunger and environmental sustainability (Headland, 1997; Crutzen & Stoermer, 2000; Crate, 2011; Haraway, 2016; Tsing, 2015).

Hunger and the environment are two powerful reasons why "everybody says *we* should reduce food waste," and both are quite specific; however, the most restrictive and specific category of all in that assertion is the "we." Forget 749 million web pages urging *you* to reduce food waste; forget the two powerful sets of alarming data they offer for the reasons why (so many hungry people, so much environmental degradation). The "we" refers to only one set of people: people who have access to so much food that they can afford to throw a not insignificant portion of it away without feeling the effects of that in their everyday lives. Shorter answer: people who live in high-income countries.

The World Bank defines "high-income countries" as those having a gross national income per capita of US$12,696 in 2020, which typically (but not always) correlates with "First World" or "developed country" status. At the time of this writing, eighty countries are in that category, and the five highest are Luxembourg, Singapore, Ireland, Qatar, and the United States. This is not to say that food is always used efficiently in "low-income countries," which the World Bank defines as those having a gross national income per capita of US$1,085 or less in 2020 (the five poorest of which at the time of this writing are Burundi, South Sudan, Somalia, Mozambique, and Malawi). The reason these data matter to the food waste conversation according to the UN's World Food Programme is because in low-income countries, where most of the world's hungriest people live, most food waste occurs during the early stages of growth, harvest, and storage (and this is often and better referred to as "food loss"), whereas in most high-income countries like the United States, up to "40 percent of food is *wasted* because people buy more food than they can consume" (UN World Food Program USA, 2024). What underlying conditions—economic, social, and historical—have come together to create a food system in which it's possible for people to be able to buy more food than they can consume, and that the most efficient thing to do with what's left over is to throw it away? I decided to investigate this question by studying a cycle in Brussels by which food *with* value (i.e., food that consumers are willing to buy, which depends on having consumers with resources to make those kinds of choices for themselves) becomes food *without* value (food that is removed from the market by sellers for a host of reasons besides the fact that it's no longer wholesome) and then, after it has been redistributed to other publics, once again becomes useful (if not profitable).

The people I met along the way—chefs, volunteers, social workers, policymakers, citizens of Brussels who were surviving on welfare benefits, migrants living transitorily in the city of Brussels, teachers, architects, urban planners, and activists—constitute the sources, the voices you will hear. I consider them alongside archival research into entanglements between food, policy, and waste in the history of Brussels, and in the history of the global north, a.k.a. the West, a.k.a. the world's high-income countries. Overlapping the lived experiences of people whose lives are most impacted by recirculating discarded food with the history of social welfare provisioning helps us apprehend not only how globalization has impacted the food system, but how local food systems can work their ways to better solutions that feed more people and waste less viable food. As the science journalist and Vanderbilt University professor Amanda Little, author of *The Fate of Food: What We'll Eat in a Bigger, Hotter, Smarter World*, puts it, "We have a growing global population. We have a growing demand for meat. We also have decreasing arable land. We have increasingly brittle and antiquated food supply chains. And all of this is combined with these increasing climate pressures. And there must be a new approach" (Little, 2019).

Part of my investigation involved trying to determine if the kinds of policies and initiatives that I saw being embraced in Brussels across the city could be generalizable in other big cities around the world. This is not because all big cities are alike, but because what it means to be a big city involves a similar set of utopian visions that reside together with what it takes to realize those dreams. In other words, and as David Boarder Giles puts it in his excellent ethnography of the anarchist Food Not Bombs movement, *A Mass Conspiracy to Feed People* (2021), world-class cities produce world-class waste. In other words, waste is a condition of being a world-class city in the first place:

> The actually existing grit and disorder of urban living are characteristic stumbling blocks for the speculative utopianisms of city planners and developers. From the ongoing influence of the "broken windows" theory of public order all the way back to the sixteenth-century French edict to lock up one's own "sullied waters" indoors rather than disposing of them in the street (described in Dominique Laporte's *History of Shit* [2000, 4]), cities have often reckoned their worth through the rejection of dirt and dereliction. But these incipient utopianisms are never very far from their erstwhile dystopias. Although the ideals of urbanists are put to work fashioning values and goods, waste is every bit as much their product: "The necessary outcome of socially profitable production, it is the inevitable by-product of cleanliness, order, and beauty." (14)

Giles points out that for every glorious outdoor food marketplace with vendors selling fresh produce trucked in from a neighboring countryside (and Brussels has more than forty), or every indoor food hall housing a dozen eating kiosks (the largest food market in Europe, created in part with funds from the brewery giant AB InBev, is scheduled to open in the fall of 2023 in the Brussels Gare Maritime, once the largest freight station in Europe), there will always be a tremendous amount of food waste. For example, consider the grapefruits from France's L'Hoste Chateau that were trucked into the weekend produce market in the leafy Watermael-Boitsfort commune of Brussels where I rented a flat. Note that grapefruits are among the most expensive items in the market, since Belgium typically does not have the climate for citrus growing and yet are among the highest citrus consumers in Europe (Food and Agriculture Organization of the United Nations, 2018). At the market close, my favorite vendor had to inventory every unsold citrus and determine what to truck back across the border to his farm in France. But what about the fruits that he determined were not in good enough condition to make the journey—after all, there had been a lot of squeezing, and the passed-over ones were less than perfect. Here's what: in the span of six hours from when the market opened to when it closed, one of his grapefruits went from being the subject of a commodity fetish to the star in a pile of garbage stacked next to the overflowing market dumpster.

There were almost always canny people who were not afraid to reach down and grab it even though it sat on old newspapers or wadded-up napkins or empty coffee cups or near a sack of dog poop (it has a peel, right?). I saw it often. Yet Giles says that the state does not insinuate itself in organized efforts to recirculate such commodities because it is "anxious to keep their scavengers and their world-class waste out of view." Giles says this is how "surplus shadow economies" form, which are places and grassroots institutions for whom those excluded items—dented fancy grapefruits, day-old loaves of bread, barely bruised fruits, bottled juices close to their "best used by" dates—are left to be found, and if recuperated, free to be circulated elsewhere in the global city (2021, 125).

In analyzing the work of Food Not Bombs, Giles finds evidence of no fewer than five global cities where officials actively work against efforts to feed people for free in public spaces—in many cases arresting Food Not Bombs group members for doing things like serving free soup in a public park. But what I saw in Brussels was a city whose policymakers were willing to stop hiding (or else relegating to the shadows) their surplus foods and peoples, particularly if it meant recuperating food that would otherwise have been wasted. Trying to discover how it came to be this way involved doing groundwork across the city to learn which initiatives worked (and to what degree, in terms of whether hungry people were being fed and also how much waste was being recuperated). It also raised the question of whether any part of these efforts, without aligning hunger and food waste, could be replicated elsewhere.

To that end, the research has been conducted for the benefit of anyone who wishes to reduce food waste; anyone who supports the value of messy trial-and-error alliances among communities that initially do not seem to have much in common; anyone who is open to the potential merits of involving corporations in efforts to improve social welfare; anyone not neoliberal enough to complain about enfolding some of the values of ecofeminism into efforts toward the same; and anyone unwilling to dismiss wholesale the idea that governments, policymakers, activists, corporate actors, and social welfare recipients can collaborate for the ends of producing measurable improvements in food justice and equity.

What Is Food? What Is Waste?

Investigating the differences between categories of "food" and "waste," and the calculus between which kinds of materials count in which category and for whom, necessitates thinking beyond taxonomic distinctions. It is tempting and perhaps even accurate to argue that it also involves thinking beyond the kinds of distinctions that customers in markets in high-income nations make. However, it is especially crucial to attend to the places in which it is not only permissible but expected to discard some, if not a lot, of "good" food (i.e., viable, wholesome, and edible) in the name of aesthetics. Why? Because if reducing food waste is a goal that policymakers and publics agree on, then doing so by as many means as possible—including and perhaps especially by recirculating food that some consumers choose against, but others would be happy to have—is an important avenue for keeping people alive and fed and, environmental activists would assert, for keeping the planet spinning.

Given the intense media attention on consumers in high-income countries doing our part to reduce food waste, I set out to discover whether community-based grassroots efforts to recirculate "wasted" food have the potential to direct, or at the very least nudge, large-scale policies toward the end of revaluing what counts as food and to learn who might be most impacted by redrawing those boundaries. The methods of recuperating surplus food and the range of divergent actors involved in these efforts in Brussels today are reshaping the materiality, affect, and politics of discarded food. My hypothesis is that knowing how their efforts work—what drives them, which methods feed the most people, which honor the local communities they are enmeshed in—could influence the kinds of messages and thus the kinds of efforts that really work, such that "Everybody says we should reduce food waste" might evolve to refer to specific people, actions, and reasons for improving relations not only between people and food but also between people and the natural environment.

My topic, which can sound quite theoretical and academic, is also quite homely. Food that people throw away is the object of my research, and the subject is how various people across social strata of a major global city—the capital of the European Union at that—deal with it (or not). By "homely," I'm being both figurative and literal. A large part of addressing such broad theoretical questions involves attempting to apprehend the quotidian decisions people make when they calculate whether a food is "good" to eat or not. To even begin to address the underlying factors in how such decisions are made, we must determine *how much* food is wasted in the world today, and to do that we must define what we mean by both food and waste. This turns out to be no easy task.

Let's take food first. To paraphrase the anthropologist Jon Holtzman's work on the entanglements between food and memory, "what is food" is "not a stupid question" (2006). Nearly every anthropologist who has written on food begins his or her findings like the formidable Sidney Mintz, the so-called Father of Food Anthropology, did in *Sweetness and Power: The Place of Sugar in Modern History* (1985), an analysis of sugar production in the Caribbean (and in his many writings beyond that, all of which combined a Marxist and historical materialist approach to social questions about food's role in the establishment of class distinctions): with the reminder that very few material objects, consumable or otherwise, are as uniting to all of humanity as food, the basic function of which is survival. It is elementary; regardless of who we are, where we live, or which resources we do and don't have access to, no matter whom we voted for or what color our skin is, we all must eat to live. Food studies as an academic area is interdisciplinary because it must be, because everything that happens after the initial fact that we must eat to survive is variable. What we eat is dependent on a tremendous number of factors that run the gamut from geography (Do you live in the mountains or on the coast? In a village or a city?) to religious affiliation (fish on Fridays?) to superstition (black-eyed peas and collards on New Year's for luck?) to idiosyncratic family customs ("We don't put ketchup on our hotdogs around here"), and all of that is dependent on the economic conditions we find ourselves bound by (by this I mean things like the unemployment rate, inflation, and fiscal and monetary policy orientations that occur in your lifetime, i.e., were you born during an economic recession? During the outbreak of a world war?), as well and perhaps most importantly of all by issues of one's social class and one's race, and of the times in which we live (the COVID-19 quarantine immediately comes to mind).

According to the latest data from the World Health Organization (WHO), each year worldwide, unsafe food causes six hundred million cases of foodborne diseases and 420,000 deaths, 30 percent of those among children under five years of age, and warns that these numbers are likely an underestimation (Sifferlin, 2015). "Food production has been industrialized and its trade and distribution have been globalized," WHO director-general Dr. Margaret Chan said at the time of the release of the statistics. "These changes introduce multiple new opportunities for food to become contaminated with harmful bacteria, viruses, parasites, or chemicals." As Chan points out, how and why people decide what to eat versus what to discard—and if they're fortunate enough to be able to decide those things for themselves—is not only a cultural or an economic issue, of course. It is also a medical one.

In general, there is one rule of thumb that applies to almost any situation in which food is discarded: food is discarded after someone determines it worthless. By worthless, I mean without value, that is, not worth being consumed (either because it is undesirable for some reason or another or because it has spoiled) or not viable to be sold on the marketplace (reasons for which could range from the fact that the food is indeed no longer wholesome to the fact that it's damaged in ways that make it unattractive to consumers, i.e., the proverbial "ugly foods").

Elementary as these taken-for-granted categories of material existence may seem—food is what we eat, waste is what we throw away—both materials' uses extend into meanings. By this I mean that food and waste do not merely symbolize certain aspects of human identity; they constitute it. For example, it's easy to grasp the idea that food is more meaningful to humans than, say, shower curtains—we can't live without one but certainly can without the other. However, the reasons why food beyond its nutritive value is not merely another commodity are highly subjective and depend on identity markers like race, gender, religion, and perhaps most importantly, socioeconomic status. In addition, when "we," a word I use for lack of a better one with the explicit acknowledgment that I can only speak from the vantage point of the Westernized and privileged experiences I have both known and observed, decide which food we want to eat and which food we dump into the trash, we are always passing judgment over that food's "goodness." This judgment is highly contextual, highly influenced by dominant (and mostly white) Westernized experiences, and highly connected to expectations of medical outcomes (since eating some spoiled foods can literally kill someone). Of course, in some places in the world the bodily impact might well be characterized not as medical but as spiritual, in which case eating something unwholesome would still count as a kind of punishment meted out by forces beyond one's choices.

How and why people eat what they do is hardly a new area of inquiry for anthropologists. In fact, social scientists have studied food since the discipline's inception. Many of the earliest researchers focused on what Mintz described as food's "utterly essential" role in human survival, and particularly on the fact that in many cultures, food is "often insufficiently available." In his annual review of the anthropology of food in 2002, Mintz expertly summarized an incredible sweep of disciplinary history and an equally vast array of research, citing more than 225 studies on food written between the years of 1888 and 2001, and showing the arc of how anthropologists have theorized the uses and meanings of food in the lives of people across the world.[1] Highlights include Franz Boas's documentation of the Kwakiutl's criteria for allocating salmon rights as well as their numerous preparations of salmon, David Sutton's intervention on the importance of culinary memory as a process of identity formation for residents of the Greek Island of Kalymnos, and Jane Guyer's economic analysis of the development of urban food supply systems in Africa. These are just three of a much larger collection of ethnographic projects that give a taste (pun intended) of the ways food theory has been formed within this discipline.

I do not—and in fact cannot—attempt to re-create Mintz's exhaustive review of a subfield that has clearly, if somewhat quietly, been thriving for more than a century. Of course, since 2002 there has been substantial subsequent work on food that even a creative thinker like Mintz could not have anticipated. For example, Mintz might be tempted to describe Marianne Lien's *Becoming Salmon: Aquaculture and the Domestication of a Fish* as a "classic food ethnography," because its subject is ostensibly the politics of salmon farming in Norway, but in its attempts to tell the story largely from the perspective of the *salmon* rather than the farmers, it probes the intersection between sentience and food farming in an intellectually heady and singular way that defies easy categorization (2015).[2] Of course, I am not writing from the perspective of a truffle or from food that has been thrown away but is still good to eat. I am, however, inspired by alternative ideas about how food extends, contradicts, and crosses boundaries of what counts as useful and valuable in the lives of eaters, which I hope to do some of here.

To illustrate the vast and sometimes even arbitrary definitions of what constitutes food, on the first day of my course Food & American Culture, I show students slides of some common things we put into our mouths every day. For each, I ask, "Is this food?" The images include a small cup of mouthwash (most say not food); a stein of beer (most say yes, it's food); a pill (most say not food); and a stick of gum (this one tends to elicit the most discussion and argument, in which some students invariably point out that gum contains calories while others highlight the fact that we don't swallow it). The point is, we regularly consume things, even things that contain calories, that are not strictly considered food. The final slide I show students is of a head of lettuce on whose ribs are little rust-brown spots. The spots are caused by ethylene gas, which occurs naturally in plants and prompts produce to soften and sweeten. The spots signal that the lettuce cells have been weakened and will rot soon, but they are harmless. Nearly all my students tend to argue that this is no longer food.

In this way, we see that contestations over food inevitably lead to contestations over waste. Anthropologists have also analyzed waste, not unlike food, since the very beginnings of the discipline, as it is perhaps the material most central to the "nature/culture" debate. Many anthropological studies throughout the history of the discipline have focused on the boundaries between pure and impure, or what we keep inside our living spaces and bodies, versus what we determine should be cast out of our homes, lives, and bodies. Such studies often sought to explain processes of separating order from chaos. In this way, waste almost always has a social life, but theories about what the life entails vary widely. In defining dirt as "matter out of place," Mary Douglas's work is almost a subgenre of its own, considering the many ways it has been used as a touchstone for examining ways in which discarded material may map social relations. Matter of place has been conceived of as a product of colonialism, that is, a material historically managed by colonial influence (Harvey, 2012), and as "distinguished from all forms of material value" (Frow, 2003). It has also been imagined as an active agent in "a regime of invisibility" (Latour, 2010) and as a "live" material for new possibilities of usefulness if not exchange (Hawkins, 2005; Gille, 2007; O'Brien, 2008; Reno, 2009; Bennett, 2010). Still other scholars imagine matter out of place as *biosemiotic*, that is, as a sign of the fact that living creatures once inhabited/visited/occupied a space—matter out of place can be proof of life (Hird, 2012; Reno, 2016). It can also be productive: matter out of place can be redistributed to populations that could not otherwise afford certain commodities and/or for whom the sense of disgust is a contestable sensory terrain that admits the discards of others (Miller, 1998; Kolnai, 2004).

Douglas is an interesting crossover figure between the two subfields of food and discard studies, because she was concerned with both, and often in how they were differentiated. Her attempt to read a meal as an exercise in structuralism, which she called "deciphering a meal," concludes that a meal is like a poem in that it has rules and rhythms that offer "the assurance to the reader [or eater] and to the poet [or cook)] himself that the poet [or cook] is in control of the disorder both outside him and within his own mind" (1974). This shows Douglas's concern with the coding of foods as acceptable and unacceptable, and how that process works for different categories of eaters. By way of example, Douglas offers a fun and funny picture of meals in her own household: She is vexed when she cannot persuade her family to make a dinner of soup—no one except her believes that soup constitutes a meal, and she wants to figure out why. "I needed to know what defines the category of meal in our home," she writes (45). In her decoding, she finds that "a meal worthy of the name supper" has a standard, of "A + 2B," in which A equals a large portion of a high-status food like meat, and B equates to two complementary foods in smaller quantities, like one starch and one green vegetable (44).[3]

For Douglas, the human is always in charge of the food, and of the waste. But in "Vibrant Matter," the political scientist and ecological philosopher Jane Bennett argues that "human hubris and our earth-destroying fantasies of conquest and consumption" can be altered if we understand that various forms of matter—including both food and waste—are life forces with the capacity to mitigate human encounters in and of themselves. For Bennett, food is a "vital" and an "actant" in producing social relations—it can do things. For example, potato chips, with their beguiling combination of saltiness and starch, can "call forth" the instinct to consume them. This she attributes to the "power of dietary fats" (2010, 40): "That food can make people larger is a fact so ordinary and obvious that it is difficult to perceive it as an example of a nonhuman agency at work," she writes (41). More grounded but along the same lines is Kathleen Millar's study of the life and labor conditions of workers in a garbage dump in Rio de Janeiro, in which she argues that waste gives the workers the chance to work for themselves and according to their own schedules.[4] The existence of waste dumps enables precarious workers "to contend with insecurities in other dimensions of their lives." In other words, despite how problematic working in a dump collecting recyclables in a burlap sack may be, it offers workers freedoms that the official state system of recognized employment does not, and thus produces a kind of value (2014).

I have discovered that when most of my students encounter the term "food waste," they first think like my son ("Everybody says we should reduce food waste"), and then when pressed to define what exactly "food waste" is, they think like George Costanza. Yes, George Costanza, the fictional character from *Seinfeld*, the self-described "show about nothing" that featured the (often hilarious, and often absurdly ignoble) microaggressions of a group of four friends living upper-middle-class lives in 1990s New York City. An episode called "The Gymnast" aired in November 1994, in which George helped his girlfriend's mother clean up after she hosted a luncheon. Alone throwing away plates in the mother's kitchen, George opens the garbage bin only to discover, sitting on top a pile of discarded magazines, an éclair still wrapped in a paper doily with a single dainty bite taken from it. Unable to resist, George picks up the éclair from the "clean" side and takes a bite—*just* as his girlfriend's mother reenters her kitchen. She spies him, éclair in hand, hunched over the garbage.

George demurs: "No, no, no, no. It was not trash."

"Adjacent to refuse, is refuse," Jerry declares.

This example from *Seinfeld* shows us two things: First, the kind of disgust that anthropologists like Douglas highlight in their theories of "matter out of place," and second, that food waste is considered a problem that occurs at a very small scale: the scale, say, of a small party in someone's aunt's apartment, when someone took a pastry and didn't eat it all. But there's one more dimension to the popular idea about food waste that this example doesn't show, and that's moral. Picture this: A strawberry ripens on the vine. It's picked, packaged in a crate, and trucked to a factory. The crate is unloaded onto a forklift and sent down an assembly line, where the strawberries are repackaged into typical clamshell containers and labeled. Next the package of berries is trucked to an airport, flown on a plane across the country, delivered to a supermarket, and shelved in the refrigerated produce section. From here, the package is chosen by a little girl and her mother, sent down the conveyor belt at the cashier, stationwagoned home, unloaded into the family fridge . . . and forgotten about until the berries have all molded. Once rediscovered in their spoiled state by the mother, the strawberries are dumped into the trash. This is no thought experiment, though. It is a literal example of the Ad Council of America's 2018 public service campaign, airing during the traditional Saturday morning cartoon-time across America. The tagline at the end of the commercial, after the moldy berries have been tossed and the screen fades to black, is this line, in white type: "Wasting food wastes everything. Water. Labor. Fuel. Money. Love. #savethefood."

The Ad Council of America is a nonprofit organization founded in 1942 that produces, distributes, and promotes public service announcements on behalf of various sponsors, including nonprofit organizations, nongovernmental organizations, and agencies of the US government. It is an effective advertisement because it stirs emotions, and it may be relatable for many people who have had the luxury of being able to buy food that they can forget to eat, but it also does not reflect the reality of what wasting food in high-income countries typically looks like. Yet it represents perhaps the most important piece of discourse around food waste and how and where it happens, which is that it's a moral failure on the part of the individual consumer. As Michel Foucault argued, discourse need not be true, and it is also capable of accruing power as it circulates—that is, the more people are exposed to it, the more they believe it's true, whether it is or not. Foucault further argues that such discourse allows new politics to emerge (1998, 100–101). According to Foucault, this is the way knowledge circulates—for example, knowledge about how food is wasted—and it becomes a strategy, a technique of self-fashioning in which a society's acceptance of certain circulated messages becomes what members of that society choose to recognize as true.

To me it's worth noting that this is not the first time that corporate concerns have aligned with American policymakers via the Ad Council of America to convince consumers that it is their job to solve social welfare–related problems. In 1971, a group of bottle-and-can companies adopted the banner "Keep America Beautiful" in their campaign to market themselves as an anti-litter organization, for which they then produced the infamous "crying Indian" public service announcement that aired around the time of the very first Earth Day. The ad featured neither a real Native American ("Iron Eyes Cody" was the stage name of an Italian American actor named Espera Oscar de Corti, who made his career portraying Indigenous Americans in films including the 1948 Bob Hope film *The Paleface*), nor did it promote a real change in efforts to combat environmental pollution (Rogers, 2005). As the environmental historian Finis Dunaway expertly describes the ad, "Cody paddles a canoe on water that seems, at first, tranquil and pristine, but that becomes increasingly polluted along his journey.... The lone Indian ponders the polluted landscape, a passenger hurls a paper bag out a car window. The bag bursts on the ground, scattering fast-food wrappers.... The narrator comments: 'Some people have a deep, abiding respect for the natural beauty that was once this country. And some people don't.' The camera zooms in on Iron Eyes Cody's face to reveal a single tear falling, ever so slowly, down his cheek" (2017). The "Keep American Beautiful Campaign" did nothing to limit the production of aluminum cans and plastic bottles. Instead, it broadcast to consumers an idea that recycling cans was their moral duty and that by performing it they could improve the environment and thus be better citizens. Dunaway points out that the ad won production awards and was so popular that by the mid-1970s, an Ad Council official noted that "TV stations have continually asked for replacement films" of the commercial "because they have literally worn out the originals from the constant showings." Closer examination reveals that the bottle and can manufacturers used this commercial to deflect consumer attention from their role in environmental pollution: "In the time leading up to the first Earth Day in 1970, environmental demonstrations across the United States focused on the issue of throwaway containers. All these protests held industry—not consumers—responsible for the proliferation of disposable items that depleted natural resources and created a solid waste crisis. Enter the Crying Indian, a new public relations effort that incorporated ecological values but deflected attention from beverage and packaging industry practices," Dunaway writes.

This is one of many messages, and thus many reasons, that most of my students, nearly all of whom are from high-income countries, think of food waste as the result of a single consumer's habits and decisions. We have been habituated to believe not only that such crises are our fault but also that we as individual citizens have the incredible power to fix them. It's not entirely untrue, of course. People throwing away unfinished food certainly could qualify as wasteful, and people should absolutely be mindful of buying more food than they need and of throwing away good food that, if they do not want to eat it, could be used by other people rather than allowed to rot and potentially degrade the environment. Those are facts, just like the fact that this conception of single-serving events, if you will—one person, one container of strawberries, one household refrigerator—fails to capture the scale of the amount of food wasted in the world today or propose an idea that would make a dent in its vastness. (Remember: according to the latest data from the UN's World Food Programme, one-third of food produced for human consumption is lost or wasted globally, amounting to 1.3 billion tons per year, worth approximately US$1 trillion. In addition, consumers in rich countries waste almost as much food as the entire net food production of sub-Saharan Africa each year.)

Something my studies in anthropology prepared me for was framing vast social and cultural questions about the role of food in people's lives: questions about what food means to people. Something my experiences in journalism prepared me for was connecting those questions to the everyday habits and practices of consumers in high-income nations: questions about how people obtain and use food. In combining these two "lives" of mine with issues of foods' uses and meanings, I realized I could think beyond the notions of surplus food demonstrated in fiction by George Costanza and exemplified in real life in discourses that encourage "smarter" grocery shopping. For instance, I could readily discern that because economic conditions play such a large role in what people eat, personal taste preferences hold less sway in how people eat than market-based capitalism does. I saw evidence of this directly when I met with one food bank volunteer, a retiree living on a generous government pension. I asked her why she'd decided to spend time volunteering at the bank, when she lived in a house in a leafy suburb just outside the city and coming to the bank meant that she had to deal with the notoriously difficult traffic and parking near it. At first, she said, "To help people," but then after a bit more talking, she added somewhat sheepishly that she also enjoyed the free box of food that the bank allowed all volunteers to take home each week. While I noticed that most of the other retirees did not take a box of free food home or else gave their share to the forklift operators, this volunteer said she considered it "a perk" that she wouldn't have been able to find in another volunteer position.

I also saw the tension between the uses and meanings of surplus foods when I interviewed a staff member of the European Union's health and food safety task force, who told me that he would *never* support any policy, even his minister's, if it involved raising the cost of food, no matter to what end. He said that this was because his own economic principles did not line up with such logic: "Food must always be cheap, so there is always enough," he said. This seems like an inarguable fact, but the truth is more complicated—chiefly because context really matters. Which foods need to be cheaper (fruits and vegetables? Sodas?) and where they need to be cheaper (are issues of food access the same in high-income countries as they are in low-income ones?) really matter to the equation. I could not resist challenging this logic, for one thing because it has been proven repeatedly and in many studies that there already exists enough food to feed everyone on the planet.[5] In fact, the United Nations reported in late 2019 that "enough food is produced to feed everyone on the planet, but hunger is on the rise in some parts of the world, and some 821 million people are considered to be chronically undernourished" (UN Global Humanities Network, 2019). So making food cheaper does not really move the needle on having "enough." This is why many economists debate market manipulation of food prices—for example, adding a "sin tax" to junk foods, or subsidizing fresh vegetable prices for low-income consumers— strategies that they argue might do more than "cheap food prices" to improve health and equity-based outcomes. That the staffer was unbending in his view of food prices is yet another clear case of the conflicts that exist between the uses and meanings of food in everyday modern life.

Journalists and anthropologists are both invested in exploring social problems like these through fieldwork. And both fields acknowledge such forms of participant-observation as often filled with contradictions and conflicting views—not only across multiple interviewees but sometimes even among individuals themselves. I expected that one of my biggest challenges would involve making sense of the nuances of people's incongruous ideas and behaviors about food waste recirculation. What I did not expect, and was not prepared for, was sifting through rotting vegetables in an outdoor market, hearing women plead for bunches of rotting fresh mint that I was not authorized to give them, or watching people working in food banks smuggling food out of it for themselves. I had no roadmap for negotiating any of these activities among people in Brussels as they attempted to find a sense of home, identity, and peace in others' discarded foods. And I encountered many such instances.

Of Moral Panics and Public Messaging

It's clear that food waste holds an imaginative sway over eaters in high-income countries not least because it is perpetually pitched (remember, more than four million organizations currently urge exactly such consumers to do their part) accordingly: throwing away food is bad, wrong, and immoral, and if you don't think so, you're someone who is willing to eat trash. This level of judgment causes many citizens of such countries, like my students and like me, to assume that the very existence of food waste is in some way our own fault—we have too much, we waste too much, and we had better stop throwing away berries. I am in no way apologizing for consumeristic behaviors and excessively materialistic patterns of wastefulness that exist in the marketplace; I am saying that the math doesn't make sense. No matter how many people in rich countries band together to stop throwing away berries, their efforts will not make a significant dent in the epic, massive problem that is food waste. The problem does not exist because people who have a lot of food choice let too much food go to waste—as I unpacked in the previous section, it exists because of the existence of excessive choice in the first place, which is an entirely different sort of problem.

And yet the pervasive need on the part of even well-meaning organizations to urge consumers to do more to reduce food waste—rather than policymakers, corporations, international food distributors, giant supermarkets, or any other large-scale player in the food system—remains. This, combined with the sheer number of efforts aimed in precisely this direction, constitutes a moral panic.

A fantastic example of a moral panic is explored in *Satanic Panic: Pop-Cultural Paranoia in the 1980s*, by the Canadian film scholar and producer

Kier-La Janisse. In the mode of the wildly popular Netflix series Stranger Things, Janisse chronicles the ways in which widespread fears of suburban Satanic conspiracies swept American culture for nearly a decade, during which MTV, the board game Dungeons & Dragons, horror movies, punk rock, and especially heavy metal music were cast in media reports as agents of the devil. "I experienced firsthand the furor surrounding heavy metal as the Eighties wore on," writes Janisse, "and the fear that covert Satanic machinations were at work everywhere around us—in our cartoons, commercials, music, movies, and most tragically of all, our daycares" (Janisse & Corupe, 2016). If nothing else, the "Satanic Panic" shows the way that ignorance, fear, and cultural anxieties can be mobilized by certain kinds of fearmongering discourse. I see this kind of fear mobilized when it comes to the ways in which excessive food waste, while undeniably an environmental problem and an example of the real challenges of a capitalist-dominant global supply chain, has come to be discussed by "experts" in media reports and consumer education campaigns from governmental agencies as a singular crisis of the modern age, and one that threatens the continued existence of the species.

First, it's important to consider how a moral panic arises, because a true moral panic (and I'll get to the distinction between a moral panic and moral outrage in a moment) has many aspects of a *real* crisis, and yet also a large dose of *fake* news. The sociologist and former social worker Stanley Cohen, whose distinguished career as a professor at the London School of Economics included groundbreaking studies on issues of emotional regulation and the connection between mass experiences of certain emotions and human rights issues, was interested in analyzing the conflicts that arose among Britain's youth culture between the Mods and Rockers in the mid-1960s and early 1970s. In so doing, his conception of a moral panic has become the most cited by scholars to date: "Societies appear to be subject, every now and then, to periods of moral panic. A condition, episode, person or groups of persons emerges to become defined as a threat to societal values and interests; its nature is presented in a stylized and stereotypical fashion by the mass media; the moral barricades are manned by editors, bishops, politicians and other right-thinking people; socially accredited experts pronounce their diagnoses and solutions; ways of coping are evolved (or more often) resorted to; the condition then disappears, submerges or deteriorates and becomes more visible" (Cohen, 1972, 9).

Following this, Cohen argues that a moral panic has five key elements: someone or something is defined as a threat to generally held social values and interests; the media depicts the threat in an easy-to-digest form; there is a build-up of public concern; there is a response from authorities; the panic results in social changes of some kind and then people move on to what they consider more pressing concerns.

Augmenting Cohen's theory in a way that is germane to my analysis of food waste is the work of late sociologist and cultural theorist Stuart Hall. In his study *Policing the Crisis* (1978), Hall argued that politicians' and police officers' characterizations of a wave of minor street robberies in London in the late '70s produced moral panics that were subversive attempts to reaffirm racism. For example, Hall investigated the way British newspapers deployed the term "mugging"—a slang term the British press borrowed from the American vernacular of the time—in articles accompanied by headlines such as "The Violent Truth of Life in London." Hall found that using a new-to-the-culture term involved an increased perception that there was in fact a major new crime wave, and one whose perpetrators were always Black youth (330).

In decoupling the facts of the robberies from the headlines about them, Hall proved that "muggings" were hardly a new crime and neither originated by nor perpetuated exclusively by Black youth. In the process, he also proved that when it comes to moral panics, the state often manipulates the media in favor of the production of narratives that serves it. The resulting moral panic produces widespread public fear, which shields state actors (including policymakers, police officers, and elected officials) from working to improve many poor social welfare outcomes. According to Hall, then, moral panics exist to distract stakeholders from real social problems.

As I mentioned earlier and wish to distinguish now, the public becoming outraged about an issue is not always a bad thing—it just depends on the nature of both the issue and the outrage, as well as the initial source of the outrage itself (the media versus stakeholders, for example). And the media are not always villainous or even duped by the state, either. It's also important to note that morally induced uproars are not in and of themselves a bad thing. For example, the race among wealthy countries to produce and then disseminate a vaccine for coronavirus during the first year of the COVID-19 pandemic is an excellent example of what a deluge of media reports around a real social danger can produce. Another striking example is the effects of the #MeToo movement in creating and amplifying violent acts against women in the workplace, which ultimately led to the conviction of film producer Harvey Weinstein in February 2020 on two charges of committing a criminal sexual act in first-degree and third-degree rape, and a sentencing of twenty-three years in a New York State prison. However, it's important to note that the activities and narratives that lead to those positive social outcomes are not exactly moral panics—they are examples of moral outrage, which a group of notable scholars including psychologists Jillian Jordan, Paul Bloom, and David G. Rand and economist Moshe Hoffman define in their groundbreaking study on public perceptions of trustworthiness, "Third-party Punishment as a Costly Signal of Trustworthiness." These scholars found that social movements whose activities demonstrate an "uncalculating" investment on the part of participants who take time and effort to condemn those who they feel have behaved baldly can serve to enhance one's own sense of well-being as well as promote cooperation by deterring defection (Jordan et al., 2016).

This is why it is crucial to note that moral outrage is not the same thing as a moral panic, and especially when it comes to an issue with as many complexities and contingencies as reducing food waste. For although Cohen and Hall both use the frame of moral panic to analyze perceptions of crimes, it became quite clear to me that their findings (and not those related to incidents of moral outrage) easily map onto discourse about food waste. For example, I first became aware of the heightened media attention on food waste reduction precisely during the time I was working in the kitchen at La Truffe Noire. In the summer of 2016 as I took the subway to work, I saw media campaigns like the Good Food Brussels initiative's flyers plastered all over the city's public transportation stations, urging people toward things they could do at home to reduce food waste, such as not to throw away ugly fruit. The posters urged people to visit a website and learn more, which is how I discovered that the project was a public policy initiative launched by the sustainability office of the Brussels-Capital regional government. The project included funding opportunities for urban gardening initiatives such as a mobile seed kiosk, a web tool with monthly information on how to make the most of seasonal vegetables, and a guide to launching a neighborhood "solidarity fridge" where communities can share food they can't use with others who might need it.

Such messaging, as moral panics do, influenced me every day as I trashed perfectly good day-old chocolate-dipped strawberries. In my efforts to learn more about the flow of food waste in the European capital where I was living at the time, I began to study Brussels itself and explore opportunities in the world of food production. For example, I volunteered at a sophisticated urban farm that was running a community-supported agriculture initiative in which produce baskets were delivered to subscribers by a fleet of bicyclists; I interviewed web developers working on an app pairing people who had bought too much produce with people who might be able to use it; and

Good Food Brussels is a government initiative sponsored by the Brussels-Capital Region and supported by multiple partner institutions (such as Brussels Environment, the region's environmental agency) and independent social groups. One of its objectives is to increase awareness of local food products, chiefly by promoting opportunities for local food production and raising awareness about ways to reduce food waste. I saw posters like this all over the city, especially in subway stations. Author photo.

I went to Belgium's largest produce auction to track what happened to unsold products after the auctioneers had bid on everything they wanted. I discovered that in most of these sites, what was called "food waste" constituted different sorts of things—in one place people used the term to describe decomposing vegetables in a compost bin, while in another it was used to mean a person's occasional grocery store shopping surplus.

Why and how had so many people, seemingly around the same time, focused their energies on talking about "food waste" in the first place? To determine if this was just a "Brussels thing," I did some additional research. It turned out that in the United States, consumer food waste was the subject of twenty-one articles in the *New York Times* alone in the calendar year 2019. In terms of other high-income nations, in 2020 in Denmark, the world's first "surplus food supermarket" opened. In the same year in Australia, a popular grassroots youth food movement sprung up called "War on Waste AU," in which farmers and environmental activists use the power and reach of social media to organize large-scale protests against the industrial food system.

What I was noticing in terms of contemporary calls to reduce food waste was, if you will, a more urgent flavor. Messages about food waste seem designed not to explain or even persuade but instead to awaken, perhaps to enrage. I traced the appearance of this urgency around food waste in the media to a key moment that has come to foreground this study, which was the release of the 2011 annual report of the Food and Agriculture Organization of the United Nations. This event marked the first time the staggering statistic I have reported to you twice already in this chapter (if you are even casually interested in food waste, this stat is ubiquitous) was widely published, that "one-third of the world's food was lost or waste every year" (Gustavsson et al., 2011). The report went on to recommend that all UN members in "industrialized nations"—at the time it was what the Council on Foreign Relations refers to as "G8," a group of eight highly industrialized nations—France, Germany, Italy, the U.K., Japan, the United States, Canada, and Russia, although Russia was suspended in 2014 following the annexation of Crimea and they withdrew in 2017—should address this by a single means: creating policies aimed at reducing consumer wastefulness. EU policymakers responded quickly, focusing their efforts on regulating their biggest sector of food distribution: supermarket chains. In early 2015, the European Union instituted a compulsory policy for these chains to donate all edible but unsellable food or face huge fines.

Across the European Union, the food producers, consumers, and distributors in member states wrestled with potential solutions to reduce food waste at the behest of the European Union's mandate to "do something" about the UN report on food waste, and Belgium was no exception. This report hit Belgium during a moment of its own precarity, as the city that is the capital of the European Union was hit hard by a range of problems including demographic shifts its social welfare benefits could not keep up with. When the European Union authorized legislation making it compulsory for supermarkets to donate all edible but unsellable food (without providing either direction or funding for doing so), Belgian politicians clearly saw this compulsion to offload some of the state's responsibilities for provisioning for newcomers. By 2016, the Belgian federal government, the Brussels-Capital Region, and each of the city's nineteen communes had all established their own food waste reduction platforms, which included strategic waste reduction goals and funding calls for local efforts. The Good Food Brussels flyers I saw all over the city in the summer of 2016 were precisely part of this newfound attention on reducing food waste in the city.

Of course, Brussels was not the only city whose officials were motivated to respond to the United Nations' report. Reuters picked up the data and circulated it to news agencies in nearly two hundred locations around the world. Discursive analysis allowed me to examine the flavor, if you will, of the ways in which this report's findings were being written about in international media. Almost immediately the *New York Times* reported on it under the headline "Food Waste Grows with the Middle Class: The Estimated One-Third of Food Left Uneaten Is a Serious Threat to the Global Environment and Economy" (February 27, 2015). Further analysis, though, showed that newspaper coverage of food waste has always had a sense of impending doom and disaster. Years before the United Nations' report was released, the *Times* published an article called "A War against Food Waste: A Substantial Portion of Food Is Thrown Away while Still Fully Edible Because of Cosmetic Blemishes or Overstocking" (Walsh, 2011), and a mere four months later printed another headline, "The Battle against Food Waste: Environmentalists Have Campaigned against the Waste of Water and Energy, but Little Attention Gets Paid to the Squandering of a Product That Uses Plenty of Both" (Galbraith, 2012).

These articles appeared almost a century after the newspaper printed its first-ever article on food waste. "Women of Wealth Fight Food Waste" describes the founding of a social welfare committee organized by "50 prominent women of New York City," including Mrs. Oliver Harriman, whose husband was heir to the fortune of one of the wealthiest private banks in New York City; and Mrs. George J. Gould, wife of the railroad executive who led the Western Pacific Railroad and the Manhattan Railway Company. The committee was founded one month after the United States entered World War I, and its mission statement included the goal to "wage war on the small minority who feel that they can continue, unmindful of conditions, in their heinous extravagance, and to fight through proper channels the food gamblers who are reaping a great harvest and who are attempting the assassination of the very life of our country." To do this, the committee took three actions immediately: it created the "Mayor's Food Garden Committee," commandeering from the city 745 acres for growing vegetables, with allotments given to each of the five boroughs; it partnered with an existent organization, the National League of Housewives, with the goal of attracting one million new members and introducing local workshops on household management strategies, including the first class to be held on techniques for canning; and it made a pledge among its own fifty members to cut their lunch meals to two courses instead of three and their dinners to three courses instead of more. "We ask the individual to eat plenty and waste nothing, for without this individual control we shall see a very perilous and difficult situation arise from an unrestricted drain on the foodstuffs of this country," according to the committee's initial minutes (May 16, 1917). From there, a standard narrative around food waste was recirculated via wire reports. It emphasized urgency, it targeted specific consumers, and it went like this: most food waste is produced in the developed world, so efforts to reduce it should focus on changing consumer behaviors there.

Returning to Hall and moral panics: Hall is an apt scholar to draw into this analysis because his work focused on the fact that mugging was not a new crime; it was just one being described in new terms, which allowed for a new scapegoat to emerge. This seemed precisely the case to me with food waste: given the amount of food being wasted in the developed world, this situation is hardly new, and one that had been operating at crisis level, if you will, for quite some time. What interested me most is the fact that this food-waste moral panic was targeting consumer wastefulness and that all the initiatives aimed at reducing it involved things that individual consumers should do differently, that the problem with food waste was a problem with shopping and consumption. Further, this problem, allegedly due to irresponsible consumer behavior, was characterized as producing two distinctly different poor social outcomes: one ecological, and the other related to human rights.

Indeed, in the wake of the release of the United Nations' report, two kinds of institutions led consumer awareness campaigns in the global north highlighting the dangers of wasting food: those whose missions alleviate hunger (e.g., the UN World Food Programme) and those whose missions promote environmental sustainability (e.g., the US Environmental Protection Agency). I could see how the moral panic throughout the developed world around the perceived problem of food waste positions it as both a cause of environmental degradation and a missed opportunity to ameliorate hunger. Advocates on both sides of the debate argue passionately, but as I learned at a meeting in the EU health minister's office in the winter of 2017, where I was invited as part of a team from the Food Bank of Brussels, these two positions are often at odds. Why? Because for people who are concerned about reducing hunger, food must remain low cost. As Marco Valletta, a member of the personal office of Commissioner Vytenis Andriukaitis, who was appointed in charge of health and food safety in November 2014, told me, "Food must always be as accessible as possible so that the people in the most difficult circumstances can afford it; otherwise, they will go hungry, and no one should go hungry in the EU." On the other hand, environmental activists often argue that farmers should use sustainable, environmentally friendly agricultural practices, such as minimizing the use of fertilizer and chemical crop protection; maximizing no-till farming and cover and catch cropping; and reducing livestock grazing and land-use intensity. Yet such practices could lead to lower yields and higher prices. As Somini Sengupta, the international climate reporter for the *New York Times*, put it, global food production has gone up while the number of undernourished people has not gone down. Sengupta argues that making food cheaper doesn't always make it more accessible, and that cash remittances are far more effective than low-price fixing: "How do remittances stack up to climate aid? In 2021, migrants sent home nearly US$590 billion, compared with the US$100 billion annual climate finance that rich countries promised to share with poor countries" (2022).

Discourse analysis shows that both causes, despite their different aims, ironically tend to aim their messages at "raising awareness." For example, the World Food Programme's "#stopthewaste" campaign urged consumers to "snap a selfie" of themselves with items in their refrigerators that they had "forgotten" to eat and then share their photos on social media—promoting themselves and their own wastefulness in the process and visibly (and voluntarily) supporting the idea that consumers are responsible for the billions of tons of food waste. Also, the EPA created an "Excess Food Opportunities Map," an interactive tool that directed consumers to places in every state such as prisons and homeless shelters where they could donate their surplus food, which effectually transfers the responsibility for providing food for such institutions onto consumers and encourages them to moderate their own

European Commissioner for Health and Food Safety Vytenis Andriukaitis invited Brussels Food Bank administrators Tony Michiels and Harry Gschwindt to a meeting to discuss food distribution solutions in the European Union during the time I was doing fieldwork. Michiels graciously invited me along. The scope of Andriukaitis's concerns centered on ameliorating hunger in the European Union, a subject close to his heart, he said, as when he was a child his own family had been deported from their native Lithuania to Siberia, where they faced serious food insecurity before they were eventually allowed to return. Author photo.

consumption so that others in less fortunate circumstances can benefit, offloading social welfare responsibilities from the state onto consumers and positioning reducing food waste as a consumer responsibility.

Capitalism and Gastropolitics and Belgium

During the time I worked at La Truffe Noire, I often marveled at the homeliness of the truffle, this knobby tuber that grows wild on woody fungi yet, through the whims of cultural tastes and values in Europe restaurants, has been elevated to the ultimate luxury ingredient. The truffle is a totem of haute cuisine, despite how closely it resembles a mound of dirt. I know, because I spent up to an hour per day there doing what Ciciriello called "brushing the truffles," which entailed removing them from individual airtight glass jars and using a special beechwood brush fitted with plant fibers to gently caress each one so as to ensure that no speck of dirt or dust was on its surface (that way, when the waiters went to grab one to shave on a customer's salad or pasta, the truffle would be in its most pristine condition). The act of brushing the dirt off mushroom-like spores may sound cruddy, but in practice it can be ethereal—meditative; peaceful, even (Stewart, 2007).[6] The truffle itself is a little hard, round, brown specimen that smells like a combination of vanilla and soil, plus the kitchen is sparkling clean. The cooks standing alongside you wear crisp, freshly laundered white jackets. The radio blasts an Adele song. It is as cossetted a zone of food production as one could ever be. Doing this very mundane thing in it gave me a lot of time to think. In fact, while I brushed the truffles I thought a lot about commodities, and of course I thought a lot about Sidney Mintz, the anthropologist who inarguably did more to trace the value of one edible commodity—sugar—than any scholar ever has.

Mintz's *Sweetness and Power* has been a guide throughout this project for good reason. The famed American nutritionist Marion Nestle once said that *Sweetness and Power* was the only book that scholars across all the interdisciplinary fields that constitute food studies—from history to romance languages, from public health to folklore—could agree upon. The slim book interrogates both the social costs of colonial sugar production and the everydayness of eating within the socioeconomics of capitalism and consumption, expertly outlining the transformation in the place of sugar in the British diet—from a rare commodity, only consumed by the upper class(es), to a form of mass food, valued for the quick energy it gave to workers who consumed it on their tea breaks (1985). In his study, Mintz attends to scalar shifts between the local and the global, and the currencies of the marketplace that balance edibility against value; in the process, he squarely centers the human production of inequality at the heart of anthropological research.

Mintz's moves in *Sweetness* offer a corrective to history, explaining how world market systems shape taste and vice versa; it is history not of "great leaders" and their triumphs but of the ways in which humble commodities were organized by corporations to in turn organize patterns of consumption in everyday life. Nestle is right: *Sweetness and Power* is a touchstone for what I consider some of anthropology's best investigations into the role of food in everyday life, the ones that investigate how certain people come to value and to discard certain foods. These include Melissa Caldwell's interpretation of events in a Moscow soup kitchen in which she finds that the clients' adaptive survival strategies developed when the liberalizing official economy stopped offering sufficient aid (2004); Julie Guthman's study of organic farming in California that assesses discourse on the benefits of small farms in order to reveal a paradoxical relationship between an agrarian populist ideology and capitalist systems of industrial food production (2004); and Brad Weiss's study of the social lives of pork vendors in a North Carolina farmers' market in which he links locality, history, and aesthetic judgments to social movements that attempt to transform the industrial food system yet inadvertently end up replicating it (2016). What these studies have in common is a critique of capitalism, and particularly its role in food systems of various scales, from global to local.

Because economic conditions play such a large role in what people eat, the most important deciding factor of what people eat versus what they do not may be market-based capitalism itself, which since the late eighteenth century has been the dominant global economic system, and since 1947, the dominant ideological system, too (Abdelfatah et al., 2021). Food and capitalism have been intertwined since the Middle Ages, yet I have discovered that even saying the word "capitalism" in one of my food studies courses will grind most discussion to a halt. One thing I never imagined becoming was a person responsible for explaining capitalism to other people. Unpack the finer points of an M. F. K. Fisher essay? I got you. Discover the way to make perfectly crisp mandelbrot? I can help. What of the perils of property ownership and the theory that the free market should set supply and demand for a society? I didn't think the query was my wheelhouse. Yet over the course of teaching food studies classes in various incarnations for more than fifteen years, I have come to realize that defining precisely how capitalism intersects with the global food system gives a useful foundation for understanding how and why it has become possible to throw away as much food as people who live in wealthy countries do today (exactly how much is staggering, and I will get to those numbers shortly).

This project is about innovative and creative ways to recirculate discarded food *before* it becomes food waste, and to do that as a way for caring for other people and for the planet, and to do that, the first step as I see it is to understand that the very existence of food waste all but depends on capitalism. This is not to say I'm satisfied with the status quo of the ways in which a capitalist system damages access to food—spoiler alert: I'm not, and in the coming pages I will suggest many amendments, policies, and actions to that end. Before I can suggest any of those interventions, I want to explore some of the ways in which capitalism affects our food system, in broad strokes and in the context of food systems in big cities so that it's clear how necessary it is that they produce so much waste in the process. Since the Middle Ages, when rug merchants hired weavers to make more rugs more quickly and borrowed from moneylenders to expand their capacity to sell more rugs, capitalism has been about competition and expansion. It has always been undergirded by the logic that any merchant needs to produce more to sell more. The easiest way to produce more was often to borrow money to do it, which the merchant would then pay back over time, with interest, before borrowing more, producing more, and selling more. The direction of capitalism is always toward more, that is, toward producing surplus.

Capitalism developed around the world at different places at around the same time, for example, with Muslim trade caravans in Europe and Chinese merchants with caravans all over Asia. And because it was a system reliant on the fact that there would be an ever-increasing demand for rugs, canny merchants eventually realized that rugs couldn't be the only commodity involved. Food came into the picture early with spices and tea, common features of capitalism by the eighteenth century, when the Dutch East India Company and the British East India Company developed their joint-stock companies to cofinance even more expansive international trade missions. This kind of financing spread out risk and increased the distribution of wealth *among its members*, a development that allowed the rising class of capitalists to separate themselves socially and economically from those who were working class—the former of which Marx would go on to call the bourgeoisie and the latter the proletariat. Because in practice capitalism created more wealth for the merchant class, it also ushered in a new kind of upper class in the form of imperialism, such that some nations quickly became wealthier than others, and with their wealth these nations could control the world simply through controlling their new mega trade routes. Control the means of production (i.e., own the boats), and you have all the stuff that everyone else needs to sell their labor to buy—that's capitalism.

Initially Britain was the best at it. In the eighteenth century, it had become the dominant world power, and with its indomitable royal navy it dominated the slave trade, moving African people to the New World and forcing them into labor for the purpose of expanding imperialistic trade—the case study Mintz gives in *Sweetness* goes into exacting detail of this process. Around the same time came what historians refer to as the second agricultural revolution, the first being in the Neolithic Era with the shift from hunting and gathering to farming. It's worth considering that although there was obviously no capitalism yet because it hadn't been invented, some scholars argue that the forces behind it were already in play. And the merits of even that revolution are hotly debated for this reason. For example, in the Introduction to Food Studies I co-teach with the viral immunologist Melinda Beck, our students are treated to contrasting views on this precise subject. One week, Dr. Vin Steponaitis, an archaeologist whose research focus is on the precolonial native cultures of the American South, argues that farming created inequalities in terms of land ownership that the world has never recovered from. The following week, Dr. Peter Coclanis, an economic historian, argues that farming improved the world tremendously by stabilizing food access and allowing for unprecedented technological advancements that benefited humankind. Both sides agree that it made it possible for farmers to invest in technologies to lead to greater crop yield, and of course the same was true the second time around in Britain. Once again, advances in technology resulted in the chance to grow more food, which led to greater population growth—because it was cheaper and easier to feed more people than it ever had been—and to even more striking inequalities. It is interesting to note that by the time of the second agricultural revolution, in wealthy areas around the world obesity had already become a bigger social problem than starvation—because people had access to consistent, stable wages and consistently priced food. Nutritionists including Marion Nestle point out that obesity is almost always a problem exclusive to industrialized nations, for whom there is much less food insecurity (Nestle, 2002). Note here that other nutritionists today argue that obesity is itself a moral panic, that across the world starvation is still a much larger problem. In *The Obesity Myth*, the American law professor Paul Campos argues that the Western medical community uses a rubric of "health" to advance class bias in favor of thin people, particularly thin women (2004). While some prominent nutrition researchers, including Barry Popkin, nutrition and obesity researcher at the Carolina Population Center and the W. R. Kenan Jr. Distinguished Professor of Nutrition at the University of North Carolina at Chapel Hill School of Public Health, where he is the director of the Interdisciplinary Center for Obesity, lauded Campos for shedding light on the covert financial interests involved in obesity research, Popkin also took care to note his opinion that Campos exhibits "selective use of research" and misunderstands epidemiological literature (Kim & Popkin, 2006). That said, what Campos succeeds in doing is demonstrating the way capitalism links to ideas about what is good to eat and what is not, and who gets to eat it.

Grievances about understanding obesity aside, most experts agree that this stability of access to affordable food created demand for more food at cheaper prices and led to industrialized food production and the Industrial Revolution—the one most people associate with the development of capitalism, the one associated with the development of the steam engine, which brought sweeping economic and social change first to Great Britain, then to the rest of the world. Now factories were taking on more and more of the work that farmers once did, and fewer people needed to work in agriculture to feed the population; in 1520 there was 80 percent of the English population working the land; by 1850 it had dropped to 25 percent (Appleby, 2010, 80). At the same time, factory owners became wealthy, while many workers lived in increasingly worse conditions of poverty, laboring for long hours under difficult and sometimes dangerous conditions.

Who wouldn't want both more and cheaper food? Perhaps people who consider the other costs that come with it. Also, perhaps people who do not realize that produce is inherently much more expensive to grow than grains. That matters because, as the science and nutrition columnist for the *Washington Post* Tamar Haspel points out, the cheaper it is to grow and harvest a food, and the less it has to be refrigerated or stored carefully as it is shipped, the more likely it is to be subsided by governments—which is one of the reasons governments do not subsidize growing blackberries (which in 2017 cost about 74 cents a cup to grow and harvest) but do subsidize growing wheat (which in 2017 cost about half-a-cent per ounce—the amount in the average slice of bread). The more likely a crop is to be subsidized by a government, the more likely it is to be grown in such a way that "adds up to huge supplies, which, as any Econ 101 student knows, drive prices down" (Haspel, 2017). What that means is, if you want food to remain cheap, you can continue to choose commodity foods (or foods made with them) in favor of fresh foods.

There are social costs to keeping foods very cheap, too. Cheaper food came by means of processes of land enclosure, whereby wealthy lords claimed privatized fields that had once been held in common among communities. Forcing peasants off land led to the creation of poverty, wage work, and the existence of commodity crops in the first place, of course. James Scott, the noted historian of agricultural systems at Yale who is firmly on the side of those who question farming's benefits for humanity, points out that enclosing land meant that commodity crops replaced a varied diet with a few starchy foods, increased the amount of hard farm labor that peasants had to do, and spread infectious disease in both humans and animals (2017). He also inadvertently proves that from the time formal states existed, there was food waste. In a chapter devoted to early state methods of population control, he points out that states needed to compel subjects to produce a grain surplus that exceeded their own needs (150–82).

Throughout history, issues involving regulating a tribe or state's food supply have led to countless fights, riots, wars, and strikes, as well as large and small acts of rebellion. You don't need me to remind you of the most famous examples, like during the so-called Golden Age of Piracy (1650–1726) when bands of pirates menaced commercial shipping in the Caribbean, frequently targeting spice-laden ships and leading to the Spice Wars of the seventeenth and eighteenth centuries. A smaller and far less deadly favorite of my own includes the uprooting of the manicured English lawn hedges of lords during the Industrial Revolution, which activist peasants enacted to protest common-land enclosure and wage slavery—the casualties of which included only topiaries (Twilley, 2021). Typically, and according to Marxist philosophy, the most effective form of worker protest is to organize into labor unions for the purpose of collective bargaining. It is worth noting Marx's idea that human beings have desires that go beyond basic self-interest and aren't always economically motivated—that collective action improved living conditions for all. This makes straightforward sense when it comes to sharing food, because if you live among a collective, it is one exceedingly easy way to use up a surplus—it's like saying, "Before I throw this away, let me see if someone else I know might want it." But that solution, which undergirds so many of the efforts at the three sites where I did fieldwork, requires willingness to share resources and sometimes a nudge (or even a shove) from policymakers, and at that point in England, there was neither.

In fact, at that point in England, capitalists owned the two factors required to produce anything: land and capital to invest in factories. Workers just had their labor. Capitalists wanted labor at the lowest possible price; workers wanted to be paid as much as possible for their work. Marx believed that work gave life material comfort but *not necessarily meaning* and that since we are social animals and we work better when we share resources, it promoted lack of collaboration—in fact that it replaced collaboration with conflict and competition. He wanted to empower workers to protect collective interests. For Marx, the solution was for the workers to stage a revolutionary class struggle so that they end up on top and remake a social order. In *The German Ideology*, Marx and Engels argue this: "Both for the production on a mass scale of this communist consciousness, and for the success of the cause itself, the alteration of men on a mass scale is necessary, an alteration which can only take place in a practical movement, a revolution; this revolution is necessary, therefore, not only because the ruling class cannot be overthrown in any other way, but also because the class overthrowing it can only in a revolution succeed in ridding itself of all the muck of ages and become fitted to found society anew" (Marx & Engels, 1970, 94–95).

Considering such an imperative, we might ask: What's good about capitalism? It aligns incentives—if you work harder, you can earn more, you can generate capital for yourself, you can improve your standard of living, you can reinvest that capital. The desire to earn (i.e., be profit driven) is a requirement. People who defend capitalism say it's a meritocracy; now, nearly everyone loves the idea of a meritocracy. Even communists had tests within the party, and people who scored highest had increased authority—what we'd now call performance-based results. Capitalism is built on the idea that if incentives are good and capital gets in the hands of people who earned it, innovations occur because the right people are handling the capital and will drive innovation. Capitalists argue for the validity of the cardinal law of political economy, which is that when you have a bunch of capitalists who can compete and innovate and drive prices down for the consumer, then the benefits should flow to the consumer. And when a capitalist, ever competitive, comes up with a better version of an existent product or else an entirely new product that suits new wants and needs of consumers (electric cars, for example), he or she will make more profits and accumulate more wealth.

I have never heard this expressed better than I did in 2016 on a tour of Brouwerij De Halve Maan in Bruges, a sixth-generation family-run brewery first opened in 1856. "We have a commitment to innovation," our guide stressed as he explained the new installation of a two-mile underground pipeline that connects the brewery in the city's historic center to its bottling plant in the suburbs. The guide explained that it was a practical solution to the logistical nightmare of having trucks thundering daily down the medieval city's cobbled streets. "Now, not a drop of beer goes to waste! And we don't burn fuel trucking beer around the city, either!" he enthused. What he didn't mention was how much easier and faster it was for the brewery now to be able to not only make more beer but, crucially, deliver it more efficiently. The other part he didn't mention was the fact that the brewery paid for the US$4.5 million "innovation" in part by crowdsourcing: the US$335,000 it raised became Belgium's most successful crowdsourcing campaign to date, and enrolled consumers in a fun effort at local bragging rights: "Cheers! The world's first beer pipeline is open!" CNN reported.

What does this show us about capitalism, about the Belgium food system, and about waste? Several things, it turns out: one, that local food is a tremendous source of local pride; two, that "innovation" is almost always to the benefit of the corporation even more than it is to the consumer; and three, that messages of capitalism can easily map onto ideas about environmental sustainability. Capitalism's benefits become less clear when one or a select few players become outright dominant in a marketplace and become so big that all the other players disappear, like a monopoly. Data show that the food system is particularly vulnerable to this. In a joint study analyzing market share data on consumer buying practices of sixty-one common grocery store food items in thousands of supermarkets across the United States, funded by *The Guardian*, the British daily newspaper, and Food and Water Watch, a Washington, D.C.–based nongovernmental organization focusing on corporate and government accountability relating to food, water, and corporate overreach, and published in *The Guardian* in July 2021, when it comes to grocery shopping in the United States, "consumer choice is largely an illusion." Citing factors of political lobbying and weak regulation in both nations, the study found that "the top [transnational] companies control an average of 64 percent of sales." Particularly striking examples are these: "PepsiCo controls 88 percent of the dip market, as it owns five of the most popular brands including Tostitos, Lay's, and Fritos. Ninety-three per cent of the sodas we drink are owned by just three companies. The same goes for 73 percent of the breakfast cereals we eat—despite the shelves stacked with different boxes." The study also noted that this kind of consolidation leads to economic power, which is often levied to create favorable policies for manufacturers: "During the 2020 election cycle, the food industry spent $175m on political contributions, including lobbying by PACs and individuals and other efforts. The money came from every part of the food chain, including dairy, eggs, poultry, meat processing, farm bureaus, sugar cane, crop production and supermarkets" (Lakhani et al., 2021).

What does analyzing capitalism have to do with food waste? For one thing, it is important for supermarket shelves to be always stocked with an array of products that give the appearance of a similar array of brands competing for our dollars but that represent a very small group of brands that need to appear more diverse—the illusion of excessive choice means there will be more food unchosen, uneaten, and discarded for shelves to be continually restocked. For another, that it is very hard if not impossible for new independent brands to get a break, and when they do get a foothold, it often can't last. For corporations to keep their foothold, they need to make sure that the consumer has the illusion of tremendous choice but that only they profit from the array of choices. Also that the economic power of the corporations contributes to their growing ability to influence policy, which in turn has led to laws that put profits before food and worker safety, consumer rights, and sustainability. The most damning finding of all is that "it's a system designed to funnel money into the hands of corporate shareholders and executives while exploiting farmers and workers and deceiving consumers about choice, abundance and efficiency" (Lakhani et al., 2021).

The problem with monopolies on food products in particular is that once all the incentives disappear, the desire to innovate disappears, too. This is unchecked capitalism, a.k.a. late-stage capitalism, when capitalism has run its course and there is no competition left, and only the big dogs—the Pepsi Co.s, the Conagras, the General Mills—remain. It also makes the market vulnerable to unexpected events, such as pandemics. When the unexpected happens, it increases the risk of shortages; when shortages happen, supermarkets are quick to increase prices to ensure profit margins remain intact, but when commodities go down, consumer prices are often much slower to decrease.

When I read the findings from the study described above, I realized that capitalism's effects on the food system are typically the most visible, even though, from the very beginning, it seems to me that capitalism has always been about food—it was about selling spices and exploiting labor, it was about dominating land ownership and controlling access to grain and other supplies, it was about automating processes to make more food to feed more people who could ensure that there would always be enough workers. In this way, capitalism itself ensures that there will be a surplus of food. Because it depends on the production of wealth, and on the existence of a marketplace that requires excessive choice, it creates consumer demand that can never be satisfied. David Boarder Giles calls this "abject capital"—a condition that exists when "massive quantities of unspoiled food and other discarded commercial goods with persistent use values" exist in the shadows of the marketplace (2021, 80). For Giles, abject capital represents the intersection of capitalist exchange and consumer aesthetics—or what happens when the market is so full of options that consumers can prioritize certain features over others and choose to purchase only those, leaving perfectly "good" things to waste.

Some scholars have argued that this "leaving aside" comes at a cost—not just to the economy but to the soul. The early twentieth-century German Jewish sociologist George Simmel was concerned with how urban environments shape their inhabitants' inner lives—in other words, how capitalism affectively shapes its consumer. For him, a city environment was the ideal place to witness human social struggles—for rights such as health care, food resources, sanitary working conditions, and fair wages but also for individual identity and a sense of self. Such struggle is the subject of the essay "The Metropolis and Mental Life," in which Simmel refers to it specifically as the "resistance of the individual to being leveled, swallowed up in the social-technological mechanism" (1964, 11). He's writing about a specific type of city—Western, industrialized—and during a very specific time, the Second Industrial Revolution/Progressive Era. Yet even then he describes a condition that would be true for people living in many such "global cities" around the world today, which is the hyperabundance of "violent stimuli" that occur with every crossing of the street (14). This includes especially the "constantly moving stream of money" that attends all commercial and social activities, as well as the relentless displays of sights and sounds that accompany one's near-constant proximity to other people. Since "the metropolis has always been the seat of money economy," Simmel says that the city dweller has little choice but to adopt a certain state of mind, a "blasé outlook" in which he or she is impressed by nothing because everything is reducible to an object and every object's worth is quantifiable in terms of money (14). Simmel's work is fruitful for my work on food waste because it brings a wide variety of the cultural artifacts of modern life into sharp relief. How it is possible to *not notice* that so much food around you goes uneaten is one effect of a blasé outlook, without which a city dweller would not be able to function.

Once I began to look around Brussels—to explore the city beyond La Truffe Noire—I began to identify various sites along a spectrum of food production and distribution. I encountered workers, citizens, and residents actively negotiating the material distinctions, sensory impacts, and economic policies of food and waste. The efforts that interested me the most were the ones that seemed to reverse capitalism, which involved recirculating food that was discarded in one area—say, removed from supermarket shelves—but still viable and wholesome. In zeroing in on a series of three sites that incorporated food waste recirculation, I saw firsthand the ways that circulating discarded food disturbs a linear capitalist model of edibility that depends on resource extraction, industrial modes of production, massive food choice and accumulation, consumption that often far exceeds human bodily needs, and waste disposal in landfills or incineration facilities. In Brussels today, attempts to create an alternative food economy marked what I saw as an innovative response to immigration, to food waste policy initiatives, and to eco-activist struggles, which I will explore a great deal in chapter 2. They also marked a new kind of intersection of social movements, state regulations, and culinary practices, a.k.a. gastropolitics (Appadurai, 1981).[7]

Within the field of anthropology, scholars have also expanded and sometimes even contested the concept of gastropolitics.[8] Of particular interest to me is María Elena García's use of it to critique the ways in which some prominent chefs in Lima, Peru, work to obscure the violence of colonialism in their claims "that gastronomy can offer a path to economic opportunity and support Indigenous livelihoods through chef-producer alliances that make possible farm to table dining" (2021). Her conclusions about the ways that chefs produce a certain kind of self-serving discourse, in what she terms a "gastropolitical machine," show a way in which a certain vision of a nation (in this case a gourmet one) intentionally undermines racialized incidences of violence. She argues that the state benefits from the ways in which some chefs appropriate Indigenous knowledges (in the form of ingredients and recipes), because such a discourse allows the government to paper over the violent revolutions that have shaped Peru's history. This analysis impacts my study here because I, too, ask readers to consider the materials, regulations, and even forms of violence that are "baked into" entanglements between a state and the food system its policymakers promote, particularly in terms of which foods reach which sets of consumers.

Of course, the gastropolitical context matters. According to Numbeo, the Serbian crowdsourced online database of perceived consumer prices, real property prices, and quality-of-life metrics, one of the largest quality-of-life information databases available for reference, Lima and Brussels are not economies of scale; according to the consumer price index, in June 2023, restaurant prices in Lima were 64 percent lower than those in Brussels, and grocery prices 42.7 percent lower (Numbeo, n.d.). Further, issues of indigeneity in one are not reflected in the other. Most importantly, only one identifies as a social welfare state that guarantees basic economic security for its citizens, a topic I will address at length in chapter 2. In researching the calculus by which people—citizens and residents alike—in a capital city in a modern European social welfare state like Brussels determine which food to eat and which food to trash, the city itself became one of my best interlocutors. If you've never been to Brussels, I can lay odds that it's not what you think it is. You would not be alone in imagining Brussels as a place where a lot of chubby white people walk around eating puffy waffles and fine chocolates and drinking beer while wishing they were as chic as their French or German or Dutch neighbors. There are so many stereotypes about Belgians circulating within Belgium itself that the stereotyping of Belgians among Belgians is the subject of an article by the late Belgian psychoanalyst Joseph Nuttin. Published in the *Journal of the American Psychological Association* in 1976, it is titled "Stereotypes of Flemish and Walloon Ethnic Groups in Belgium" and forefronts the theory that Brussels natives complain equally about familiar insults hurled at them by the Dutch, who ridicule them as fat and lazy, as well as by the French, who call them stupid and lazy. There are so many stereotypes about Belgians circulating within Belgium itself that the European Union's "Youth Portal," which is an online portal designed for young professionals new to working in the European Union, has a page on its website called "Belgian Cultural Clichés" that states, "Belgian people are the subject of a huge amount of jokes and clichés—they eat fries at every meal, have beer running through their veins, and only read comic books" (Bertulot, 2019). I felt I had to write the chapter that follows this one—appropriately titled "Why Belgium?"—because so many stereotypes of Belgians exist *outside* Belgium that in nearly every instance that I told other anthropologists where I was conducting fieldwork, they responded with that precise question.

I devote the next chapter to the "Why Belgium?" question, including the history of how its capital city, Brussels, came to be the capital of the European Union, its precise history of occupations and how those occupations affect the food system there today, and the precarious nature of city life there in the present. I also consider why so little anthropological work has been done there. To be fair, when it comes to Belgium, anthropologists have historically been interested in the flow of people in and out of the country, considering Belgium's role as the (often brutal) colonizers of the Congo, and the fear that I'd ignore that past in favor of innovative food waste politics seemed to come through. Having chosen to work in a country with lots of chocolate and even some air conditioning (though not as much as you'd think), I address the Belgian context because the most damning stereotype of all is the idea that Belgian politics are insignificant when it comes to the measure of global affairs.

It was difficult not to feel a little sensitive about the "Why Belgium" question, but over time I have ultimately come to embrace the query. This study is not concerned with waste itself, but specifically with ways in which the waste is operationalized by a network of scrappy semi-state-funded organizations;

indeed, this study is about redistribution and recirculation of food that is in fact *not* waste but that also cannot be sold in the traditional marketplace. One key to this argument has to do with the fact that Belgium is a social welfare state but also one with a uniquely complicated trilingual and multibranched governmental structure. Studying these recirculation efforts there, as chapter 2 will show, was not incidental; it has been essential. And yet it still necessarily involves unpacking both global and local stereotypes about the nation of Belgium and what everyday life is like in its capital city.

In her masterful discussion of the ways in which stereotypes of Black people and fried chicken have come to have political weight and meaning in the United States both among community members and among outsiders of the community, American studies scholar Psyche Williams-Forson argues that stereotypes can both contribute to and resist a community's own process of self-definition. "One engages in the process of self-definition by identifying, utilizing, and, more importantly, redefining symbols" that are commonly related to that community (2006, 343). In the case of Brussels, and of the ways in which outsiders have come to associate symbols like waffles and fries with the city, it is my contention that these depictions partially emerged as a way for Belgium's neighbors to control the identity of its city dwellers, such that a "Belgian" identity meant a person who was prone to overeating fatty foods. Doing this made it more likely and even politically and economically advantageous for a person to identify more strongly with his or her French or Dutch roots and to associate with other, more flattering stereotypes, that is, either with people who had classier tastes (the French) or with those who had more rigorous ideas about self-regulation (the Dutch). What these stereotypes do is align Belgians with people with nothing better to do than eat.

It is undeniably true that stereotypes can give rise to toxic prejudices about race, gender, and many other social distinctions. And yet, as Yale psychologist Paul Bloom explains, in some cases in which people "have experience with things and people in the world that fall into categories and we could use our experience to make generalizations of novel instances of these categories," they can also enlighten debates ("Paul Bloom: Why Do We Create Stereotypes," 2014). It is true that Belgium, and particularly the city of Brussels, can be considered a "foodie" place. This is in fact historic: the city of Ghent contains the remains of one of the world's first food halls, the Vleeshuis (Meat House), which was built in 1251, rebuilt in 1884, and renovated in 1912 and in 2002, respectively. The market is open and bustling to this day, and its initial existence marks the beginning of an age of food markets in villages and towns across Europe that is very much alive to this day. For example, the Brussels Zuidmarkt/Marche du Midi is one of the busiest outdoor food markets in Europe.

One enduring source of "foodie pride" for Belgians is one of those stereotypes rooted in fact. Nearly every Belgian I've ever met has been proud to tell me that French fries were an invention of their own ancestors. According to historian Peter Scholliers, professor of contemporary history at the Vrije Universiteit Brussel, carts selling thin fried potatoes began appearing on commercial streets throughout Belgium and particularly in Brussels in the 1840s. By the last quarter of the nineteenth century, the carts were parked outside most railroad stations in the country—which remains the case today. The operations initially consisted of one man with a pushcart, a pot of boiling beef grease over a little coal fire, and handfuls of hand-cut potatoes. This was a quick, cheap treat for working Belgians long before they became "French." Of that process, Scholliers offers the most widely circulated origin story, which holds that fries were "discovered" during World War I by American soldiers stationed in the area who mistakenly thought, given that the people all around them were speaking French, that they were in France. "No one, except a few French people, would claim that fries are French and not Belgian (there is no *frites* culture south of Paris)," writes Scholliers (2009).

The pride in fries is almost quaint considering that food access has become a dire concern in Brussels, one that often surprises those unfamiliar with the city beyond its historic gastronomic charms. In fact, the city's once almost universally prosperous population has precipitously shifted from less prosperous to more precarious over the last thirty years. While many political conservatives are quick to blame immigration, other scholars cite the limits of a social welfare state's ability to live up to its promises in a world dominated by late-stage capitalism. On the one hand, Brussels's lavish gastronomic tradition is still on display in temples of cuisine such as La Truffe Noire and 128 others over the last one hundred years that have earned *Guide Michelin* star ratings. On the other, its all-volunteer food bank—the largest of nine in Belgium—serves the 33 percent of the city's population who were, pre-COVID and according to the Brussels Health and Social Issues Observatory, living below the poverty line against the daunting backdrop of a 25 percent unemployment rate (*Brussels Times*, 2015). There are also some things about Brussels that have not changed: the city's religious history drives politics in ways that I have come to believe most city dwellers do not see but express in their everyday attitudes. Since the sixteenth-century Counter-Reformation, also known as the Catholic Reformation, Belgium has been "a country permeated by a Catholic identity while maintaining a strong secular tradition nonetheless." Citizens express that dichotomy in their everyday lives: 75 percent of Belgians identify as Catholic, while only 11 percent of them attend Mass (Blainey, 2016). A connection to Catholic ideology may not be visible in church services, but it is felt in church-sponsored soup kitchens and food banks in all the city's nineteen communes. In this way, the city still has vestiges of the religious view of food as the agent for "making the stranger welcome in order to better know God" (Rudy, 1997).

Ultimately, I found that Brussels is ideally suited for this study because of the unique model for reducing food waste that is emerging there. Bound by small-scale, policy-driven, citizen-supported efforts to recuperate food scheduled for incineration, the objective is to redistribute this still-edible food to those individuals and communities in Brussels struggling with hunger. Since Brussels is the principal seat of the European Union and the European Parliament, recuperating food waste there has the potential to influence policymakers and grassroots organizations in other European cities, and beyond. I found that the city's rich Catholic history laid the foundation for a strong network of charity that was designed after World War I to distribute food to the poor. I noticed that after the European Union instituted its compulsory mandate aimed at supermarkets and requiring them to donate their unsold surplus, food waste recirculation was being mapped onto this network.

Throughout the following chapters, I take care to pay special consideration to the people of color with whom I worked both for and alongside in all three organizations. To acknowledge my own positionality, I entered the sites as an outsider of privilege: a white American Jewish woman whose academic work was funded by a private university. In these sites, I frequently worked with—both alongside directly and on behalf of organizations designed to serve—African-descended, Turkish, and other Muslim peoples. Some of these were organization administrators, some were fellow volunteers, and others were recipients of state-supported care. I do not presume to speak for the complexities of anyone's experiences in the world of food distribution efforts in Brussels except my own. What I have intentionally sought to offer here are ethnographic snapshots of incidences I either observed directly or learned about firsthand through interviews. I was often astonished at the trust placed in me with the experiences and stories of the people willing to speak with me for this study, and in it I share only what I was expressly given permission by these sources to share.

In addition, I have worked to forefront the voices and experiences of people of color in Brussels, many of whom visit, volunteer, work in repurposing, and receive the surplus discarded but still viable food from these sites. In my view, Brussels is a city whose history with racial violence must also be attended to. The people I worked with who are featured in this study all still contend in various ways with the horrors of the Belgian king Leopold's brutal colonization and occupation of the Congo, from 1908 until 1960, and of the Belgian state's subsequent and ongoing treatment of African and African-descended people both on that continent and at home. I saw firsthand that this particularly extends to the state provisioning of state leadership and support. For example, the first African mayor of a commune in Brussels, Congolese-born Pierre Kompany, was elected in 2018 while I was doing my fieldwork. His election was a watershed event with celebrations spilling out into the streets.

Conflicts involving race in Brussels today are not especially central to the work in food waste redistribution, but the three sites on which I focus do each have their own internal conflicts that often feature racial politics, and I have attempted to attend to them as sensitively as possible. A challenge is that interwoven into a history of oppression are modern challenges vis-à-vis the concomitant crises of immigration and economic downturns the European Union faces. These conflicts certainly impact policy goals of putting food in the hands of fragile populations and affect the ways in which people across the city make decisions about what to eat on the day-to-day level. The issues of accessibility, affordability, and freshness that they consider when they make those choices have changed now that food that would once have been unavailable to them *must* be recirculated. Up for debate now are which foods get to count as good, why, and for whom. Life without compulsory policies directing supermarkets to recirculate rather than discard food they didn't wish to sell was generally organized around a binary: food versus waste. But now there is a new spectrum of edibility, on which a range of options from pristine and perfect edible specimens coexists with nearly rotting varieties of the same. As the chapters that follow will address, this spectrum prompts policy reconsiderations for food resource redistribution in high-income countries across the globe. It also disrupts discourse that places the individual consumer at the center of the social life of food, offering exciting new possibilities for collaboration.

CHAPTER TWO

Why Belgium?

"Here's some advice," began a friend, a mentor in the field of anthropology who is a tenured professor at a university across the country from where I live. I liked him because he wrote in a way that I felt challenged anthropological trends toward the philosophical and the excessively jargonistic. "Don't do your next project *in Belgium*."

I had to laugh, mostly because he said what so many people had told me about this project in its inception. The general theme was that nobody cares about what happens in a rich country that holds the record as one of the most brutal colonial empires ever to have existed. This fact alone makes it impossible to defend Belgium as a historical entity, but I have always wondered when anthropologists were ever in the business of defending any empire in the first place. It struck me that not studying people who lived in places that had once been oppressive regimes would be nearly impossible—not to mention a ridiculous position for a field whose earliest practitioners included folks who argued that "savagery, barbarism, and civilization" were the three bona fide phases of human development and, if properly understood, could be used as the basis for the reform of society.

Yet every grant proposal I wrote came back with the "Why Belgium?" question. And frankly, "Why Belgium?" is a legitimate question. Food waste is a global issue, and choosing a tiny nation where people assume that everyone has enough to eat seems strange. Indeed, there is a lot about Belgium that is strange, and especially the fact that its capital city is nothing like the rest of it. In my experiences of living and working back and forth between Brussels and the United States for six years, people in Belgium were keenly aware of how unlike the rest of their nation their capital city is—in terms of diversity, linguistic tensions, and even preferred fast food (kebab shops versus burger joints)—but most people I talked with about Belgium in the United States were not.

For this reason—and with the acknowledgment that the context of any research project always matters—specific details about the history and culture of Belgium matters just a little bit more. Therefore, to contextualize the food recirculation schemes treated in the subsequent chapters, in this one I offer three important things: the history of and current demographic statistics on immigrants in Belgium and Brussels, especially in relation to the legacy of

Belgium's colonial past; Brussels's and Belgium's current economic and employment conditions, especially in light of the 2008 recession and European austerity policies; and the history, structure, and extent of Belgium's social welfare program especially as it pertains to food resources in Brussels.

This is also important context given the European Union's attention to food waste in the wake of the release of the report by the Food and Agriculture Organization of the United Nations (Gustavsson et al., 2011). For example, I could have chosen any number of cities in which to conduct the project. I chose Brussels because in the summer of 2015 while I was exploring a project on human and nonhuman relations in a world-famous truffle restaurant there, I observed a vibrant, active local network of people working on the goal of reducing food waste by one specific and shared method: recirculating discarded but still edible food. These efforts were guided by different groups, logics, and modes, and yet were all accomplishing the task to different ends. It was this combination of a shared goal with unique methods for working toward it and diverse outcomes that suggested the grounds for an ideal comparative study. And comparative studies are the foundation of anthropological research. In the process of working with the three organizations highlighted in this study, I discovered that Brussels is not only a good place but a distinctively excellent one in which to observe and participate in food waste reduction initiatives. What follows, then, is an analysis of the context of my fieldwork so that you can see it, too: the crucial aspects of Brussels's history and economy that have made it the unusual city it is today, and a great window into food waste as a sociopolitical crisis that can, in fact, be managed.

To connect Belgium and its capital's history to the current efforts of its citizens to recirculate food waste in Brussels today, it is essential to understand how the Belgian government has been established and has evolved since Belgium became a nation in 1830. That setup is what makes Brussels a capital city four times over, what has allowed for a government with a giant superstructure and multiple avenues for social welfare funding, and what makes social welfare projects there easy to develop. In addition, the many divisions of the Belgian government, as I attempt to describe, allow for the creation of so many such offices. Of course, no offices of any kind would need to exist if there weren't people in this city who could benefit from such social services. To understand the need for the programs I immersed myself in, it is also crucial to understand the facts behind the current migration waves of peoples into Brussels as well as the way the prolonged European debt crisis continues to affect both the country and the city.

CONTINENTAL EUROPE

BELGIUM

The Southern Netherlands rebelled during the 1830 Belgian Revolution, establishing the modern Belgian state, officially recognized at the London Conference of 1830. The nation shares borders with Germany, Luxembourg, and France. Although the geographic size of the state of Maryland, its central location means that since its inception it has been an urban and economic nerve section of all of Europe. Map by Louis Bruges Davidson.

It is also crucial to understand the ways in which the nation's unique geography and history have set in motion the conditions for its current politics of food and waste. At 11,781 square miles, Belgium is about the size of the US state of Maryland, which makes it the fifth-smallest country in the European Union (behind Malta, Luxembourg, Cyprus, and Slovenia). It is both very old—archaeological records show that people have been living on this land since 20,000 B.C.—and very young, as it only became an independent state in 1830. It gets its name from a band of fierce Celtic warriors, the Belgae, who swept across Western Europe in 250 B.C., settling across the continent and in the British Isles, forging weapons from iron, building wooden boats, and trading with tribes on the Mediterranean Sea to the south. What the country is known for most of all on the global stage is its extraordinary history of occupations. I offer a brief historical snapshot of them below because it lays the groundwork for the food waste recirculation initiatives that exist today. This is not an exhaustive or encyclopedic account, by any means, but it is my own summary of the most important events that shape everyday politics in Belgium and especially in Brussels today. For legibility's sake, I have collected all the references for this brief note on Belgian history in the appendix rather than include citations here, and so encourage readers to investigate them.

Since its inception, Belgium has been invaded by the following peoples:

- The Romans. When Caesar invaded in 57 B.C., he wrote, "Of all the people of Gaul, the Belgae are the bravest." The Romans went on to dominate the lowlands of Europe for nearly five hundred years, during which they built roads linking Belgae to the rest of the empire and established Tongeren as the first Belgian city.

- The Frankish Germans. They spoke the Germanic language that is the root of the modern Dutch, and thus of Flemish. In the areas that retained Celtic culture and traditions, though, the Belgae were simultaneously developing a language that combined their own tongue with the Latin spoken by the Romans. This language would later evolve into French, which shows us how early the two distinct languages of Belgium were taking shape. During this time, the early fifth century, the Roman Empire began to crumble. As its troops pulled out, the Franks poured in, led by Claudine. His great-grandson, Clovis, inherited his land and became a powerful king who in 481 invaded Gaul and stretched his empire into Germany. During his rule, Celtic monks from Ireland and Scotland brought Christianity to Belgium. Clovis became the first Germanic king to convert to Christianity. Following him, Belgians converted in great numbers. Meatless Wednesdays and Fridays were widely introduced, along with the practice of keeping Lent. Clovis directed the construction of the first monasteries, convents, and abbeys, which have played important roles in everyday Belgian life ever since. Also in this period, the Cistercians became one of Belgium's largest religious orders. Cistercian monks took a vow of silence and spoke only when necessary and were known for their farming techniques, especially early hydraulic engineering. One branch of the Cistercians were the Trappists, who not only are still active in Belgium today but have become admired globally for their fine beer-making recipes and techniques.

- The Burgundians. In 1384, a royal family from Burgundy began to unite Belgium and the Netherlands into a single state. But these Burgundians had quite a different character from the Netherlandish. They were rich, and they lived opulently. To cement their rule, the Duke of Burgundy, Philip the Bold, married the daughter of the Count of Flanders. Family ties did not prevent Philip from leading his army against the Flemish, which allowed him to gain control of almost all of Flanders and inherit the title from his father-in-law. The "Great Dukes of the West," as the Burgundian princes were called, were effectively considered national sovereigns. The urban and other textile industries, which had developed in the Belgian territories since the twelfth century, became under the Burgundians the economic mainstay of northwestern Europe. Philip's rule marked the beginning of almost a century of peace, prosperity, and artistic achievement in the Low Countries, now referred to as the Burgundian Netherlands. Under Philip's successors, Belgium became one of the richest states in Europe. The most well-known of these rulers was Philip III, known as "Philip the Good," who ruled from 1419 to 1467. This Philip promoted the port of Antwerp as good for trading to merchants all over Europe, and his efforts paid off: by 1490, Antwerp was the commercial heart of Europe. But although Antwerp was economically important to his empire, Philip chose to hold court in Brussels, a move that foreshadowed Brussels's development as a seat of governance. Burgundian rule ended when Philip the Good's son Charles died in the Battle of Nancy while trying to siege the capital of Lorraine for the Burgundians. His heir and daughter Mary married Maximilian, a member of the powerful Austrian family Hapsburg. After Mary's death just a few years later, Maximilian tried to assert his control over the Low Countries. The Flemings in particular resisted Maximilian, but they could not hold him off. After a few years of struggle, Belgium became an official part of the Hapsburg Netherlands.

- The Spanish. Maximilian's grandson, Charles V, inherited the Burgundian lands from his father's family and the vast Spanish lands, which included territory in Italy and colonies in the New World, from his mother's. By 1520, Charles ruled over more than thirteen million Europeans. Charles was born in the city of Ghent and raised in the city of Mechelen, and so had a soft spot for Belgium. Under him, while Belgium was referred to as the Spanish Lowlands it became a hotbed for European art and learning. Religious conflicts plagued Charles. In 1517, the sect of Martin Luther broke away from the Roman Catholic Church. Belgium was caught in the middle of religious disputes raging across Europe, as the new Protestant religions were gaining strength in the lowlands. While Charles V was able to unite the Netherlands with Spain in 1519, his son Philip, a devout Catholic, assumed the throne in 1555, and religious warfare erupted. Unlike his father, Philip had no ties to the Low Countries and did not hesitate to use force against the Protestants. In 1567, while some nobles urged Spain to tolerate Protestants, Philip sent his army into Belgium. They arrested thousands and executed many. The lucky fled to Holland, where rebels were fighting for their independence from Spain. By 1579, the rebels had won, in the process forming the Netherlands. In the end, the Dutch republic was able to hold onto the northern provinces, which became the Netherlands, while the Spanish maintained control of the southern provinces, which (more or less) became today's Belgium. This period was pivotal for the city of Brussels, which began its rise to prominence after the Dutch revolt. Already a court city for royal families, it became a center of trade as well. When the revolts officially ended in 1585, Brussels became capital of the new region called the Spanish Netherlands. The Spanish rulers gave all Flemish Protestants remaining in the Belgium two years to settle their affairs and leave the country or face certain death. While most of Europe did not experience such intense religious conflict until the Thirty Years War began in 1618, in the Low Countries bloody battles had been going on for fifty years prior. Although the Netherlands became a nation in 1579, Spain would not recognize its independence until 1648.

- The Austrians. In 1695, French forces attacked the Netherlands to annex Belgium, bombarding Brussels and burning down the center of the city and its Grand Place in addition to more than four thousand homes. But the Dutch prevailed: by 1713 in the Peace of Utrecht, the French were to give up their claims to Belgium, while the Spanish were required to cede Belgium to the Austrian Empire. What had been the Spanish Netherlands became the Austrian Netherlands.

- The French. The French Revolution ended Europe's rule of kings. The Belgians felt the spirit of freedom. In 1790, the people proclaimed their independence from Austria and established the United States of Belgium. The Austrian army, however, quickly quashed their efforts. But only a few years later, in 1794, in a battle near Charleroi, French forces defeated the Austrians. The next year, France took control of Belgium. At first, many Belgians welcomed the French, but soon enough began to resent Napoleon's leadership. In 1815, joint forces from England and Prussia defeated Napoleon near the small Belgian town of Waterloo, just outside Brussels. Many Belgians thought they had won their independence in the process, but instead an alliance of European nations influenced mainly by Great Britain placed them under Dutch control.

- The Dutch. In 1830, the Belgians revolted against the Dutch, with the rebels defeating the Dutch forces in Brussels. The Belgians declared independence on October 4, 1830. To avoid another war, European superpowers recognized the new country in 1831; in February 1831, the leaders of Belgium passed the country's first constitution. For their constitutional monarchy, the Belgians chose as king Leopold I, a German prince and an uncle of England's Queen Victoria. In what historians have come to describe as a process of "casting about for nobility," the Belgians were strategic. They did not wish to choose a French person, because they felt the French had designs on their land; they did not wish to choose a Dutch person, because they were in the process of breaking from the Netherlands. Instead, they chose someone with royal ties and established relationships with important houses in Europe.

- The Germans. When World War I began in 1914, Belgium declared itself neutral. Germany ignored the proclamation, invading Belgium on its way to France. King Albert I, Leopold II's descendant, led troops in counterattacks. Some of the worst fighting in World War I took place around the Belgian city of Ypres; more than eighty thousand Belgians died before the war ended in 1918. One of the most famous battle poems of all time,

"In Flanders Fields" by John McCrae, commemorates soldiers who paid the ultimate price in those battles. After the war, the Belgians worked to rebuild their factories and increase farm production; nonetheless, the country entered an economic depression (much like the Great Depression in the United States), and then came World War II.

- During the second World War, Belgium was invaded by Germany twice, the worst on May 10, 1940. Hitler's troops waged an eighteen-day campaign, after which King Leopold III surrendered to their forces. Thousands of Belgians were imprisoned in a concentration camp in Breedonk; others became forced laborers of German factories. Belgian resistance groups helped to save downed American and British pilots. In September 1944, Allied forces drove the Germans out of Belgium, but the war was not over. In late December, Germany launched a last massive counterattack during which planes bombed Antwerp and Liege. In the forest of the Ardennes, German tanks struck hard in what became known as "the Battle of the Bulge" (because the Germans took control of a "bulge" of territory in an Allied region). The turning point of the battle came near the town of Bastogne, when a small US force held off the Germans until reinforcements arrived. The German region of Belgium, which is a small strip of land between the German border and the city of Liege with a population of approximately seventy thousand, was controlled by Nazi Germany during the war but returned to Belgian rule in 1944. Many of the German-speaking Belgians were later suspected of being traitors during the war. Although since the war the minority German-speaking Belgians have neither protested nor used politics to gain rights for their community, they have received many of the social and political privileges the Flemings and Walloons have. Since 1963, German has been Belgium's third official language.

- Immediately post–World War II, the Belgian monarchy was in trouble. King Leopold III had been criticized for his actions during the war. Some Belgians thought he had not done enough to resist the German invader; he was widely accused of being a Nazi sympathizer, and some factions demanded an end to the monarchy altogether. In 1951, Leopold stepped down as king. His son, Baudoin, took the throne on his twenty-first birthday. During the next forty-two years, Baudoin restored the honor of the Belgian monarchy. Fluent in both French and Flemish, he helped mitigate Belgium's age-old language conflicts. The country once again became a center of industry and trade for Europe. Membership in the first of two new international organizations added to the country's status: NATO, a military alliance created by the United States, which it joined in 1949.

Running counter to this dizzying array of occupations is Belgium's own history not as the occupied but as the occupier. In 1835, Belgium's King Leopold proved good for the new Belgian economy, leading the nation's railway development. In 1883, Leopold's successor, his son, Leopold II, hired the Welsh explorer Sir Henry Morton Stanley, who had failed to get support from the British government to develop the Congo region himself, to set up a Belgian colony in central Africa. The idea was to export and exploit cocoa (and other) crops. The US Senate adopted a resolution in support of Leopold's eventual claim to the Congolese territory. By 1885, the "Congo Free State" (later the "Belgian Congo") was established. Rather than control the Congo as a colony, though, as other European powers did throughout Africa, Leopold II arranged to privately "own" the region, chiefly by financing development projects with money loaned to him from the Belgian government. For eighty years, the Belgians exercised destructive colonial rule over a landmass seventy-five times its size, while the Congo proved to be a tremendous asset to the economy by sending valuable natural resources such as ivory, minerals, and rubber into Belgium. It was also a human rights catastrophe. While Belgian industries from chocolate to diamonds developed and then prospered thanks to Congolese imports, entire Congolese villages were dragooned into manual labor tasks including tapping rubber, and if they refused to comply, or complied but failed to meet quotas, people were brutally punished by having limbs amputated. The hands of dead Congolese were severed and kept by militias to account to their quartermasters for spent ammunition.

Several rebellions staged by Congolese were successfully put down by Leopold's armies. By far the greatest number of deaths, however, were caused by sickness and starvation. The savagery resulted in what most historians estimate as the loss of ten million Congolese lives. Leopold, who himself never once set foot in Congo, funneled profits into building monuments, parks, and buildings in Brussels. However, as the suffering in the Congo became known and reported on publicly and globally in presses around the world, demonstrations and protests both in Belgium and around the globe virtually forced Leopold to end the occupation. In 1908 and due to intense international pressure, the king turned the Congo over to the country of Belgium. The "Belgian

Congo" remained a colony until the Democratic Republic of Congo (DRC) gained independence in 1960.

Even then, it was not a peaceful transition. In the months leading up to independence, the Congolese had elected a president, Joseph Kasavubu, and a prime minister, Patrice Lumumba, in addition to a senate and to other governing bodies throughout the Congo's provinces. In the United States, the Eisenhower administration had high hopes that the Republic of the Congo would form a stable, pro-Western, central government, but in a matter of days the situation on the ground in the newly independent nation descended into chaos. On July 5, Congolese soldiers in the Force Publique mutinied against their white Belgian commanders at the Thysville military base, demanding increased authority. Violence soon broke out across the nation as thousands of Europeans (primarily Belgians) fled, and stories of atrocities against whites surfaced in newspapers around the globe. Unable to control the Indigenous Congolese National Army, the Belgians sent troops to restore order but without seeking permission to do so from the new Congolese government. In response, the Congolese government appealed directly to the United Nations, demanding the removal of the Belgians. On July 13, the United Nations approved creation of an intervention force, the Organisations des Nations Unies au Congo (ONUC), and called for the withdrawal of all Belgian troops (Haskin, 2005, 101).

On October 15, 2018, Belgian voters made history in electing their first-ever Black mayor, Pierre Kompany, a Congolese refugee who fled the DRC with his family in 1975 to lead the commune of Gashoren, an overwhelmingly white community. Kompany drove a taxi to support himself while he studied for an engineering degree and became a Belgian citizen. His son is an international soccer star who plays in Manchester, England, as well as on the Belgian national team. Kompany's platform included policies directed at supporting social welfare reform in favor of the elderly, expanding daycare availability, and improving commune soccer fields. Only a handful of people with sub-Saharan roots have ever been elected to offices in Belgium, including two women who won seats on city councils in the same election cycle as Kompany. "I think one has to regard this as a victory for humanity as a whole," Kompany told the *New York Times*.

Today's Belgium reflects influences of all these historical developments, and more that I didn't mention. It remains both a constitutional monarchy and a federal state; it has a king (largely ceremonial) and a parliament (sometimes functional). The nation's official internal borders divide it into three regions: Flanders, Wallonia, and the Brussels-Capital Region. These regions have considerable powers: each has its own economic, trade, employment, housing, agriculture, environment, energy, and transport policies, while the federal state takes care of foreign affairs, defense, justice, health, and social security. In addition, the population of Belgium is divided into three linguistic communities: in the north is the Flemish-speaking community, which constitutes more than half of Belgium's population (the language is the equivalent of a local dialectic of Dutch); in the south is the French-speaking community of Wallonia; and on the eastern border of Belgium where it connects to Germany is the smallest language community, which consists of several communes whose official language remains German. The city of Brussels is officially bilingual, although most of the population is French speaking. Why the division into language communities matters when it comes to social welfare is because fiscal support for education, health care, and cultural initiatives are in fact the responsibility of the language communities, and each one of them has a separate administration.

Finally, each region has its own communes, or local municipal authorities. There are 581 of these, with 300 Flemish communes spread over five provinces, 262 communes spread over five provinces, and, in the Brussels-Capital Region, 19 communes. I have heard many Belgian politicians reference "communal autonomy," but that does not mean that the local politicians can do anything they like—merely that they can exercise powers over local issues like when and how often the recycling is collected. That said, local communes have an impressive range of services, including regulating matters as diverse as public parks, street-cleaning services, local tax regulations, local voting and polling initiatives, and key to this study, the administration of social welfare services (for which they work with the language communities). Simply put, the commune is the political body that is closest to a citizen's everyday life.

The linguistic tensions are the single biggest political issue the nation faces, and it has been this way since the beginning. About one-tenth of the Belgian population is bilingual, but a majority has a working knowledge of both French and Flemish. On the ground level in my experience and based on my interviews and observances, what that looks like in Brussels is that everyone speaks French; native Flemish speakers are in the serious minority. This is a historical fact: as the new capital, Brussels experienced a population explosion. In 1830 Brussels had 50,000 inhabitants; in 1875 it had grown to 250,000; in 1914 to 750,000, and in 2022 reached 1.22 million, a slight increase from the previous year and the highest in the recorded period ("United Nations, Department of Economic and Social Affairs," 2022). As the political and economic center of the nation, Brussels had a French-speaking upper and middle class, and because primary and secondary education was only provided in French, the French language gradually came to permeate the lower social classes. Many immigrants to the city whose families came from Flanders were forced to speak French if they wanted to climb the social and economic ladders, which I heard both anecdotally from many people I interviewed and which is substantiated in the historical record. This caused what the Flemish refer to as the "French-ification" of Brussels, and which remains true today: although there are more Flemish speakers in the nation than French speakers, there are far more French speakers than Flemish speakers in Brussels. A lot of Flemish people are not only keenly aware of this but annoyed about it, and their annoyance in turn annoys the French. This is such an established truth that Babbel, the German-based language-learning subscription service, learning software, and e-learning platform, publishes this on its website:

> There's one thing concerning the languages spoken in Belgium we can't stress enough: If you are in Wallonia, you should *never* address anyone in Flemish right off the bat. Not only is there a great chance that you won't be understood (knowledge of Flemish among French-speaking Belgians is low), but you will also likely be met with silence. Likewise, if you are in Flanders then you should refrain from addressing people in French (despite knowledge of French being very high in this region). Such is the resolve of the two groups to protect the status of their respective mother tongues. Neither the Walloons nor the Flemish take kindly to being addressed by strangers on the street in the "wrong" language. (Sumner, 2022)

Brussels is not only exceptional in terms of its linguistic tensions; it is exceptional in almost every other way, too. The largest city in Belgium, since the heyday of Bruges and Antwerp in the Middle Ages, it has been the country's center of commerce, industry, and intellectual life. It is a four-time capital: capital city of the country of Belgium, capital of the government of the Flanders region, capital of the Brussels-Capital Region's nineteen communes, and de facto capital of the European Union. It is also home to embassies and consulates of most of the world's countries, to offices housing delegations from most of Europe's major substate regions (e.g., Catalonia and Bavaria), and to more than one thousand nongovernmental organizations associated with the United Nations. Although far more Bruxelloises speak French than Flemish, Brussels is the capital of Flanders, and although since 1980 when Brussels was declared a bilingual city, and all street signs and restaurant menus were required to be printed in two languages, 80 percent of the city's population speaks French as the primary language. "The Francization of Brussels," as the evolution of the French language in the city despite the fact that it was historically Dutch-speaking is referred, is fascinating and has to do with immigration patterns; what it has to do with this study is that it emphasizes the internal political tensions and tangents of power that run through Brussels and that must be contended with in order to address any political issue, great or small. For instance, it comes into play when food waste recirculation efforts are concerned because the separation of resources according to linguistic communities within the city means that organizations that can communicate in both languages have twice as many chances to get funding from an already-large pool of organizations working to address food waste.

This alone should have been a great justification for conducting my research in Belgium and particularly in Brussels. However, few anthropologists have historically been interested in the nation beyond its role and terrible legacy as the colonizers of the Congo. I could find very few studies situated in Belgium, with a couple of notable exceptions. Sociologist Renée C. Fox offers a functionalist perspective on ways in which divisions of language and class affect local social life in Belgium (1978), which she followed with a memoir of her thirty-five years spent researching Belgians, *In the Belgian Château* (1994). Second, Marc Blainey, a scholar of Indigenous American societies, argued in an article in *American Ethnologist* for the need for more ethnographic research to be conducted . . . in Belgium, especially if ethnographers wish to apprehend the ways in which "enduring linguistic-cultural discord parallels a broader rift that has long existed across the European continent" (2016, 480).[1]

Even less than the little scholarly attention that has been paid to Belgium has been paid to Brussels. And yet here is a city overflowing with tensions over the sorts of issues anthropologists care about, especially those having to do with equity, labor, and belonging. I asked Filip De Boeck, a renowned anthropologist of the Congo and theories of postcolonial identity and memory in Africa, about this. De Boeck is a Brussels native and a lifelong resident. "I have always wondered about why anthropologists don't study Belgians, too," he said. "Perhaps we are just too easy to overlook. And perhaps we should keep it that way" (De Boeck, 2017). I agree with him about the potential merits of being undervalued and quietly overachieving, but I also think such misperceptions of Belgium come with consequences. In my view, ignoring this city means ignoring the full measure of Europe's role in global affairs.

It is not only stereotypes that detract from taking Belgium seriously; there are more than a few operational data of the nation's governmental malfunctions, and plenty of European historians and media analysts at the ready to point out each instance. As the Belgian political scientists Lieven De Winter and Kris Deschouwer wrote in an essay that became a contribution to a collection called *Où va La Belgique: Les Soubresauts d'une Petite Démocratie Européenne?* (Whither Belgium: The Upheavals of a Small European Democracy?), coming late to statehood when it did has done Belgium no favors in terms of establishing legitimacy either globally or locally. When Belgium declared its independence from the Dutch and became a nation in 1830, it did so as a kind of cultural mash-up—an "artificial country" composed of Flanders, where people speak Flemish and share common ancestors and some cultural customs with the Dutch, and Wallonia, where people speak French and share some common ancestors and some cultural customs with the French.

How these two sides ever came to agree on anything is mysterious, especially since both misunderstood the other's aims from the beginning. A rough summary of how it happened—if not exactly why—is that the original idea for Belgium to separate from the Netherlands was an impulsive move on the part of a group of Belgian elites who were exasperated by the Calvinist domination. Following that, the new Belgium was initially a homogeneous Catholic state. However, this irritated the liberal elites, who supported the creation of Belgium because they hoped to create a more democratic regime specifically by ridding themselves of the burden of the Dutch administrative language that had been imposed on them. Even if this aspiration of a linguistic nature was shared by both Catholics and liberals, De Winter and Deschouwer note that the factions quickly realized that they each envisaged a very different Belgian state, such that "the Church clings to its power as Liberals attempt to secularize state and society" (1989, 141). For though Belgium's liberal elite threw off Dutch rule in 1830, they could neither uproot nor supplant attachments to the Catholic Church or the Dutch language. Thus, the formal structure of the Belgian state existed—but was still deeply ensconced in the cultural, social, and welfare structures of the church, which now became what the authors call a "state within a state." That was eventually followed by the development of a socialist/labor movement, which came with its own rival structures for mutual aid assurance, cultural associations, the French language, and even newspapers—in some cases, all under one roof, like in the grand Bond Moyson Building on Ghent's Vrijdagmarkt.

Then a third faction emerged. Situating itself against both the Christian Democrats and the liberal socialists were the anticlerical and middle-class liberals, who constituted the third corner in Belgium's political triangle. They did not have the same popular support, or the equivalent social structures, but they did succeed in creating a world within a world, with *their* own political parties, cultural centers, and, yes, newspapers.

What these party divisions yielded was nothing less than a formal state that developed its services—education, health care, and other expressions of the welfare state—not only including but using the structures of its political parties. De Winter and Deschouwer delineate the ways in which these parties then came to assert control over public services funding and to extend their influences across semipublic and quasi-autonomous organizations, too, ranging from holding sway over who got the job of administering a publicly run kindergarten program to who became the CEO of Sabena, the now-defunct national airline. The bottom line is that the history of the subdivisions in the Belgian state mirrors a subdivision of Belgian culture and society; of course, these divisions then affect everyday life in Belgium in many ways, but especially in terms of how citizens access public services. As the state is divided into regions and communes, access to the state is through these very divisions. And right in the middle of the divisions sits an array of political parties, which means that political patronage in Belgium is more than a typical case of "government by parties," because the parties do more than exercise a predominant influence in the process of making government policies: "Political parties have also invaded, in depth and breadth, the public sector." In other words, Belgium has been and remains haunted by intense parochialism, which they describe as "the feeling of belonging to a very local entity" and the sense among its people as experiencing not new but already-existing allegiances; if you want political power, you must be willing to exchange access to goods and services for support (1989, 140).

Note that there have been attempts at reforms—mostly in the form of revisions to the constitution, which has been amended four times between 1970 and 1993. These reforms have been in all cases designed to accommodate religious differences and reduce tensions between the language communities. Birnbaum notes that in many cases those reforms involved "formalizing the division of spoils," which only further instantiated systems of patronage, for instance, to allocate control of certain jobs between different political parties. This shows that Belgium's linguistic differences continue to add extra layers of complexity to the allocation of public services, particularly in and around Brussels, which was first designated as a bilingual region in 1962 (its borders and bilingual status were reconfirmed most recently in 1989). Parallel structures were created to cater to the different language groups.

The myriad of regions, languages, communes, and governments that form the loose union of a nation support all descriptions of the "artificiality" of the Belgian state. The lack of national identity that such "artificiality" produced is the reason, I believe, that Brussels was easy for international policymakers to select as de facto capital for the European Union. After all, most Belgians in both the regions of Wallonia and Flanders feel far more loyal to their like-speaking locals than to "Belgians" as a whole. From the outside, it often feels like a state that has never really come together (Bailey, 1972). That Belgium is not a nation with a tremendous identity of its own, let alone a felt sense of national pride, is not a new theory, of course. It's been in circulation at least since the days of Austrian parliamentarian Franz Joseph, prince of Dietrichstein (1767–1854), who termed Belgium "a political attempt rather than an observable political reality" (Belien, 2005).

Such constructivist views remain alive today and are often repurposed by both policymakers and journalists—often as derogatory, yet sometimes as evidence for how good Belgium is at integrating people from a wide variety of backgrounds. This logic holds that since being "a Belgian" is not a particularly meaningful category to most Belgians—Blainey argues that Belgium only exists at all thanks to "a mutual rejection of a coherent Belgian inheritance that unites many Flemings and Walloons alike"—it is relatively easy for newcomers to establish themselves (2016, 481). Note that in my observations of social activities in the nineteen communes that constitute Brussels, being good at integrating people from disparate backgrounds often simply means tolerating their presences. In other words, most people I saw living and working in Brussels seem not to care if newcomers can trace their heritages to these lands or not, a quality that apparently can be easily mistaken for promotion of diversity.

Yet even if longtime citizens don't actively encourage people from diverse backgrounds to move to Brussels, no one can deny the fact that it has become, since World War II and as Belgian prime minister Wilfried Martens described it, "the prototype of Europe": "The Federal Belgian State is a prefiguration of a Europe of Peoples, united in their organized diversity," he said (Rodriguez, 2007). In fact, Brussels is recognized today as one of the most diverse cities in the world, "the beating heart of multiculturalism in Europe," as it has been depicted in the French press, who support the claim with the evidence that 180 nationalities and one hundred languages thrive within city borders (Bourgeois, 2018). Further is the fact that close to half of the 1.1 million documented residents of the city today were born elsewhere, mostly in Turkey and Africa, specifically Morocco. This diversity alone would have been a good reason to make Brussels the capital of the European Union, but in fact it had nothing to do with it. Brussels did not become the capital of the European Union as part of any strategic leadership decision or as the result of a heated battle among other cities for the honor. Rather, it happened through a series of political and financial alignments that began in the ashes of World War II.

To set the stage, and as I mentioned earlier in this chapter in the list of Belgium's magnificent history as occupied land, it is crucial when considering how Belgium changed after World War II to recall that the Belgian royal family is not in fact made up of Belgians. When the state was formed in 1831, local dignitaries and elected officials formed the government as a "constitutional parliamentary monarchy" alongside the principle of ministerial responsibility. This means that although there is a king, the elected prime minister and his cabinet of ministers are responsible for the legislative and executive acts; according to the official online portal of the Belgian government, maintained by the Federal Public Service (FPS) Chancellery of the Prime Minister and the FPS Policy and Support in cooperation with Regional and Community public services offices. The king "serves as the symbol of unity and permanence of the nation" and swears an oath "to maintain the national independence and the integrity of the territory" (Belgium Federal Government Informational Website, n.d.) But how does a newly formed nation acquire royalty?

Its founding politicians determined that a royal family would legitimize their new nation and help become a global power. However, they were wary of selecting existing royal lineage from France or the Netherlands, because they felt such a decision might leave them vulnerable to future occupation. So, the National Congress of Belgium chose a German prince with close ties to the British monarchy instead; a choice that felt safe, did not seem to threaten the European balance of power created in 1815 by the Congress of Vienna, and yet felt sufficiently "royal." Prince Leopold of Saxe-Coburg, the fourth son of Francis, duke of Saxe-Coburg-Saalfeld, who served with the allies against Napoleon's forces during the Napoleonic Wars, was the uncle of England's Queen Victoria, and had previously turned down an invitation to be the king of Greece, became the first king to be chosen directly by the elected representatives of a nation. In fact, rather than be known as "King of Belgium," the Belgian crown's official title is "King of the Belgians." History knows Leopold I for two things: fighting off, with the assistance of France and England, the attack attempts of William I of the Netherlands (who refused until 1839 to recognize Belgium as an independent nation) and using marriages to strengthen Belgium's political position in the world (he himself married the daughter of French king Louis-Philippe, and one of his daughters married the archduke of Austria).

By the time World War II was over, Belgium was on to its third Leopold (there had been an Albert in between). When the war initially broke out, Belgium declared itself neutral, a position strongly supported by the king himself, who expressed wishes to keep his nation out of the conflict. Alas, he couldn't. On May 10, 1940, German troops invaded Belgium, the Netherlands, Luxembourg, and France. While the entire civil government fled to Paris and later to London, Leopold chose to remain in Brussels and surrender to Hitler's Wehrmacht—against the advice of his parliament, who urged him not to do so and attempted to remind him capitulation was a governmental and not a monarchical decision. The Belgian government, in France, stripped him of his constitutional powers. It was not just his ministers whom Leopold upset; Winston Churchill was furious with him, declaring the following in the House of Commons on June 4, 1940: "At the last moment when Belgium was already invaded, King Leopold called upon us to come to his aid, and even at the last moment we came. He and his brave, efficient army, nearly half a million strong, guarded our left flank and thus kept open our only line of retreat to the sea. Suddenly, without prior consultation, with the least possible notice, without the advice of his ministers and upon his own personal act, he sent a plenipotentiary to the German Command, surrendered his army and exposed our whole flank and means of retreat" (Stengers, 1980, 28).

Initially this was a wildly divisive series of events. While some Belgians viewed Leopold's decision as one that prevented further humanitarian disasters and lives lost in Belgium itself, others were quick to brand Leopold as a Nazi sympathizer and even quicker to remind the public that during the war he had in fact personally visited Adolf Hitler in Berchtesgaden. In hindsight, what it all amounts to is the fact that Leopold, perhaps given his own personal politics and certainly given his bloodline, picked the wrong side. A few months in advance of when Allied forces entered Belgium on September 2, 1944, Hitler had ordered Leopold and the rest of the Belgian royal family to be deported to Germany, where they were put up in castles in Saxony and then Austria. By the time Belgium was officially liberated in February of 1945, American forces found the Belgian royal family in Strobl guarded by about seventy *Waffen-SS* with watchdogs, surrounded by a high fence with barbed wire: "The news that Germany had surrendered unconditionally the same day may have reached them in time. After lining up before their former captives and the American liberators, they made the Nazi salute and were quickly put on trucks and led away" (Vanderstappen, 2017).

How to proceed became known as "the royal question" throughout Belgium, with other world leaders, many of whom had decried Leopold's decisions, watching carefully. In the interim, the king's brother Charles was appointed as regent, a title designated for ceremonial purposes only; the king agreed not to return due to political unrest, and a date for a public referendum was set (Vanderstappen, 2017). Overall, 58 percent voted in favor of the king. However, most of these votes came from the Catholic Party, and the regions were sharply divided: in Flanders, 78 percent said yes; in Brussels, 48 percent; and in Wallonia, 42 percent. Parliament thus allowed the king to return home, but the country itself was on the brink of a civil war. As Van den Dungen, the rector of the Free University of Brussels, wrote to Leopold on June 25, 1945: "The question is not if the accusations against you are right or not [but that...] you are no longer a symbol of Belgian unity" (Velaers & Van Goethem, 1994). The day Leopold returned home, July 22, 1950, one of the most violent protests in the nation's history occurred in the city of Liege, in which three protesters were killed when the police opened fire (Destatte, 1997, 235). To avoid tearing the nation apart and in the face of Wallonian threats to abandon Belgium in favor of France, Leopold abdicated on July 16, 1951, in favor of his son Baudouin.

While Leopold traveled the world, often collecting geological specimens and acting as amateur zoologist (two species of reptiles are named after him) and speaking out politically in favor of authoritarian causes (while visiting Senegal he strongly criticized the French decolonization process), Belgium was a mess, and Europe remained reeling from the destruction of the war (Hochschild, 1998). It was a moment ripe for a stabilizing force, and Jean-Baptiste Nicolas Robert Schuman (1886–1963) was just the man to lead the way. Twice the prime minister of France in addition to having been France's minister of finance as well as its foreign minister, the Luxembourg-born Schuman was a dominant political figure in Europe, and he had a backstory to match. Before he entered politics, he had been an attorney; during the war, he was arrested by the German Gestapo in 1940, escaped in 1942, and worked for the Résistance until France was liberated in 1944. After becoming a statesman, he published the "Schuman Plan" in 1949, with his vision of promoting a Franco-German rapprochement, leaning heavily on anti-nationalist ideals, and promoting a spirit of collaboration. As he described it in a speech delivered in Strasbourg on May 6, 1949,

> We are carrying out a great experiment, the fulfillment of the same recurrent dream that for ten centuries has revisited the peoples of Europe: creating between them an organization putting an end to war

and guaranteeing an eternal peace. The Roman church of the Middle Ages failed finally in its attempts that were inspired by humane and human preoccupations. Another idea, that of a world empire constituted under the auspices of German emperors was less disinterested; it already relied on the unacceptable pretensions of a "Führertum" (domination by dictatorship) whose "charms" we have all experienced.

Audacious minds, such as Dante, Erasmus, Abbé de St. Pierre, Rousseau, Kant and Proudhon, had created in the abstract the framework for systems that were both ingenious and generous. The title of one of these systems became the synonym of all that is impractical: *Utopia*, itself a work of genius, written by Thomas More, the Chancellor of Henry VIII, King of England.

The European spirit signifies being conscious of belonging to a cultural family and to have a willingness to serve that community in the spirit of total mutuality, without any hidden motives of hegemony or the selfish exploitation of others. The 19th century saw feudal ideas being opposed and, with the rise of a national spirit, nationalities asserting themselves. Our century, that has witnessed the catastrophes resulting in the unending clash of nationalities and nationalisms, must attempt and succeed in reconciling nations in a supranational association. This would safeguard the diversities and aspirations of each nation while coordinating them in the same manner as the regions are coordinated within the unity of the nation. (Schuman, 1950)

Schuman's plan was subsequently used as the foundation for the European Union when Belgium, France, Germany, Luxemburg, Italy, and the Netherlands agreed. For it, Schuman would go on to become one of the most influential figures in the shaping of modern Europe, often referred to today as "the Father of Europe," based on this declaration. Of course, the heart of his argument was that European countries should come together to control their coal and steel industries. His position was that this step would ensure the greater financial benefit of all involved. Schuman could not have been a better person to articulate a strong economic position, considering how deeply respected he was as a political leader: Accordingly, and by 1951, all the European allies had signed the Treaty of Paris, which established the European Coal and Steel Community. A few years later, in March 1957, the Treaty of Rome built upon Schuman's vision by establishing the European Economic Community and the European Community for Atomic Energy.

Now that there were real financial stakes at play, policymakers realized the need for a headquarters and nominated several cities to host the new initiatives. From the beginning, Brussels was included, but consensus among members, all of whom supported their own hometowns first, could not be reached. The failure to compromise worked in Brussels's favor. By January 1, 1958, when the first *fonctionnaires* (civil servants) had been hired and the institutions were set to start operating, a decision had still not been made. An emergency meeting held among representatives from all member nations was held in Paris, after which it was concluded that the institutions would be chaired in turn by the ministers of each of the six member states. The EU capital would rotate, all agreed. Based on alphabetical order, Belgium would go first. In this case, going first also turned out to mean going last. Whether due to inertia or what some historians have called "a massive snowball process," no one mounted a campaign to move the proceedings, except, most memorably, Charles de Gaulle in 1962, and even he couldn't muster the support to do it; therefore and henceforth, Brussels's entrenchment as EU capital was complete (Van Parijs, 2014).

Since the beginning of the European Union's life as a global institution, the goal of the European Union's founders in the decades following the devastation and suffering of World War II was to build a new idea of the Old Empire, or as the charter put it, "an ever-closer union" that would be tied together through economic and political integration, as well as a shared set of values about the importance of social welfare (Fimister, 2008). The commitment to supporting governments that would in turn aid individuals and families in need was baked into the very foundation of the new alliance. The new Europe would be one providing social welfare in the form of publicly accessible health care, housing, and other programs geared toward assisting the poor, unemployed, and marginalized in society. Many theorists have argued that Europeans felt a responsibility to atone for their colonial pasts, and the social welfare state's existence was their answer (Obinger et al., 2022; Taylor-Gooby, 2004). Despite the turmoil associated with various global events over the subsequent years, including the European debt crisis of 2008, the most recent large-scale public surveys conducted across member countries still show that Europeans still believe in the goals upon which the European Union was founded, especially promoting peace and economic unity throughout the regions (Wike et al., 2019).

However, over the course of the last few years in the wake of financial and immigration challenges, that perception of what the welfare state can achieve outside of the European Union is changing. If discourse in *New York Times* headlines is a measure, right now Europe is experiencing "crisis." In 2019, 972 articles proclaimed it so, focusing on, among other topics, the ongoing struggles of Brexit; the yellow vest movement in France; migration patterns into the continent from citizens of African countries who arrive seeking asylum, such as the many Rwandans trapped in Libya hoping to reach Italian shores; and the threat of a global recession. This last has become a deeply moral concern, highlighted in May 2019 by Pope Francis's visit to Bulgaria, the poorest nation in the European Union, during which he spread his message to all Catholics warning them against turning their back on immigrants. The Pope compared their perilous journeys to Europe to the suffering of Christ and said the immigrants bore the "cross of humanity" (Dzhambazova, 2019). Perhaps unsurprisingly, some Bulgarians strongly disagreed, including a high-ranking bishop in the Bulgarian branch of the Russian Orthodox Church, Metropolitan Nikolai, who dismissed the Pope's visit as "political" and condemned his comments). If nothing else, the Pope shed light on the fact that the uptick in migration patterns brought with it dramatic change to European politics and contributed perhaps more than anything else to the rise of anti-migrant force in Europe and elsewhere.

These events show that for even an idea as seemingly equity based as the social welfare state, time marches on—and attempts to update with the original formula are not only smart but required. Since the end of the Cold War and rise of the European Union, member countries have seemed to be among the most stable in the world, and yet such immigration patterns challenge not only a global imaginary of European life as welfare-minded and "progressive" but also the weft and weave of everyday life, from working conditions and access to health care and food to aspirations and imaginations for what the future holds.[2] Wealthy countries like Belgium that for decades enjoyed stellar reputations around the world for their livability and impressive array of resources for citizens have had to adjust policies and practices to keep up with not only immigration but various economic transitions.

Taking keen notice of this are scholars across disciplines. Some historians and anthropologists especially have become interested not only in the lives of those peoples colonized by Europeans but also in the ways in which European colonization and annexation of territories have affected the everyday lives of Europeans themselves. For example, in *Tight Knit: Global Families and the Social Life of Fast Fashion*, Elizabeth Krause explores the tensions—over family, capital, forms of ownership, and craft production—at play in the historic hub of textile production in Prato, Tuscany, as the "Made in Italy" label designation becomes a global phenomenon and Chinese migrants to Italy now work in factories that were once owned by local families. In exploring the ethics of fast fashion, Krause also explores the question of belonging in contemporary European life (2018).

In this project, I have sought to investigate the everyday processes of eating and procuring food in Brussels during a time when the city's political arrangements and demographics have been upended by global economic events. In discovering and then volunteering with a network of people working to recirculate food waste, I saw a whole lot of food being moved from institutions in which it was deemed unsellable and into ones in which it was conceived of as highly useful. This "food journey" I beheld was new to me, but I discovered that it wasn't new to European everyday experiences. In fact, from the beginning of the European Union's existence, its policies as set by Schuman have laid the groundwork for the existence of precisely this kind of network. As I noted in the previous chapter, after the FAO "alarm bell" report about food waste was released in 2011, the European Union compelled its members to tackle the problem, which was identified as being twofold. The first is economic and related to hunger: disposal of food waste in the European Union costs an estimated €143 billion (US$153 billion) per year (European Commission Special Report, 2019). This is food that activists argue could feed the fifty-five million people living in food poverty in Europe more than nine times over (Bacchi, 2017). The second is environmental and related to climate change and sustainability: the production and disposal of EU food waste leads to the emission of 170 million metric tons of carbon dioxide, which accelerates global climate change (Zweynert, 2017). Although there is not uniform data collection across the EU member countries, the data that emerged from an EU-wide study published in 2013 identified the Netherlands, Belgium, Cyprus, and Estonia as the largest food wasters among member states, and that food waste in the bloc on a whole is estimated to total 173 kg (381 lbs) per person per year, almost two and half times the average weight of an EU citizen (Zweynert, 2017). Given these findings, EU policymakers began focusing their initial efforts on reducing waste in the largest sector of food distribution: supermarket chains. In 2015 the European Union began to institute a compulsory policy for supermarkets to donate all edible but unsellable food or face huge fines, identifying food waste as a "key priority" in the European Union's "Circular Economy Package," a then-new legal framework designed to foster sustainable growth throughout the union (Larmer, 2018). This package also set forth the European Union's commitment to halve, by 2030, an estimated eighty-eight million metric tons of food waste generated annually in the European Union. Simply put, this project could not have existed without that piece of policy, because its ripple effect into everyday life in Brussels changed the shape of food waste on the ground almost overnight: what was once reserved for a handful of dumpster divers around the city became the material for building a new infrastructure of food distribution.

Note that this wasn't the case only for Belgium. Although all the European Union's member countries have had to comply with these new policies, the European Union provided neither a roadmap nor a funding guide for how to accomplish the goal it set. Instead, each state has been on its own to sort out a solution, and, predictably there has been a wide range of approaches. For example, in Germany increased support for food banks has been the main answer. However, with the rising number of migrant clients, some of the charitable food organizations decided to prioritize German citizens and not allow foreigners to sign up for aid, setting off ongoing national debates on refugees and poverty (Schuetze, 2018). By contrast, the French government has moved beyond regulating supermarkets from discarding food and now requires *all* food vendors to earmark surplus products for charities or face fines (Beardsley, 2018). In Poland, a country solely responsible for 10 percent of the European Union's total food waste, the government has been slow to institute the proposed VAT tax reforms for recirculated foodstuffs, which so far has kept many supermarkets and restaurants from participating in the recirculation efforts (Zimmermann, 2021; Figurska, 2022).

Belgium typically ranks among both the European Union's wealthiest countries and its most socially progressive, which are sources of local pride; as one EU official noted in conversation with me, neither its leaders nor its general populace liked being high on the list of countries that waste a lot of food. That's why by 2016, the Belgian federal government, the Brussels-Capital Region, and each of the Capital Region's nineteen communes had all established their own food waste reduction platforms—which means that at every level of the Belgian government from the most national to the most local, there were new strategic food waste reduction goals. These goals lead directly to the creation of new government grants specifically earmarked for food waste reduction projects. My research offers three examples of institutions that benefited directly from these new policy directives and the attendant funding opportunities.

As I came to learn, the complexity of Belgium's government often makes it hard for politicians to get things done. For example, this is how hard it can be: From May 2010 until December 2011, Belgium went 589 days without an elected government. This occurred after a national election failed to produce a parliamentary majority, and while the leading parties in Flanders and Wallonia refused to form a coalition and remained locked in a stalemate. It set a world record for the country in existence the longest without a formal government; instead, a temporary caretaker government functioned during the crisis. As former *Washington Post* European bureau chief Michael Birnbaum

THE 19 COMMUNES OF BRUSSELS

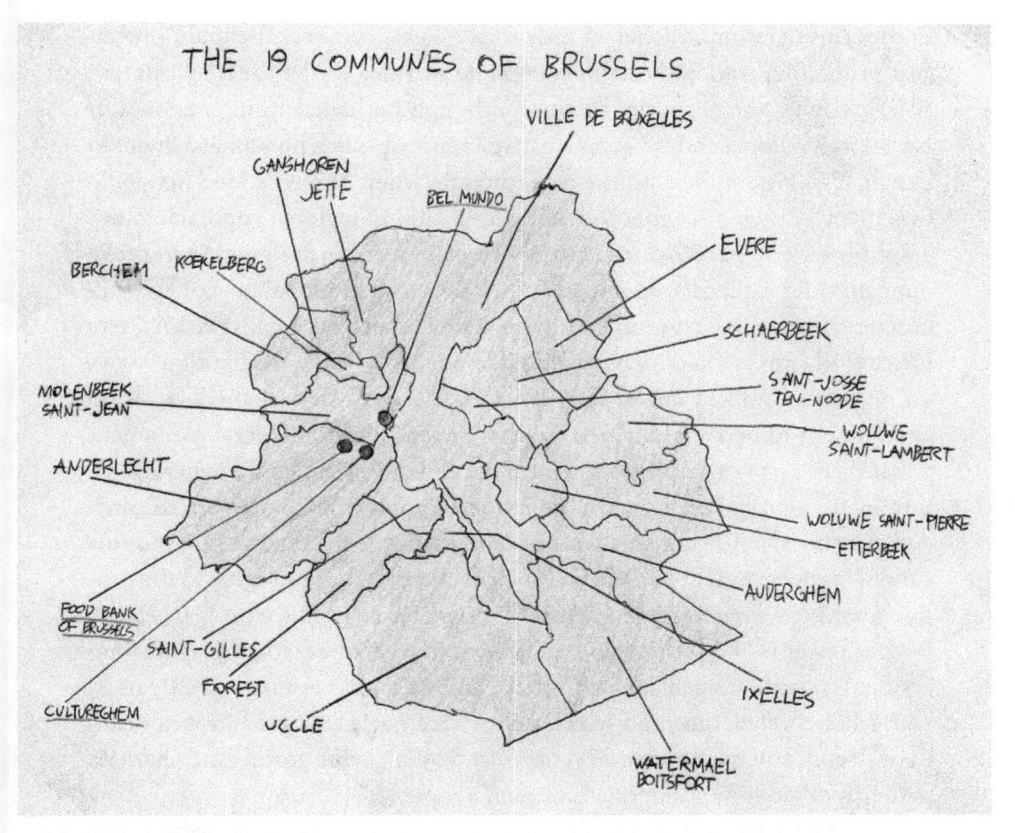

[Map of Brussels showing the 19 communes with labels: Ville de Bruxelles, Ganshoren, Jette, Bel Mundo, Evere, Berchem, Koekelberg, Schaerbeek, Molenbeek Saint-Jean, Saint-Josse Ten-Noode, Woluwe Saint-Lambert, Anderlecht, Woluwe Saint-Pierre, Etterbeek, Auderghem, Food Bank of Brussels, Saint-Gilles, Forest, Ixelles, Cultureghem, Uccle, Watermael Boitsfort]

In Brussels, the level of civic administration that is closest to the individual is the commune. The city's nineteen communes constitute the most local level of authority, administering traffic, fire safety, and, crucial to this project, social services. Most food waste recirculation in the city is concentrated in the poorer pockets of Molenbeek and Anderlecht. Map by Louis Bruges Davidson.

described a subsequent stalemate in 2019, "The prime minister's office is occupied by a caretaker. She has little power. Lawmakers show up to work, but the Parliament doesn't pass ambitious legislation. Civil servants keep their heads down. Last year's budget serves as this year's guide. Washington is consumed by the impeachment battle, but in Belgium there isn't anyone worth impeaching. Some Belgians say they haven't even noticed a difference. The trains keep running—just as tardy as usual."

The lack of willingness to form a government is not the only recent splotch on Belgium's reputation as a disorganized, haphazardly operating nation. On December 18, 2019, the Belgian prime minister Charles Michel abruptly resigned amid loss of national support in a very public, and global, fight over

European migration. Michel, at only thirty-eight, had been Belgium's youngest prime minister. Early in his tenure, he was cast in the press as a potentially unifying force, mostly because although he hailed from the town of Namur in Wallonia and thus was a native French speaker, he was also fluent in Dutch. The bloom blew off the rose, though, when Michel added his signature to a UN migration pact providing for a common global approach to migrant flows. The pact included twenty-three objectives designed to improve opportunities for legal migration and better manage a global flow of 250 million people on the European continent. The Flemish nationalist N-VA Party (Nieuw-Vlaamse Alliantie/New Flemish Alliance), which has hardline views on migration, walked out of the parliament. This caused Michel's coalition government to become unglued. Michel appealed to the federal parliament to back a minority administration until the country could hold a general election in six months, asking for a "coalition of good will" to see him through and warning that the country would be otherwise left rudderless for months should his government fall, but the Socialist Party refused to agree to the proposal, and the king accepted Michel's resignation (Boffey, 2018). In classic Belgian fashion, two protests immediately followed, one featuring right wingers demonstrating against the United Nations' pact because it still passed with Michel's signature, and which police had to use tear gas and water cannons to end, and a counterprotest organized by left-wing groups and charities in the city that drew about one thousand people (BBC, 2018).

Despite these ongoing complications, I have come to believe that it is just this porousness of government, this stubbornness in the face of attempts at organization and streamlining of services that has enabled food waste recirculation initiatives in this city to thrive.[3] This at first seems counterintuitive, I know: How can a tiny nation with a governmental structure that is both so vast and so disorganized be doing a good job at anything, let alone a gnarly, deeply difficult problem to solve like reducing food waste? From what I have observed, though, it may have been the vastness of the governmental structure and the concomitant inability to act quickly that enabled Belgium to survive the second most important factor of EU life affecting this study, which is the European Union's so-called debt crisis, a term that references the European Union's struggle to pay back debts it has accumulated over the past couple of decades, largely due to five of the member countries' failure to generate economic growth after the global recession of 2008–9. The debt burden necessitated a series of bailouts by the European Union and the European Central Bank, and although Belgium is not one of the five countries—Greece, Ireland, Italy, Portugal, and Spain are—it was far closer to becoming one than most outside prognosticators, with their focus on the overspending in Greece in particular, failed to emphasize.

Before 2008, Belgium's economy grew faster than average for the EU bloc and had a huge increase in housing prices, an uptick in domestic investment, and banks secured by cheap debt (Klein, 2015). Despite those boom times, Belgium also had soaring labor costs, zero productivity growth, an extremely indebted corporate sector, and a persistently wide government budget deficit; by 2010, Belgium's public debt was 100 percent of its GDP, the third highest in the European Union after Greece and Italy, which engendered serious doubts about the stability of its banks. After the disastrous failure of French- and Flemish-speaking factions to form a coalition government in the wake of the split-party elections of June 2010, by November 2011 when a caretaker government was still in charge, financial analysts forecast that Belgium would be the next country hit hard by the crisis.

However, luck prevailed for the Belgians: the government deficit of 5 percent was relatively modest, and Belgian government ten-year bond yields in November 2010 of 3.7 percent were still below those of Ireland (9.2 percent), Portugal (7 percent), and Spain (5.2 percent) (Robinson, 2010). Furthermore, thanks to Belgium's high net foreign asset position—meaning that Belgium had proportionately high financial claims on the outside world—the Belgian government was able to avoid the spikes in borrowing costs that Spain and Greece experienced, making it less prone to the fluctuations of international credit markets. Belgium survived, but barely, and because it did not experience a housing bust, which allowed the country to avoid the downturn in employment that other countries—notably the United States—experienced. Even then, on November 25, 2011, Belgium's long-term sovereign credit rating was downgraded from AA+ to AA by Standard and Poor's. It was only then that negotiating parties reached an agreement to form a new government. The deal included spending cuts and tax raises worth about €11 billion (about $11.7 USD), which brought the budget deficit down to 2.8 percent of GDP by 2012 (Martens & Clapham, 2012). How Belgium missed experiencing the crisis in a bigger way is put down to the fact that it could not act quickly to change its position—paradoxically, the country's paralysis in forming a government meant that it did not enact the austerity measures other countries implemented, and the ensuing months allowed residential investment spending to grow, which forestalled a housing bust. In addition, a relatively healthy private sector was able to keep lending rates to banks and households stable, allowing Belgium to remain a major partner to German high-end manufacturing firms. Today, analysts laud Belgium's

Social assistance growth in Brussels

	2006	2007	2008	2009	2010	2011	2012	2013	2014	2015	2016
Population	1,018,804	1,031,215	1,048,491	1,068,532	1,089,538	1,119,088	1,138,854	1,154,635	1,163,486	1,175,173	1,187,890
GDP growth	2.6%*	3.7%*	0.4%	−2.0%	2.9%*	1.7%*	0.7%	0.5%	1.6%*	2.0%*	1.5%*
Supplemental Security Income recipients	20,887	21,836	23,034	24,189	26,591	26,881	27,570	28,467	29,902	31,584	34,605
Supplemental Security Income recipient Percentage	2.05%	2.12%	2.20%	2.26%	2.44%	2.40%	2.42%	2.47%	2.57%	2.69%	2.91%

Note: GDP growth is represented with an asterisk when it is above +1.0 percent and underlined when it is below. The percentage of Supplemental Security Income recipients grew steadily through the ten-year period, regardless of whether GDP growth was above or below 1 percent. Data from the Brussels Bureau of Statistics show a steady rise in populations seeking social assistance from 2006 to 2016, indicating the emergence of a new class of working poor.

"incredible resilience," which is not incredible so much as the result of the slow-moving nature of its large government (Klein, 2015).

Despite managing to avoid severe consequences, Belgium's topsy-turvy economic status during what the head of the Bank of England, Sir Mervyn King, referred to as "the most serious financial crisis at least since the 1930s, if not ever," took a toll on its capital region. At its height in 2013, unemployment in the Brussels region was 20 percent (compared with 11 percent in Wallonia and 5 percent in Flanders), and the number of people seeking social assistance in the capital soared. Based on my analysis of the data (for the years 2005, 2013, 2018—right before, during, and following the crisis) provided for this study by the Brussels Institute for Statistics and Analysis, even when unemployment fell, the number of beneficiaries of social integration services (including provisions for free health care and food) continued to rise. Also, although the number of "unemployed job seekers" remained stable and even dipped a bit between 2005 and 2018, the number of "beneficiaries of the right to social integration" during that same time period increased by more than twenty thousand people—a difference that shows that having a job is no longer the protection against poverty in Brussels that it once was. These data support claims I heard from several sources in this study—including an official on the EU Sustainability desk—that "the working poor" didn't used to exist in Brussels but are very much a feature of it today. The new existence of this class is essential to this study, because the people who constitute this class are precisely the people who seek food assistance in Brussels today.

Precarious Brussels

As the de facto capital of the European Union, Brussels in the 2020s finds itself plunging into crises of demographic and economic displacements, heightened expressions of political nationalism, and general social unrest. Given the level of unemployment in the city juxtaposed against the high level of people seeking social assistance, it is fair to use what Anne Allison calls "a word of the times" to describe work prospects in today's Brussels: precarious (2013, 6). *Precarite* was embraced and then deployed by European socialist movements—including Belgium's own two socialist parties (a French-speaking one and a Flemish-speaking one)—in the 1970s, to describe a shift in late-stage capitalism toward conditions of work that are "uncertain, unpredictable, and risky from the point of view of the worker" (7). Given that most workforces throughout human history have labor markets that in fact qualified as precarious, this term today is most pertinent to those industrialized countries where workers once could reasonably expect long-term, regular employment and now face issues of gig economies. In the United States, for example, it was not until the government stepped in after the Great Depression with the New Deal to create jobs and establish social welfare protections that an idea of secure jobs for all citizens became the rule rather than the exception. Belgium, however, avoided the need for this as for many, many years, the fact that it was a small wealthy country meant that there were enough jobs for its citizens. It was only since 1960 and the waves of immigration, combined with the failure of the coal and steel industries in Wallonia, that conditions changed, making work scarce in the capital. It was these conditions that were exacerbated by the European Union's economic crisis.

Now finding themselves in a situation in which work in the capital is no longer guaranteed, the citizens and residents of Brussels must face what it means to be precarious: "Precarity references a particular notion of, and social contract around, work. Work that is secure; work that secures not only income and job but identity and lifestyle, linking capitalism and intimacy in an affective desire for security itself" (Allison, 2013; Berlant, 2011). Precarity marks the loss of a secure job and the dreams and hopes that accompany it—as Allison points out, it is a loss that only certain countries at certain historical periods and certain workers ever had in the first place.[4] Unlike Japan, the focus of Allison's research, Belgium is *not* one of those countries. Brussels, however, is one of those cities.

To explore the effects of what crises and precarity mean to people living in them, particularly the ways in which everyday life in the European Union is being remade to accommodate the new period of economic troubles, I look to the question of who gets to eat what kind of food and under what conditions. In the three sites where I conducted fieldwork, I found people who reduce food waste through projects that recirculate discarded still-edible food from people and places in the city where it was not valued to people and places where it can find utility. Such projects tackle neither large-scale issues of industrial food production nor small-scale issues of individual food accumulation. Instead, they focus on creating new utility for food that has already been put to waste. In the process, they address issues of hunger and environmental sustainability.

As I have noted, Brussels is also the capital of a particularly small country with a particularly large multilayered governmental structure. So, amid that structure, how do precarious people access care? The path is through social services, which are accessed at the commune level but organized at the national one. Belgium may be the world's sixty-first-smallest country by area, a few kilometers smaller than Lesotho and a few kilometers larger than Moldova, but its government is the world's second highest per-capita spender—with 29 percent of its GDP going to public social services, ranking it just behind France and just ahead of Finland. Such services are defined as cash benefits, direct in-kind provision of goods and services, and tax breaks for social purposes. Benefits included are those targeting low-income households, the elderly, disabled, sick, unemployed, and youth populations. To be considered "social" by economic indices, programs must involve either redistribution of resources across households or compulsory participation. Social benefits are classified as public when a general government (that is central, state, and local governments, including social security funds) controls the relevant financial flows (OECD, 2019). When it comes to food resources, it is not *just* the large per-capita spending on social programs that enables food waste recirculation programs to thrive in Brussels. It is the conjunction of the size and scope of the government itself. The multiple layers of government whose functions come together in Belgium's capital—including the European Union, the state, the three regions plus the three language communities, and the city's nineteen municipalities—all promote pathways and allocate funding to social programming and to food waste reduction efforts that involve recirculation.

One way to note the disparity in how people live is to measure how they eat. While twenty-five restaurants in Brussels earned Michelin stars in 2018, about 33 percent of residents live below the poverty line (FPS Economy, 2016). Brussels is home base for the offices that oversee national public assistance programs such as citizens' universal health care and retirement pensions. The city now faces critical challenges in maintaining these programs. Brussels contends with feeding a rising class of the working poor, who are the recipients of the efforts to recirculate food waste outlined in this study.

This demographic shift is concurrent with the EU developments recognizing food waste as a social welfare and environmental problem. After the big policy announcement from the European Union prioritizing food waste reduction in 2011, fighting food waste became "a top priority" in Brussels, too, according to Josephine Henrion, the director of the food and consumption unit for the Brussels-Capital Region's Office of the Environment. In a press conference on food waste, Henrion highlighted a rating system devised by the Netherlands' Wageningen University & Research that her office has adopted. The system ranks the European Union's food waste reduction priorities: preventing waste at its source is first, redirecting it to human consumption (through food aid or transformation) is next, redirecting it toward animal consumption is third, turning it into raw materials for industry is fourth, and burning it is considered the last resort. In dealing with the huge food surplus among the million-plus residents of the Belgian capital, Henrion said the best-case scenario is either redistributing food waste as food aid or else transforming it before it is trashed (Belin, 2019).

What decides? Logistics is the biggest challenge, she said. "On the expiration date indicated (for packed food) or when it has to be removed and replaced (for fresh food), you have very little time to grab what's left before it is dumped" (Belin, 2019). The best places to turn, she said, are food banks, such as the Food Bank of Brussels, because the only associated costs with delivering food are vans and drivers; social welfare programs, such as the social restaurant Bel Mundo, because the region can then work with additional funding streams from municipal centers for social support to aid food distribution; and finally, initiatives that offer cooking lessons and programs for schoolchildren, which are good because they address food waste at its source in homes, one of which is Cultureghem. Thus, the people operating all three of those sites mark the focus of this study.

CHAPTER THREE

Church, State, Food, Waste

A central question I had about food waste recirculation from the beginning involved food banks. Since no food products *begin* their lives in such places—food banks aren't factories that *produce* food, and they aren't groceries where consumers first encounter it—it is possible to theorize them all as repositories of "food waste." How were food banks managing the aftereffects of the European Union's compulsory policy mandating that supermarkets donate instead of toss food they don't wish to sell? Was there a surplus of surplus? And if so, which populations in the city were benefiting from it? The answers, I discovered, had less to do with how much food a food bank has to give than with how religious its clients are and how much its mission connects to a city's other social welfare programs that involve economic incentives rather than charitable donations.

The first thing I had to figure out is why food banks exist in places where there is a lot of food. This leads immediately to histories about religion in cities. For instance, I learned while volunteering at the Food Bank of Brussels that there are very few food banks free of religious ties—upon investigation in Europe and the United States in an informal survey of one hundred food banks, even some of the ones that think they are nonsectarian and/or purport to be turn out not to be—and that those religious ties map onto ancient ideas about charity and philanthropy that pit wealthy citizens against needy "others."

Informal "food banks"—by which I mean places where poor people could go to get free food and that were stocked with community donations—have been features of cities pretty much since cities have existed. Historians have been able to prove that in ancient Mesopotamia, hunger was rare but existed, in a form "less than famine, but more than a temporary inconvenience"—and alongside it, evidence of "the political management of hunger by early states . . . as providers of security and political membership as a rational economic choice" (Richardson, 2016, 750). There is even evidence that politicians in these early cities may have purposefully cast apart the hungry among them "to 'prove' the efficacy of the very system that had marginalized them" (752). Today, to meet the needs of hungry people in a major global city, a food bank needs to offer both something for the state and something to attract volunteer laborers, too. While the state ostensibly benefits from not having to fund poor health outcomes for people if it keeps them fed, volunteers at food banks are looking for ways to fill their time in meaningful ways. To that end, I discovered tensions and contestations not only between church and state but also among volunteers, since they were people who could afford not to work and thus could spend their time helping others. Conflicts among volunteers at the bank were staged on several scales, including between race and class and between young and old. There were also issues over who exactly had the right to material expressions of care. Could a volunteer take home a "free" candy bar from the food bank for her grandchild, or would this mean taking food from the mouth of a child who otherwise would not have access to such a treat? This specific type of conflict struck me not only as opposed to the general concept of what a social welfare state is supposed to be but also a reflection of the ways in which both age-old religious and new neoliberal politics slip so easily into moral debates about what "doing good" means, and for whom.

That's not to say that the function of a food bank can be reduced to candy bar access; food banks are hardly irrelevant to the major concerns that face a city. Far from it, especially in Belgium today. According to the latest statistics taken by Flemish newspaper *Het Laatste Nieuws*, in 2021 in Belgium, nearly 20 percent of the population (2.2 million people) were at risk of poverty or social exclusion, and these rates are much higher in the Brussels region, where inequality is more acute. Since 1995, there has been a 153 percent increase in national food bank use (Carter, 2022). Unsurprisingly, then, of the three sites I study here, the Food Bank of Brussels is the one that actually "does good" the best, if we're measuring in terms of the amount of food waste recirculated and the number of hungry people who benefit from it.

Here is what it was like to volunteer there: Sporadically over the course of five years, I went into the bank for a few days a week. Ninety percent of the time, I sorted food from the giant grocery store boxes it arrived in, which involved checking that the food was still wholesome—boxes were unopened, cans were intact, and so forth; then organizing and stacking the food by type (condiments all together, cookies all together, cereals all together, etc.); repacking it into boxes with other products in its category; and, finally, weighing the boxes (they were required to be 10 kilograms each or less, or about 22 pounds) and labeling them for their redistribution in food pantries. Occasionally I was asked to assist administrators with various language-related tasks, such as copyediting documents originally written in French or Dutch that had been translated into English, or to help with running the bank's own

Church, State, Food, Waste 89

The Food Bank of Brussels. Since it was established in 1985, the city's largest clearinghouse of surplus food operated out of an old Lipton tea factory in Anderlecht. Despite its loading docks, the building wasn't large enough and didn't have enough cold storage for all of the incoming food, and the bank was increasingly hindered in its capacity. In early 2020, officials relocated the bank to a new space for the express purpose of meeting the growing demand for food caused by increases in local poverty. Author photo.

weekly internal food distribution for its employees (but not its administrators or volunteers).

Housed in a former Lipton Tea packaging plant, the Food Bank of Brussels is the largest clearinghouse of edible but unsellable food in Belgium, so it was an obvious place to track surplus supermarket food waste—so much of it, after all, came here. It was a much larger operation than I had expected. The building itself takes up an entire city block in the commune of Anderlecht. International sports fans know Anderlecht for its soccer club, which is Belgium's most successful not only in its domestic league competitions but also in Union of European Football Association (UEFA) competitions. Anderlecht was also one of the first of Brussels's nineteen communes to industrialize, in the early

1800s. Of course, that industrial history ensures the presence of old factories; this one shares a block with a Leonidas chocolate factory and a Renault car mechanic shop, which in turn ensured that the street always smelled like a strange combination of hot chocolate, gasoline, and rotting food.

Inside the bank, a staff of twelve employees and thirty-four volunteers manages the rerouting of discarded edible food to more than six hundred charities and welfare organizations throughout the city, who work to redistribute it to fragile populations they service; annually, these efforts feed an estimated twenty-six thousand people—making it by far the most effective food distribution organization in the city (Gschwindt, 2016). To become a client, charitable organizations must apply and meet criteria, including the fact that they serve people who are at or below the city's poverty level. To ensure that the organizations' reports are honest, bank administrators visit all clients biannually, meeting with the directors, observing the food distributions, and ensuring that the food goes where the clients claim.

The employees at the bank included forklift operators, truck drivers, a couple of secretaries and administrative assistants, an orders coordinator, and two logistics managers who oversaw the operations of the building. All of these are men of color, and they span racial and ethnic categories that include Moroccan and Turkish migrants to Brussels (both recent and second generation), plus second- and even third-generation African-descended Belgians (especially those whose ancestors were from the Congo, although Ghana and Senegal were both also represented)—except for one: a white Flemish woman is the onsite liaison from the European Union's FEAD program (Fund for European Aid to the Most Deprived), whose job involves managing a specific selection of EU-sponsored and -funded products (applesauce, various canned goods) that is earmarked for specific distribution channels to manage cases of "extreme deprivation and poverty." The salaries and benefits for the twelve employees are paid from employment contracts issued by the regional and communal social welfare services offices. The administrators of the bank, who include an executive director, a communications manager, a human resources officer, a finance manager, and a supply controller, are all volunteers and all retired white people, of whom two are women. The administrative staff set their own hours but tend to show up at least three days a week and for the usual nine-to-five workday; their offices are on the second floor of the old factory; the employees, who punch clocks to be paid, work downstairs in a shared office and on the floor with the forklifts, pallets, and boxes. This space seems multicultural when you first encounter it, but when you spend time volunteering in it day in and day out, it would be impossible not to note that the people making decisions have very little if anything in common with the bank's stakeholders, while the people who are employed by means of social welfare state-sponsored contracts there do.

What I learned from the administrators is that the compulsory EU policy mandating all supermarkets donate rather than discard surplus food did not change *the source* of food at the bank very much—most of the food had always come from supermarkets' unsellable but still edible goods, plus a handful of "new" products the bank receives as part of the European Union's FEAD initiative (Michiels, 2016). What changed was the volume: supermarkets that had been throwing food away suddenly looked for community partners to avoid fines, and the bank acquired so many new partners that when I worked there it no longer had the capacity to take on new ones, even though the food pantries that relied on the bank could easily have taken more food.

Operationally, the bank had two trucks, both donated by corporations, both quite old but functional. The trucks were in near constant use. As soon as one dumped food from a supermarket, it was reloaded and sent out to get more—but the trucks weren't refrigerated, which limited how far they could travel to pick up food. In addition, the special license required for driving a truck is a special category and requires proof of special training. The bank's administrators found that most qualified truck drivers worked for companies that could pay them a whole lot more than the state could in addition to offering them permanent employment rather than renewable contracts. The drivers who were looking for state-sponsored social welfare contracts *and* had truck licenses often had some strikes already against them. Some who applied had criminal records or suspended licenses due to moving violations or failure to renew or pay the licensing fees and were hoping the bank might pay to reinstate their licenses for them (in one case the bank did). The issue of finding additional truck drivers haunted the bank the entire time I was there in a seemingly endless loop of frustration for the administrators as well as for the two maxed-out truck drivers, who often complained that they didn't get enough breaks between runs.

The legal and social obstacles that prevented the bank from finding a pool of viable drivers turned out to connect to the same obstacles that many of the banks' clients face when they try to access social welfare benefits. There used to not be so many people in Brussels who qualified for social services, but now there were, and the state had not adjusted to making things like truckers' licenses or access to employment services more accessible. The very model of the bank speaks to a dated foundation of food distribution, too: this kind of food bank represents the "warehouse model" of food banks (Fisher,

2017). Unlike "frontline" food distribution models that distribute food directly to consumers in need—which is generally what food pantries do— warehouse-model food banks function as storage and distribution depots accessed by agencies such as civic charities as well as church groups who pick up and then distribute food to the local and/or faith-based communities they are designated to serve (Fisher, 2017, 228). According to Harry Gschwindt, the secretary of the bank who has been volunteering in it since a few years after its inception, there were so few people in need of food in Belgium until very recently—he cited the last twenty years as the tipping point—that starving in Brussels "was unheard of . . . you never read that someone in Brussels starved to death" (2016). Gschwindt has a short white pompadour, a steady supply of blue cashmere sweaters, and a gold watch. You can often find him standing outside on the bank's stoop, smoking a good cigar. A retired director of Belgium's Department of Economic and Employment Development, he was forced into early retirement due to a serious heart condition. He found it did not suit him. "I was bored to death," he said; he noted that the work at the bank is fulfilling and keeps him out of his wife's way. "I like to feel I'm doing something beneficial to society with my time anyway," he added.

Gschwindt is of Swiss descent and ended up in Brussels because of his work in international diplomacy; his wife is German. Although he spoke more languages than he could remember—literally, he stopped counting them off to me at six—Dutch is not one of them. That said, his impeccable French was extremely useful to the bank, and he was the communications director. If documents had to be translated into Dutch, he gave them to someone else to manage. Even though Brussels is officially a bilingual city, "Brussels has always done its official business in French; it's not a problem," he said. According to Gschwindt, the bank has one goal: to help feed the 20 percent of people living below the poverty line in Brussels. To do this, he said the bank has three rules of operation: "We never buy food; we only receive food for free; and we only give away food for free." The bank is permitted to receive monetary donations, which according to its statutes must be used strictly to cover operational costs.

As the bank deals in food, it also deals in valuations. As Gschwindt explained, "Our job is to create value where there was none before, to take food that was given to us, make sure it's viable for consumption, and then distribute it to people living on the margins of society." Value at the bank, then, is understood as being "created" (to use Gschwindt's term) in two ways: first, by means of sorting discarded food into which items might be repurposed versus which could not (say, a can of beans that had been pried open in

Food Bank of Brussels sorting room. Each week the bank sends drivers to its supermarket partners to pick up large boxes filled with a dizzying, and entirely disorganized, array of surplus foods. Once back at the bank, volunteers inspect and sort the contents, discarding damaged or opened packages and organizing new boxes according to type (cereals, condiments, etc.). These new boxes are picked up by client organizations. Author photo.

transit); and second, in the efforts of volunteers like himself who sought to make a positive difference in the lives of the poor of Brussels (thereby providing a valuable service that otherwise would not exist).

Another way the bank trades in value is in the fact that it does not have to pay for its labor. The bank has no labor costs because the twelve salaried employees were paid directly from regional and communal social services programs. The rest were volunteers and like Gschwindt, all those happened to also be pensioners. Not only were all the pensioners white Belgian citizens, but all were also worldly (trilingual is the norm), well-traveled, and well-heeled. One gentleman was the former vice president of Austrian Airlines. Their upstairs offices contained old, donated desktop computers, from which they used email to reach out to clients (directors of charities, food pantry administrators, and others) about new needs, create materials and mailings to solicit donors, take data for and produce an annual report, respond to requests, negotiate with and prepare the necessary paperwork for the social services offices in order to be able to continue employing the paid staff, communicate with EU officials of the FED program, and other tasks. The employees were all social service recipients, the vast majority from other countries, mostly Morocco, Romania, and Tunisia; they wore work boots and jeans.

To acquire a supermarket's food, the bank's first step was sending a representative, often if not always Gschwindt, to meet the manager and set up a delivery schedule. Gschwindt said this process was more onerous than it should have been thanks to the truck driver situation. Gschwindt reported that since 2014, supermarket managers had been happier to see him than they used to be. He also noted that unsellable foods often come in many forms. Gschwindt recalls receiving one hundred crates of whole milk (that's about four hundred gallon-sized cartons) that had been mislabeled as skim, which meant the milks could not be sold in stores even though their contents were wholesome. The milks presented a unique challenge, because most of the bank's food is packaged goods, which of course are not nearly as perishable as fresh food. The bank received far less fresh food from the supermarkets—that's been another change since the recent policy, because it used to receive next to none but now will take fresh unexpired food (usually things like packages of deli meats that are close to expiring, unsold fruit and vegetables that were picked over because of bruising, and meats and cheeses that had been reduced to sale prices that they no longer had refrigerated shelving space to hold), but it was often enough to make up a pallet. Whatever fresh foods on hand were distributed to the charities and social institutions who arrive to pick them up three times a week and were divided evenly between them. One of the logistics managers, Karim, organized this by counting which organizations showed up on those three distribution times and letting them have lottery-style picks from the pallets of what they needed. When I observed this fresh food distribution, I noticed that the demand for fresh goods varied wildly; some days there would be close to twenty food pantries sending in vans and cars to try to pick up fresh food, but other pantries were only open nine months a year and closed for the summer; still others were in the habit of visiting more than one food bank in the city, and when their vans were full didn't bother braving the traffic into the southwestern part of Brussels where Anderlecht is located. In the end, Gschwindt and his team cold-called their six hundred clients and got as many of them to come to the bank to pick up the milks as they could; he said only about twenty-five cartons had to be emptied and recycled.

Gschwindt recalled another, easier sort of crisis, which occurred when a supermarket employee intending to order two hundred boxes of pasta accidentally ordered twenty thousand, and the store did not have room to stock them all. The bank sent a truck for them and dispersed them to the food pantries evenly. With some pride, Gschwindt said, "If these foods had not been donated to the bank, they would have ended up in an incineration facility." Because Belgium was settled on the inland rivers and waterways of the North Sea, the nation and thus the city of Brussels do not have enough land depth to sustain burying trash—there can simply be no landfills. Thus, the city's waste is incinerated—at very high temperatures, until it becomes ash (Brussels Environment, 2010). Curious about what happened before incineration facilities existed, I discovered that Brussels has a sewer museum. It was founded at an underground sluice in Anderlecht in 1998, in response to regular requests to the city's Sewer Department to organize visits from public and parochial schools; it has been maintained by the city's Department of Culture since 2015. Musée de Égots/Riolenmuseum is devoted to celebrating the ways in which one city barely above sea level in many places has found a way since its existence to deal with its waste, including highlighting the way sewers were built and *explaining* the city's water cycle. A highlight of the visit is the underground tour and a chance to walk along the (newly clean) waterways. The main thing I learned there is that like many cities developed in the Middle Ages, Brussels used the river it was built on, the Senne, to drive mills, produce beer, and dye fabrics—and for centuries, get rid of waste. Of course, a city with an open sewer means refuse of all kinds, everywhere. People threw their filth directly into the water, including dead bodies. And as everyone who knows anything about Belgium knows, it rains a lot there, which meant that the Senne (and its refuse) were frequently overflowing. The first underground sewer system did a lot to ameliorate this, but eventually the Senne itself was diverted to the outskirts of town from directly through the center of the city. Today's Brussels operates with two water filtration treatment plants, one in the north, and the other in the south of the city; it takes twenty-four hours to purify the water and discharge it, cleaner, into the river.

Gschwindt was quite proud of the fact that the food bank reduces negative impacts to the environment in Brussels because it reduces not only usable food from being incinerated but particularly the number of aluminum cans that are incinerated. Why? Because incinerators are combustion devices that create toxic by-products known as dioxins, which accumulate in fatty tissue and increase in concentration at each successive level of the food chain (National Research Council, 2000). Because dioxins are known cancer-causing agents, there is substantial pressure on the European Union from its growing number of environmental "green" parties to reduce incineration (Harrabin, 2007). Another problem is that incineration is costly. According to Gschwindt, it costs about 60 cents to incinerate just one can. But Gschwindt said that upper- and middle-class consumers were luckier to discard cans of food if the outside of the cans were dented, even if the can was otherwise unpunctured or harmed. In his ethnography of the lives of workers in a Detroit landfill, Reno reported that he saw a lot of canned food in perfectly good condition save for a small dent that did not compromise the cans' contents—and these cans were unnecessarily buried underground. Reno concluded that a lot of waste exists for the preservation of consumer ideals of what products should look like rather than the quality of the products themselves (2016, 56). I saw a lot of slightly dented cans on shelves at the bank, which meant that grocery shoppers passed them over for precisely the same reason Reno cited—why buy a can of food with a small dent in it when the one right behind it is perfect?[1]

Another thing Gschwindt was proud to see surprised me, which was his confident assurance that food banks such as this one "were invented in America." Given the bank's basic framework, though, I wondered how that could be. I knew that at least since the Middle Ages, medieval church congregations would collect food from their wealthiest congregants and make rounds delivering it to the neediest in their villages and towns. Upon research, I discovered what Gschwindt meant, which is that food banks *as separate entities from religious institutions* that donate food to the poor were "invented" in America. In that, he was right: most historians agree that the existence of nonprofit, nonreligious organizations that distribute food to those in need did indeed begin in the United States in 1967 (Poppendieck, 1999, 112). And most of them cite community activists in Phoenix, Arizona, led by a relocated businessman named John Van Hangel and initially stocked with gleaned fruits and vegetables from local orchards, as the formers of the first such nonreligious bank. At the time, Phoenix was in the midst of a serious economic downturn and a sharp spike in local hunger, as a result of the United States ending the free distribution of federal food surpluses in favor of food stamps (Riches, 1986, 20). With more produce than he had room for, Van Hangel got some help from the pastor of nearby St. Mary's Church, who lent him the use of a five-thousand-square-foot abandoned bakery that had been donated to the parish. With that, he formed the St. Mary's Food Bank Alliance. From here, food banks spread across the United States and into Canada, reaching Europe by the early 1980s. In 1985, the first food bank in Belgium opened in

Brussels, a city whose citizens had managed to feed the poor and the needy among them courtesy of their churches for centuries (Poppendieck, 1999). There are nine banks now, but the Brussels branch is still the biggest and the only one open five days a week. However, what it delivers along with rations of food to poor people in the city of Brussels includes some old-fashioned moral-inflected ideas about charity and some hidden power dynamics that anyone outside the bank cannot see.

Where God Meets Frozen Lasagna

Site One is a bank client located in the Brussels neighborhood of Laeken, which is also where the Royal Palace and Royal Gardens are located. Laeken also boasts one of the city's premiere tourist attractions, the Atomium, a building constructed for the 1958 world's fair in the shape of, yes, an atom, and that today houses a museum and cultural exhibition space. There are lots of public parks here, mostly in the northern part of the neighborhood; the southern part has industrial areas and a canal. Like a lot of Brussels, it's a decidedly mixed area.

The site itself is on a leafy block lined with brownstones. Once a church, for the last ten years it has housed a Protestant congregant whose lay leaders, a retired couple whom I will refer to as Hugo and Anna Peeters, run an on-site food distribution three days a week. Of the food bank's six hundred clients, this is the one director Tony Michiels mentions as a special favorite. He even spoke of it when he was invited to the European Union's health minister's office to discuss the future of food banks in the European Union, calling it "one of the best-run organizations we have, period" (Michiels, 2017).

Anna Peeters has white permed hair, round glasses, and a beleaguered smile. She's tall, pale, and doughy in a way that reminded me of a stereotypical Midwestern American grandmother, but even well in her seventies, she can adeptly balance an infant on one hip and a box filled with cans of soup on the other. That was what she was doing when I met her one summer day. She was the only white person in a sea of hijab-clad, much younger women in the rec room of the church, all of whom were setting up the food distribution. Soon recipients would begin to arrive, then queue up to present their identification cards indicating they were entitled to social welfare aid in the form of food. Once they showed their papers (effectively a kind of laminated permission slip from the communal social services office stating they were entitled to receive food by the state as officially registered social welfare recipients), they would each receive a ticket allowing them to enter the rec room and pick up some food. I asked Anna what happened if someone showed up looking for

Before recipients at Site One can enter the weekly food distribution, they are strongly encouraged to attend a sermon in the adjacent sanctuary. Even if they chose not to, there would be no other place to stand, since the rooms are connected. In addition, church members "run" the various stations at the bank on a volunteer basis, but they do so in exchange for having first pick of the foods on offer. Author photo.

aid *without* the required paperwork. She looked at me long and hard before deciding to answer: "I do not turn away. They must wait until everyone with the paper has gone through, and then we allow them to enter." This showed me that documents entitling the poor to state social welfare benefits from food banks were important, but not always essential. It also showed me that Anna felt she could bend the state rules when necessary.

Before I got here, Michiels had told me a bit about Anna and Hugo, notably that they were both widowed when they met and fell in love more than twenty-five years ago (Michiels, 2017). Back then on weekends Anna spent her time making sandwiches in her home kitchen and then taking them to give them away to homeless people near the city's largest train station. When she got together with Hugo, she brought him along, too (2017). She told him about her dream to have a building for her then-fledgling Protestant church congregation, and with his help and connections—Hugo was a car mechanic who for years ran a successful and well-regarded autobody shop—she has succeeded. "I started all of this with my tears and my God," she said as she pointed her index finger up, toward heaven.

The site's food distribution turned out to be unlike many of the others run by the bank's clients whom I visited. Instead of handing out presorted food packages that volunteers arranged in advance, carefully rationing out supplies so that all weekly aid boxes contained roughly the same amount of food, recipients here were allowed to choose foods from an array of items at stations manned by volunteers. Michiels said he preferred this way of doing things: "If people can choose their own food, they are more likely to feel that they are a part of their community" (Michiels, 2017). There were tables devoted to the usual assortment of packaged foods—pastas, condiments, cereals—and several piled high with day-old (or more) baked goods, mostly cakes, pastries, and loaves of bread. The pastries were all in boxes that bore the telltale yellow discount stickers, indicating that they'd been marked down and nearly expired, but I noticed that a lot of the items themselves were in pristine condition. For example, I may never forget the temptation of a strawberry meringue tart that looked so good it defied stereotypes of food waste. Others, though, did bear the telltale signs: tattered boxes carrying smudged and damaged goods, such as a heaved-in raspberry cake that resembled a pile of pink mush. The volunteers at that table were busy arranging the offerings to look attractive, pushing the nicest-looking items to the front, exactly the way I've seen supermarket workers do.

"You will help us today," Anna said, steering me toward a station. "Heb je kinderen?" she asked as we walked. I nodded and told her that I have two sons. "Ah, you are a mother, good," she said, patting my hand and introducing me to a volunteer named Fatma before moving on to other tasks. Fatma smiled warmly and asked me where I was from and how old I was; she said she was thirty-five years old, and I noticed that she also looked about thirty-five weeks pregnant. She was clad head to toe in pale purple, including the hijab wrapped tightly under her chin. Fatma's two small daughters played by her feet—ages six and three, they wore matching pink Barbie t-shirts. Fatma motioned for me to stand with her at this station, which consisted of a large foldout table loaded with all kinds of yogurts and cheeses. Of the twenty volunteers behind other folding tables, I noticed that 90 percent were women.

Fatma chatted away, saying she was eager to practice her English. She told me that she came to Brussels ten years ago from her native Morocco to join her cousins here; their parents were part of a wave of Moroccan guestworkers who emigrated to Belgium at the invitation of the government in the '60s to help the nation ameliorate worker shortages in their then-booming coal industry (Schoonvaere, 2014). Fatma met her husband here; he is also Moroccan but was born and raised in Belgium. She said he quit high school to help run his uncle's convenience store, but it had gone out of business, and now they were both unemployed and received welfare benefits. Fatma said volunteering here was good because the site's policy allowed her and other volunteers to "shop" for food before the other food recipients did. She pointed behind us to show me that she had already gotten a cart full of food before she began setting up our station. She then explained that our first job was to transfer shredded Emmental cheese from five-pound bulk bags into small individual bags so that more people could have some. We donned rubber clothes to do this. "I know I am having a boy; I feel it!" Fatma said as we worked.

As we stuffed bags with cheese, I spied what was on offer at the table next to ours: an unlucky volunteer, another woman in a hijab, was tasked with distributing boxes of frozen lasagna. I say "unlucky" because it was summertime and thus not lasagna season, and because half of the three hundred or so boxes piled on her table were both rapidly defrosting and contained meat sauce with pork, which observant Muslims, many of whom attended this food distribution, do not eat. I walked over and said hello, then checked out the boxes to see how many of them were vegetarian. That's when I saw that more than a few of the lasagnas had expired. The Food Bank of Brussels is prohibited from distributing any food that exceeds its "use by" date. However, sometimes items slip through the cracks—especially if they weren't checked by an experienced volunteer at the bank or, as was the case with these lasagnas, if they came not from the bank but from one of the smaller local grocery stores that also deliver unsold foods directly to the site. Bypassing the bank sometimes saves smaller stores labor and money, but it does not ensure any level of food inspection (Michiels, 2017).

I went back to my table. Fatma said that she heard 206 tickets had been handed out today—not the most this bank has served (that would be nearly four hundred), but according to Jeanine it was on the high side. As the distribution began, the volunteers directed recipients from table to table, telling people how many of each thing they were allowed to take. I learned that each table was supposed to see how many items they had, find out how many tickets were given out, and then determine how much an individual could have. Today that meant two loaves of bread, a packet of cheese, two containers of yogurt, one frozen lasagna, et cetera. As Fatma and I managed the cheeses and yogurts, I glanced at the lasagna station. Sure enough, more and more people picked up packages, inspected them, and then turned them down. Halfway through the distribution, Anna told the volunteer there to tell people who wanted lasagna to take two.

One thing required of recipients here is a method to carry their own food. Most used the kind of pushcarts that urban grocery shoppers use—I saw those for sale on streetcorners in lots of Brussels neighborhoods. In the crowd on this day, there were also plenty of people pushing food carts and baby strollers simultaneously, as well as many elderly people seemingly using their food carts as walkers. Some recipients were models of efficient consumer strategy, meaning they did not linger as they flowed from station to station; it was almost as if they had created mental shopping lists. Most attendees, though, treated this bank as a social event and were chatting away with other recipients while seeming to browse the stations; it looked like a lot of them were neighbors or else had become acquaintances from weekly visits here. It felt lively and loud to be in that rec room, kind of like a whole bunch of grownups were playing "grocery store" with real food. I noticed that some folks were pretty dressed up, too: women wore makeup and trendy jewelry and had their nails done. If people think of food distribution sites as sad places where poverty is on display, that was certainly not the case here. To be sure, there were people who did not look well-to-do, but the conviviality was unmistakable.

From setup to breakdown, the food distribution here takes about three hours. Our table of cheeses and yogurts was totally wiped out. The lasagna indeed proved a challenge. After telling people they could take two, Anna had also told the volunteer to try to convince recipients to take it. I heard her say, "You have to convince them to take it; they need the food. Tell them it's good. Tell them it will feed the whole family. Tell them you have vegetarian," she advised. The last bit of wisdom occasionally did the trick: "Vegetarian lasagna, no meat!" the volunteer said to each person who approached. And as Anna predicted, there were many more takers.

The thing I noticed that was the most surprising happened about five minutes before the distribution began. It was when Anna stood in the center of the room and said that the sermon in the adjacent sanctuary would begin in five minutes. In this site, all food recipients are "strongly encouraged" to listen to a short sermon before they receive food. I later asked Michiels if that was legal. He was perplexed by the question. "Is it legal? I don't know. But this is Anna's concern and condition," he responded (Michiels, 2017). So even though attendance at a sermon cannot formally be required by the state for a person to receive social welfare benefits like food, and even though the Food Bank of Brussels that supplies this distribution site is a nonprofit, state-funded, nonreligious institution, attending the sermon before receiving food was clearly an expectation. And not just for the recipients. As Fatma took my hand and gently pulled me into the sanctuary with her and her daughters, I noted that everyone here, all the volunteers and all the recipients, were being ushered in as well. Most people were taking spots at pews in the far back, near the door. Fatma, a self-described Muslim, took her girls right up to the front, so I went along. There we stood in the third row before a pastor, who was old, white, round, and already sweating through his short-sleeved plaid shirt. After everyone got settled—more than two hundred people in the tight sanctuary—he began speaking in impassioned French to this audience. I turned around to spy more than a few people who were not as dedicated as Fatma. These folks sat sideways in their chairs; some carried on their own conversations as he spoke, and others were unashamedly on their cellphones. Anna stood in the front row, holding her hands over her heart. If the pastor noticed that so many people weren't paying attention, he remained undeterred and focused on the small contingent of folks who were. He then proceeded to deliver a twenty-minute sermon to a room full of mostly Muslim people about the dangers of divorce:

"*And he left there and went to the region of Judea and beyond the Jordan, and crowds gathered to him again. And again, as was his custom, he taught them,*" the pastor thundered loudly, closing his eyes, quoting from the New Testament, Mark 10:1–52. He took a breath, wiped his sweaty brow, then continued:

"*And Pharisees came up and in order to test him asked, 'Is it lawful for a man to divorce his wife?' He answered them, 'What did Moses command you?'*"

The pastor looked up into the crowd. I had to wonder: What did he think as he saw the sea of headscarves and strollers in his sanctuary, the people obviously waiting for him to finish talking so they could pick up some food? He seemed only to focus his gaze on the front pew as he continued:

"*They said, 'Moses allowed a man to write a certificate of divorce and to send her away.' And Jesus said to them, 'Because of your hardness of heart he wrote you this commandment. Hardness of heart. Hardness of heart!*"

At the last "*hardness of heart*"—*dureté de cœur!*—the pastor pounded his fist on the lectern. The sound prompted some of the disinterested folks to look up. He resumed: "*But from the beginning of creation, 'God made them male and female. Therefore, a man shall leave his father and mother and hold fast to his wife, and the two shall become one flesh.' So, they are no longer two but one flesh. What therefore God has joined together, let not man separate. Let not man separate!*" he thundered. "*Whoever divorces his wife and marries another commits adultery against her, and if she divorces her husband and marries another, she commits adultery*," the pastor concluded. With this, he fished a handkerchief from his pocket and wiped his brow. I spotted Anna wiping her eyes with her own handkerchief. "God zegene jullie allemaal," she said, loudly and in her native Flemish: *God bless you all*.

As if on cue, a volunteer began calling out numbers for the first wave of people to enter the food distribution room.

Where Pork Meets Fish

"The problem is that the Muslim people do not eat pork," Hien said to me as we set up the meat station at Site Two's food pantry. She was a tiny Vietnamese woman of indiscernible age, although the long and white-gray braid floating down her back gave a clue. Hien and I were assigned to hand out packages of fresh but nearly expired meat and fish at this site, another Food Bank of Brussels client, this one a social welfare housing development in an abandoned hospital with its own in-house tri-weekly food distribution. Michiels sent me here because Site Two is one of the food bank's largest clients, serving an average of 1,400 clients each week—more than four times as many as the ones served in Site One. Hien told me that she had lived on the premises for more than fifteen years, and as a condition of her occupancy, for which she uses funds from social services to pay the small rent, she is also required to help organize food distribution.

I already knew, of course, that observant Muslims do not eat pork, and yet I was not sure what to do with the giant boxes of frozen pork chops and loins at our station. In my time volunteering in Brussels food distribution centers, I came across an enormous amount of it. Almost always, it was there because it was close to expiring. I almost never saw chicken, beef, or fish. On one hand, it wasn't surprising to see them there—Belgium has a long history as a pork-producing nation and pork is still the most popular meat sold in grocery stores there—but on the other hand, 25 percent of people who live in the city of Brussels identify as Muslim, and the number is growing (Scholliers, 2009, 41). Based on what I had seen at other food bank distributions, I knew that most Muslims who come through food banks flatly refuse pork products or else, if they take them anyway, go somewhere right outside the distribution facility and attempt to trade them with non-Muslims for other items. I observed that these would-be traders were sometimes successful, but oftentimes their attempts were futile. Conducting such trades required two skills in short supply among immigrant and refugee committees: confidence and the ability to speak Flemish.

Interestingly, though, on this day at Site Two there were as many packages of frozen calamari, shrimp, and salmon as there were of pork. I felt happy to see them, because it meant more people would have access to some types of food that they might not only be able to use but also enjoy; fish and shellfish are popular parts of dishes in many Muslim-majority countries. I suggested to Hien: Instead of handing Muslims packages of pork they could not eat, why not give them the fish, and save the pork for those without religious prohibitions against it? Hien shrugged. "We can try it," she said hesitantly. In the moment, I was unsure about why she would even hesitate—my arrogance at having come up with what I thought was a great plan—but I would soon learn.

Before Hien and I set up our table, I discovered more about Site Two's operations from its director, whom I will refer to as Christina Alonto. It is not far from the Food Bank of Brussels in the Anderlecht commune, whose complicated economic and industrial history in Brussels I discuss more in chapter 5. In its brochures, the site bills itself as "an Intercultural Christian community that seeks to provide and achieve care, reception, integration, and education of immigrants and other people in need" (Alonto, 2018). In practice, it is an old, run-down hospital housing a multicultural assortment of people, all of whom are subsidized by social welfare benefits. Since a beloved and civic-minded local priest bought the deserted hospital from the city and converted it to low-income housing with the cooperation of city social services in 1994, it has also been running a food distribution program, for which it receives additional funds from the city.

Vestiges of the care facility that was once here are everywhere, and I found them unsettling. For example, the food distribution area used to be an ambulance bay, and it still has an enormous red "EMERGENCY" sign over its doorway. About three hundred people live in the apartments here, all of which were once hospital rooms—and rather than apartments, they look like hospital rooms—one room, one bed, one small bathroom with a rail installed in the cement wall, one small refrigerator in the corner, shared communal kitchens down the hall.

Most residents here have jobs they're required to do, like chores—some are on maintenance duty and sweep and mop floors and wash dishes; others are required to staff the food distribution. Hien noted that this was a good job because it meant that workers were allowed first pick of the food before the other recipients, who had to form a line outside the old ambulance bay and wait to be invited inside. To qualify to attend this food distribution, an Anderlecht resident would have had to meet the requirements of the commune's social welfare office, the Centre Public d'Action Sociale (CPAS), which include having more than one factor making it difficult to access the job market (no language skills, no high school diploma, etc.), and would have to be living at or below the poverty line. In addition, some part-time workers who held jobs but did not meet the state standard of living requirements for salary were allowed to attend, too—just less frequently, for example, once a month rather than once a week.

Since the community's founding priest died of a heart attack in 2011, Christina Alonto told me that she has been the chief administrator here, and Michiels told me that in his view she was the ideal director because she had intense personal ties to the place. Alonto told me that her family emigrated to Brussels when she was a child; they were "rescued," as she put it, from poverty in their native Philippines thanks to the missionary efforts of the founding priest, whom she spoke of in reverential terms (Alonto, 2018). Alonto effectively grew up in this site, where she still lives today with her husband and five children, the oldest of whom was eighteen. In addition to managing the site's operations, she also held an "outside" job in administrative affairs at the Brussels Airport. Despite how busy she is, Alonto is soft-spoken and humble. I have seen her mop floors, assist her clients as they filed official social services documents with the state using her own computer, and meet on-site in her crowded office with philanthropists who serve on Site Two's board—and I mean I have seen her do all of this on the same day, and with the same quiet determination.

On this food distribution day, I stepped outside to see the crowd gathering by the door. There were still thirty minutes before it was scheduled to begin, but already I counted 250 people gathered around. From the looks of it, there were many Muslim women, plus many women of African descent and, in the minority, some elderly white people. Food distribution is like that in Site One in that there are "stations" of food, but it's not in a rec room or in a U-shaped area; instead, it takes place down the long hallway that was once not only an ambulance bay but also a waiting area for an emergency room, and it stretches into what were emergency exam rooms, too. Also like at Site One, when recipients entered, they were required to show their commune-issued eligibility cards to a person doing check-in. Here Christina was stricter than Anna: no card, no entry, no exceptions—people without the documents would be turned away, which Christina said she didn't like but was required by the commune to do. She did have boxes of chocolates on hand—they arrived from the bank as part of a promotion whose date had expired—and told the person attending the desk to be sure to offer one to each person upon entry. Inside, a resident oversees each food station.

Hien and I had the most expensive ingredients on offer here today—meat and fish, and we had separated them out into boxes on two sides of our long table. At first my idea seemed smart and was working: as recipients came through the line, we held up two packages—one pork, one fish—and let them choose. What surprised me was that to a person and no matter what their ethnicity appeared, every recipient chose the fish (which was filets of frozen cod). When I handed a package of the fish to one of the women passing through, she was so happy that she hugged it to her breast—"Voilà, poission!" she said. A friend of hers farther back in the line saw this and began gesticulating toward Hien and me—the friend clearly wanted a similar package of fish. I saw no harm and indicated I would set one aside for her.

Maintaining a steady flow of recipients moving from station to station in a food distribution is crucial to keeping it running smoothly, but it can be hard. Sometimes, recipients linger at tables and ask for more of something or try to barter—"I won't take cereal if I can have two jams," that kind of thing, which was something I could easily imagine doing myself. Other times, people tried to bargain and trade items in the line, which held up everything. At Site Two's food distribution, flow was monitored by two big African men, both residents and both who told me they were from Congo, whom Christina stationed on either side of the wide entrance. These "guards" regulated how many people entered at a time and mitigated any conflicts that arose (such as if a person without a benefits card refused to leave). They were an intimidating presence, but Christina told me she felt these men were "proud to protect [Site Two] because it is their home."

As people flowed through the line, Hien and I were running out of fish. The woman for whom I had set aside the cod eventually reached us at last. I gave her the fish; she took my hands in hers and kissed them. It seemed to me at that moment like it might have been a long time since anyone had done anything *just* for her. Unfortunately for Hien and me, she was not the only one to notice the kindness. A white Flemish-speaking woman was standing right behind her. This woman wore a frayed trench coat and had short gray hair, and she looked tired. She had seen me pull the fish from the "hidden" spot where I had set it aside and had seen my hands kissed in gratitude. I smiled and, almost out of fish and as this lady was not obviously Muslim, offered her pork. "Waar is de vis?" she said loudly. Where is the fish? She began pointing at the Muslim woman standing in front of her, who was still clutching the package of frozen cod.

Stunned, I did not know how to respond. There were only a couple of packages of fish left in the boxes we had been given for this distribution.

I stuttered. The lady asked again, this time louder: "WAAR IS DE VIS?" She continued to point at the Muslim woman, who was now hunching over the package of fish as if it was about to swim away. Meanwhile, I was as frozen as the fish was: I saw my mistake in an instant. I wanted to explain that this issue was my fault; I wanted to tell the Flemish woman to leave the Muslim woman alone, but I could not manage words. I also could not figure out why the woman was mad at the lady holding the fish instead of at me, since I was the one who had given it to her. Hien stepped in, calling over the security guys for help.

By this time, the trench-coated woman was attempting to take the package of fish from the woman holding it; there was a little tug-of-war going on. Meanwhile, I was waving one of the last packages of fish at her to try to get her to let go. When the security guy, a man named Henri, got to us, he moved his body in between the two women and held up a hand in front of the woman in the trench coat. She let go of the other woman's fish. Then Henri took the other package of fish from me, handed it to the woman in the trench coat, and said, "Tu, pas!" You, leave. The woman in the trench coat turned around abruptly and strutted out of the Raphael Center while waving the frozen fish over her head like a trophy.

"Vous obtenez ce que vous obtenez!" Henri said for all to hear. Then he turned to me and quietly repeated it. You get what you get. Hien patted me on the back. I had been curious about why the food distribution centers in Brussels did not differentiate foodstuffs for the many Muslim people who visited them. Now I knew.

Where Perks Meet Rights

The first floor of the Food Bank of Brussels is a loading dock lined with boxes coming in and going out; inside there is a small office for the forklift operators with a punch-clock in it, and an adjacent large, open room with a scale and prefolded boxes where the sorting of the goods takes place. Farther in, there is also a small room, maybe once a foreman's office when the place was still a tea factory, that looks like a one-room miniature grocery store. This space is referred to by its French name, Le Magasin. I thought it looked rather like an exhibit of a grocery store, like the kind they have in children's museums that are lined with fake fruits and vegetables and pretend jars of jam, only with real items. In it are two little aisles whose shelves are lined with jars of jam—including some fancy brands like Bonne Maman, imported from the South of France, but mostly store brands from local grocery chains—as well

One of the most interesting features of the Food Bank of Brussels is the faux grocery store (*le magasin*), set up with aisles and departments like a "real" market complete with an ancient cash register (which doesn't work), which bank workers are allowed to visit once a week for the purpose of selecting a box of free food from the bank's inventory to take home for themselves. The conversation about whether this is "a perk" or "a right" was one of the most tense ones at the bank. Author photo.

several varieties of coffee, including sacks of ground as well as whole beans and Nespresso machine pods. Stock also includes canned soups, boxed cereals and pastas, and many jars of condiments. There is even a "sundries" section, with dishwashing liquids, feminine hygiene products, and cat food. The only thing missing is fresh produce; the refrigerated shelves where you'd find the apples, oranges, and tomatoes instead held (unrefrigerated) boxes of tea bags and jars of honey. There is even a counter with an ancient cash register on it. I often overheard visitors to the bank, such as tour groups of high school students or social services administrators, remark curiously about "the store" inside the bank.

Gschwindt, as a former diplomat, gives all the bank tours, and he would always answer: "This is a 'store' for our workers; as a perk, they visit it once a week and take a parcel of food—for free—as a courtesy gift," he says as he ushers them past. The visitors smile, nod, and move on, but the store was an ongoing mystery for me. Except for one hour each week, the door to it was always locked. Eventually and after volunteering for a few weeks, I asked Michiels what it was all about. He began by explaining that communal and regional social services offices fund employment contracts for the twelve workers here, but the "store" was for them, and they were allowed to get one ten-kilogram-sized box of free food, about twenty-two pounds, from it each week, in what he described as "a perk."

I was curious: Because they draw salaries and receive benefits, how did it come about that they also got a box of free food from the bank? The workers' social services contracts ensure that the twelve workers receive the Belgium minimum wage, which was fixed at €1,859.81 per month (about US$1,781), making it one of the highest in Europe, which has a range from €500 in Bulgaria and Romania to €2,000 in Luxembourg (Fleming, 2020). However, Michiels pointed out that this relatively high minimum wage is still less than 10 percent above the poverty line. In fact, during a union of trade workers strike in 2019, the spokesperson for the socialist national trade union (officially the General Federation of Belgian Labor, known as the FGTB), Nicholas Depret, said that this was not enough to meet the expenses of everyday life. "Is it logical to have to choose between health care and proper meals?" he asked (*Brussels Times*, 2019). Michiels explained: "Over the years, our workers have told us that they are surrounded by food they give away to others, and that they want this perk. We found that they were taking food from the bank anyway, so we made a little store and allowed it, mostly so they feel they should not just take food." He told me that the internal distribution happens every Thursday at one o'clock. "Go and see it for yourself," he said.

When I arrived at the store on Thursday at ten minutes to one, there was a line at the locked door—the forklift operators, truck drivers, and administrative assistants were in it. One person was inside: Bruno, the bank's controller. Bruno oversaw a lot of the inventory coming in from the groceries and kept spreadsheets noting which store partners sent what. He was also, each Thursday, in charge of the bank's internal store. I spent a lot of time sorting food with Bruno and came to know and love him. He was a Ghanaian immigrant to Brussels who had worked as a biomedical engineer until kidney cancer and the burden of biweekly dialysis forced him into retirement when he was just forty and even then, in frail health. Well into his sixties during the time I worked at the bank, he occupied a unique position as a person everyone could agree on: he was beloved by the bank's directors as well as its workers.

He was also unpaid; he survived on his disability income and his pension and thus, officially speaking, was a volunteer, yet I often saw him eating lunch and hanging out with the other African and African-descended people at the bank, rather than with the administrators (who were all also volunteers). He was about five feet tall, and his clothes were perpetually too big for his thin frame. From his engineering days, he was partial to wearing a starched white lab coat, which he brought with him to the bank each day. It occurred to me that Bruno was about the size of my twelve-year-old son. He said he came to feel useful and give himself something to do: "I have five children and nineteen grandchildren, and many of them live with me and visit me all the time; I have to get out of the house!" he told me (Owusu, 2017). Michiels told me that volunteers are not allowed to use the store—it is only for the workers, who ostensibly need it while the volunteers do not, but that Bruno was the only exception (Michiels, 2016). The bank directors agreed many years ago that he could take home a weekly food package, too. Bruno told me that he relies on the cereals, jams, boxes of sugar cubes, and tea bags to feed his many grandchildren.

It is hard to believe that bank director Michiels was the same age as Bruno, because he was as robust as Bruno was fragile, and not at all in need of help feeding his grandchildren. Although Michiels retired from the corporate sector as a director of an international pharmaceuticals company, he had humble beginnings as the son of a railway worker. He told me he never went to college and instead had been working since he was in his late teens, steadily climbing the corporate ladder, first for the same railway company that employed his dad and eventually getting bigger jobs in bigger companies—in a way that he says would be unimaginable for a non–college graduate in America (Michiels, 2017). After he retired, though, Michiels said he came to volunteer at the bank for the same reason Bruno did: "I wanted to do something good with my time, and a friend told me they needed a new director. I thought, 'I have handled the distribution of pharmaceuticals to international suppliers; surely I can do this'" (Michiels, 2017). Michiels owns a lovely home in Waterloo, just outside Brussels in Wallonia. He says he likes volunteering in part because doing so allows him to maintain ties to the city he loves but might not visit as often if not for the gig.

Inside the store, Bruno was almost finished lining up the boxes for the workers to come in and fill with the foods they choose for themselves. I learned that the Food Bank of Brussels is not the only food bank in the city institution that allows the people who work in it to keep some of the food intended for the neediest recipients; most of the other nine banks do, too,

The food bank's longest-term volunteer runs "the store," a weekly opportunity for bank workers to take home a box of surplus food for themselves. This volunteer acts as a middleman between administrators and employees. Author photo.

according to Bruno. "There is a fine line between people who work here and people we serve," he noted (Owusu, 2017). At one o'clock on the dot, Bruno began letting people into the store, three at a time. The first was Pascal, a forklift operator. Pascal is the size of an NFL linebacker; he has big muscles and big, brown eyes and says very little when he passes the administrators in the halls of the bank—unfortunate for me, because I was often being chaperoned by one or another of the administrators, even when I was sorting food. I say unfortunate because my only chances to observe Pascal were when he was driving a forklift and thus unable to talk with me, or when he was in *le magasin*. When I was alone writing in my notebooks or taking a coffee break, though, he often smiled at me in a more friendly way; I wished I'd had a chance to ask him about his experiences. Because Pascal was one of the few people at the bank whose state contract meant he punched a time clock and because he did not eat lunch in the dining room but instead took his food downstairs, I did not ask to infringe on his paid work time. I did, however, ask Michiels what he could tell me about this large yet mysterious presence around the place. He told me that Pascal was thirty-four and immigrated to Brussels from the Democratic Republic of the Congo (DRC) when he was a kid (Michiels, 2017).

The DRC, the second-largest country in Africa and eighty times the land size of Belgium, was Belgium's official colony from 1908 until 1960. Given this history, Pascal's story is hardly an unfamiliar one in Brussels. As of June 30, 2020, when the DRC celebrated sixty years of independence, more than 280,000 people had emigrated from the DRC to Belgium, and more than 120,000 live in Brussels today. The first wave to arrive in Brussels, students looking to live near the Free University of Brussels, established a now-thriving Congolese community in the Matonge neighborhood, which they immediately renamed upon settling there after a district in the DRC's capital Kinshasa (De Lorenzo, 2020). The tortured, exploitative legacy of Belgium's forced occupation of the Congo, in which the colonizers took advantage of the country's vast natural resources in addition to forcing its people into what the first prime minister of the DRC, Patrice Lumumba, referred to in a historic independence speech as "humiliating slavery," means at least two things when it comes to Pascal: one, he speaks perfect French; two, like many of his compatriots, he feels Belgium owes him some recognition. Here is one example of how this feeling is demonstrated in everyday city life: In the wake of Black Lives Matter protests in Brussels that resulted in violence against Black protesters in 2018, the local organization Reparons L'Histoire (Let's Repair History) launched a high-profile, media-backed petition to remove all statues of former Belgian king Leopold in Brussels; in response to the demand, the state secretary for city planning and heritage for the Brussels region created a working group to decide the fate of the statues and other signs of colonialism in public spaces, for which debates are ongoing, and the education minister proposed making courses on the history of the DRC and colonialism compulsory, which is also still in the process of debate at the time of this writing and as the modification of school curricula in Brussels can take up to two years (DeLorenzo, 2020). As these conflicts play out in Brussels today, Belgian-Congolese and other pan-African organizations claim they have the patience to stay the course. As Gia Abrassart, an activist and the founder of the cultural organization I Congo, a library and art space dedicated to Belgians of African descent, told the German newspaper *Deutsche Welle* in 2020 in an article on activism in the Matonge, "We do not fear this moment will end, we have understood that we need to put continuous pressure on the Belgian government" (De Lorenzo, 2020).

Taking down statues may be an eventual step in what turns out to be a long process of rewriting the shared history of Belgium and Congo, but for now Pascal clearly needed food. Even though he, like all bank employees, was allowed to take a box of food, he took four boxes from the stack and began filling them, quickly loading in boxes of cereal.

"Pascal, c'est assez! That is enough!" Bruno said, pointing to the boxes.

"I have four children to feed. Get out of my way, old man," Pascal responded, not stopping as he stuffed another box with bags of potato chips.

I did not expect to see much intrigue at the bank's internal food distribution to its employees, but I was intrigued. Bruno was technically Pascal's superior. The bank had rules about how much food its employees could take, but the only person who seemed to be enforcing them was a frail old Ghanaian immigrant—someone who ostensibly had more in common with the people of color who used the bank's internal bank than with its wealthy white administrators. I was intrigued that Pascal did not stop even after Bruno had warned him, and thought of my own children, then eleven and eight attending an art class. I knew that if I had to worry about them having enough food, I would do exactly what Pascal was doing: ignore the warnings of a person who had no power to fire me or enforce artificial rules and continue to fill as many boxes of food as I could carry.

Pascal was now up against time; his colleagues—the other forklift workers, truck drivers, and maintenance and cleaning staff at the bank—were growing impatient behind him and telling him to hurry up. "Allez! Allez!" a few said. "Come on." I saw that sweat had formed on Pascal's brow as he grabbed an expensive raspberry jam—exactly, in fact, the one I would have chosen had it been available to me—with one arm and several sleeves of crackers with the other. Into the box they went. Bruno shook his head.

I thought back to Michiels telling me that Pascal has been enrolled in the city's social welfare system since he arrived in the country as a child. That meant that his primary education, like that of many Congolese who grew up under Belgian rule, was overseen not only by the state but especially by the Catholic Church (De Boeck, 2017). This arrangement in which the church was enrolled in an official educational capacity had been in place for centuries before the government sought to sever the ties, but vestiges of it remain today. For example, the Belgian Constitution (art. 24 §1) states that public education is free, but this does not only mean that parents can choose a school for their children; it also implies that (non)religious communities are free to set up their own schools with state support if they meet the criteria about the quality of education. In fact, according to a study conducted by Patrick Loobuyck, a political philosophy professor at the University of Ghent, and Leni Franken, an expert researcher on the freedom of education at the University of Antwerp, even though all religions in Belgium have the legal opportunity to set up church-based schools, the only extended network of such schools in the nation is Catholic, with a few Jewish schools and almost no Muslim schools: "In fact, approximately 70 percent of all Flemish and 60 percent of all Walloon schools are non-public, Catholic schools, which is a unique situation in all of the European Union" (Loobuyck & Franken, 2011). When it comes to educating the children of Congolese, after the Belgian parliament assumed control of the Congo in 1908, Catholic mission schools there were afforded government subsidies and given a privileged official status. This meant that primary education was not only associated with evangelization (and an emphasis on morality rather than knowledge acquisition) but remained that way for decades despite waves of nationalism that threatened to return schools to the jurisdiction of the Congolese state (DePaepe, 2010).

What this meant for Pascal is that by the time he immigrated to Brussels, where his family registered for social services such as unemployment benefits because they arrived without jobs, he was already less qualified to attend primary schools. I was not surprised, then, when Michiels told me that Pascal had dropped out of high school in favor of working to support his family. Once he reached adulthood with no high school diploma, Pascal had little choice but to register himself for communal social services—which is how and why his social worker offered him a contract to work at the food bank. In accordance with the bank's renewable eighteen-month contracts, Pascal is required by communal social services to do two things while working this job, both designed to make him a more attractive prospect on the job market: learn to speak Dutch by speaking with bank coworkers (only some of whom actually speak Dutch—the administrators, most of whom he had little contact with), and learn how to operate a forklift (which he in fact learned and became certified to do while on the job).

In addition to being caught in the crosshairs of Belgium's ongoing attempts to contend with extending new forms of justice to its Congolese population, Pascal is also an example of a person in Brussels who contends with the city's enduring linguistic-cultural discord, which itself mirrors a broader rift that has long existed across the European continent (Blainey, 2016). In his wide-ranging study of the politics and ethics of nation building via the institution of a lingua franca, the KU-Leuven (Katholieke Universiteit Leuven)–based political philosopher Philippe van Parijs argues that the European Union, which has twenty-four official languages and an official language policy objective for every EU citizen to master two other languages in addition to their mother tongue, operates "a highly coercive territorially differentiated linguistic regime" (2014, 137). His example of why he became interested in the issue has to do with living in Brussels, which he describes, correctly, as "the officially bilingual capital city of an officially trilingual country; a city that has now also become, by chance far more than by design, the capital of the European Union, a weird political entity of an unprecedented kind committed to granting equal status to the official languages of all its national components and hence forced to develop the bulkiest interpretating and translating services in the history of mankind" (1).

What does this mean to Pascal, on his designated day to take home one box of free food from the Food Bank of Brussels where he works as part of his state-funded welfare benefits? It means that in a largely French-speaking city, he is required to conduct business in Dutch, a language he has affinity for and that is in fact one of languages of his colonizers, and even required to speak it on the job if he wishes to conform to the terms of the state. This is more than weird or bulky or awkward; it's arguably abusive. It also means that while all bank workers are given an allotment of free food to take home each week, they must do so under the gaze of the all-white bank administrators. This is yet another example of processes of surveillance and regulation, like those described by American studies scholar Psyche Williams-Forson in her study *Eating While Black: Food and Race in America* (2022). In numerous observances of real-world encounters, Williams-Forson articulates powerful ways in which instances of food shaming, surveillance, and regulation happen every day in American social life, particularly in the context of food procurement for Black people. One generalizable point of Williams-Forson's work that transcends American culture is that in the absence of knowing other people's personal and social histories, many times passersby make judgments about the ways in which Black people consume food without bearing in mind the numerous factors that affect the single moment they are witnessing (2022). For example, without understanding anything about Pascal's personal story, not to mention the history of the relations between the Belgians and the Congo, it is impossible to grasp the meaning of Pascal's activities.

Williams-Forson argues for the value of what the feminist anthropologist Donna Haraway refers to as "situated knowledges," or, in essence, the value of taking the standpoints and contexts of people into account as you seek to understand their worlds (1988). Haraway's premise is that knowledge about how people live is always personal and subjective, so it would be impossible to analyze any social interaction from a neutral, external standpoint (which she refers to as playing "the god trick"). Instead, and according to her, the only fair and just way to apprehend any perspective other than one's own is to carefully attend to all the power relations at play not only in observing other people but also in the processes of knowledge production itself. In other words, Haraway urges us to consider questions like, What external forces contribute to what we think we know about a person, and in which ways? In the case of Pascal in the food bank, it might be tempting to see him in this situation with Bruno as a person who "should" be taking one box instead of four, but such a perspective fails to account for the history of Pascal's culture as it developed in Brussels, nor does it consider his own standpoint as a bank worker in the near-constant presence of wealthier, more powerful bank volunteers who run the place yet do not require its services, whereas he works at the place and does. This more nuanced perspective underscores why Pascal might have felt that it was his right to take more food than the bank's allotment—which to begin with was arbitrary and not based on need. Bruno, caught between understanding the needs of his colleagues and the demands of his supervisors, stood shaking his head mournfully and seemed to neither agree with Pascal's actions nor be willing to do anything to stop them.

In watching all this play out, I asked myself: Did it matter that one bank employee took food that otherwise could have gone to recipients, and if so, for whom did it matter? I did not have to wait long to discover that one person it mattered to was director Michiels, who, after I asked him if it was all right that some bank workers left with more than one box per week, told me that he believed the *magasin* itself had exceeded its intended purpose. "It was originally supposed to be a perk, but to them [the bank workers who access it weekly] it has become a *right*." This was a complicated argument, not least because it was the government providing the food in the first place, in the form of a social service, which itself is in fact a *right*. If the bank workers are employed by means of a government contract, why should that not also get a ration of the government-supported food assistance? I asked Michiels. He responded that the employees of the bank are already receiving work contracts and thus should not also need food, but they were, in his view, resentful, and thus prone to acts of petty thievery. "Look around," he told me. "You will see food is hidden everywhere. Some workers say they need it as much as the people who receive it, but we don't know that" (Michiels, 2017).

Over the next few weeks, I followed Michiels's suggestion and looked for "hidden food"—which turned out to be a difficult pursuit because there are literally tons of nonhidden foods at the bank, mostly overflowing from gigantic boxes that are stacked all over the place. However, I discovered that Michiels was right. In the bank's small laundry room, I spotted two brown paper shopping bags stuffed with jars of spaghetti sauce and boxes of pasta. Behind the forklifts I discovered several smaller cargo boxes filled with bars of good chocolate. And I noticed that sometimes when I was in the sorting room going through the daily pickups from supermarkets, various workers would enter the space, peer into the newly delivered boxes, then take out a few items—a box of cookies here, a bottle of olive oil there—and then leave, the new items in their apron pockets. Some walked out as if nothing had ever happened; others winked at me knowingly. I felt that it was beyond my position as a researcher to intervene, but I was also confused about whether they had in fact done anything untoward. If they also needed food, this seemed like the place to get it—in a liminal space where the food in question held no official value, since it had been removed from the marketplace and yet had not been reassigned to any new population who would miss it.

Michiels and other administrators had a different perspective, though, and theirs was based on events beyond those that took place weekly at the *magasin*. I was there for one. On July 19, 2018, I came into the bank early one morning to meet with Michiels for an interview session, of which we had many scheduled that summer. Usually impeccably groomed and well attired, the former pharmaceutical executive was pacing in his office, disheveled and clearly annoyed. "Are you all right?" I asked. "Ah well, I hate to tell you about this," he began. "But you are now speaking with someone who is the subject of a criminal investigation."

As Michiels explained it, in the late afternoon of the previous day, he had received a summons from the commune of Anderlecht's police department requiring him to appear at the station for questioning. Apparently, an anonymous source had tipped off the commune police that a worker at the bank (I should note that it was not Pascal but in fact a white man of French descent) was running a black-market operation in a nearby apartment building, selling foods he had taken from the bank to building dwellers and their friends. Michiels told me that the police wanted to know if the bank had allowed this and was profiting from it; Michiels swore that this occasion was the first he'd heard of it, and then explained that all bank workers were allowed to take home one box of "free food" per week. After the police were satisfied with this explanation, Michiels then hightailed it back to the bank, where he called the worker's social services supervisor and explained the situation. The social services supervisor told Michiels that he couldn't just "fire" the bank worker and that there were a series of disciplinary actions he should take first. "I said 'No way, he cannot return, and if he does, I'm going to turn him over the police," he told me. This, apparently, was enough for the social services supervisor, who agreed to place the offender elsewhere. By the time Michiels finished telling me all of this, he was exasperated and red-faced: "We turned a blind eye! We thought we were giving a perk!" he practically shouted.

Catholicism, Care, and Chips

What do these scenes of food distribution at Site One, Site Two, and the "store" inside the Food Bank of Brussels tell us about food waste in Brussels today? For one thing, all three are laden with culture clashes. At Site One, a Protestant preacher hectored a roomful of Muslim women against the dangers of divorce while they were required to bide their time listening in order receive allocations of food assistance promised by the nation of Belgium, a social welfare state that has prided itself globally on the assistance it offers its citizens and residents. At Site Two, one food bank recipient challenged the rights of another to a package of frozen fish in an emotional confrontation that pitted the role of religious prohibitions on foods against the conditions of deprivation. At the "store" inside the bank, one worker took his stated perk but was criticized for taking too much by the same people who offered it but did not require it, while another deployed the perk in illegal black-market activities that required administrators to answer for offering the perk in the first place.

Activities in these three sites reveal the tensions simmering at the surface of the oldest form of food distribution in this and almost every other global city: charitable donation of food to those in need. More than merely showing how charitable donations of food can be emotional and full of intense feeling and conflict, these scenes represent the ways in which religious expressions of care reinforce certain class-based ideas about the worthiness and value not only of food but of people. They reminded me very much of the conclusions that Rebecca De Souza draws in her analysis of the operations of two food pantries in Duluth, Minnesota: *Feeding the Other: Whiteness, Privilege, and Neoliberal Stigma in Food Pantries* (2019). Food pantries are clients of food banks—the "middlemen," as it were, between the places where food is collected and sorted (banks) and the people to whom it ultimately will belong. At first blush, the pantries De Souza studied seemed quite different from one another: one was funded in part by government and private grants and used an "entrepreneurial" distribution scheme, which means it charged very low prices for the food on its shelves, kind of like a low-cost secondhand grocery store; and the other was a faith-based pantry run by an evangelical church that operated entirely without state support and used a more traditional method where recipients got food for free. What De Souza found, though, was that both were spaces in which clients were routinely stigmatized through discourses that emphasized hard work, self-help, and economic productivity. De Souza notes that "charitable food assistance programs have come to stand in for the state and function as arms of the government," which is certainly the case when it comes to the Food Bank of Brussels (Poppendieck, 1999; Riches & Silvasti, 2014). She also notes that in the process the way most such organizations run food distributions create and emphasize the social distance and difference between the people who work or volunteer in them and the populations they serve, such that "a problem like hunger becomes a problem of *the hungry* and suspicions about the morals and motives of the recipients follow Calvinist ideas about the deserving workforce versus the undeserving poor" (De Souza, 2019, 22).

De Souza is not the first scholar to note the way clients of food pantries are generally treated, as if they are to blame for much larger systemic causes of hunger and are not working hard or enough or otherwise doing their best to succeed. As she readily acknowledges, her claim that "stigmatizing ideologies about the hungry hold the food system in place" sits on the shoulders of other scholars and activists (2019, 17). For instance, sociologist Janet Poppendieck noted that most charitable food distribution she observed over the course of thirty years of hunger in America "normalizes destitution and legitimizes personal generosity as a response to major social and economic dislocation" (1999, 5). In addition, Andrew Fisher, who worked in the anti-hunger field for twenty-five years as the director of national and local food groups, and as a researcher, organizer, policy advocate, and coalition builder, coined the phrase "hunger industrial complex" precisely to describe the inequalities at play when "private, public, corporate, and community actors come together to deliver, distribute, or cook food for the hungry and food insecure" (2017).

Thinking with De Souza, Fisher, and Poppendieck means acknowledging that even the best-run food pantries are not neutral spaces where food is shared and community is created; they are places where stigma is front and center. What my observations in Brussels can add to their discussions is such determinations about worthiness of food *as well as of people* happen further up the chain and are not relegated just to the spaces where food is distributed to clients. It also happens prior to those encounters in the warehouses where food is sorted, in the grocery stores where certain foods are abandoned by certain classes of consumers and left for others, and even among food distribution workers who argue among themselves and their colleagues over rights to food meant for other populations. Of course, this proves the larger point outlined in *First World Hunger, Revisited*, that "in rich, food secure, industrialized nations there coexists institutionalization, corporatization, and globalization of charitable food banking" (Riches & Silvasti, 2014, 48). It also proves a lack of real commitment to reducing social inequalities as they play out in the allocation of food resources.

It is easy to see the ways in which faith-based food distribution efforts, rather than legal entitlements, have become a cornerstone of a government's efforts to end hunger. That the efforts to ensure that all people regardless of income have access to fresh, healthy food so often happen in churches is a function of classic Judeo-Christian logics of hospitality and care. There are many ways, though, that members of different religions in high-income countries choose to practice such acts. For example, in Judaism, it is considered a legal obligation to offer food to strangers in need and a mitzvah of *gemilut hasadim* (the giving of loving kindness); for example, at a traditional Seder on Passover, the service specifies the issuance of an invitation to the hungry and needy: "Whoever is in need let him come and eat" (Ta'anit, 20b). The Talmud even specifies rules of engagement for sharing food between those who have a lot of it and those who do not. While hosts may not make guests feel unwelcome, guests are also obligated to express gratitude for the labors of the host (Eisenberg, 2004). In the Lutheran Christian tradition of Norway, to which more than 75 percent of Norwegians belong, a tenet of the underlying ethic of universalism, which emphasizes the idea that all will be saved, it is considered a public and civic responsibility of all citizens in a society to reduce inequities, including by feeding the hungry (Silvasti & Karjalainen, 2014).

In Belgium, the prevailing logic is Catholic based. Providing free food to the poor has been an important mission of the network of Catholic churches in Brussels for hundreds of years. Since the sixteenth-century Counter-Reformation, also known as the Catholic Reformation, Belgium has been "a country permeated by a Catholic identity while nevertheless maintaining a strong secular tradition" (Blainey, 2016). In practice this means that 75 percent of Belgians identify as Catholic, yet only 11 percent of them say they regularly attend Mass (Anderson, 2015). In my experience, it takes an outsider to see the ways in which expressions of Catholicism connect to everyday life in this city—most Belgians I asked about whether the church played a role in their everyday lives said no, and yet five of the official ten state holidays are in fact not only religious but specifically Catholic, including Whit Monday (*Pinkstermandaag/Lundi de Petecote*; "Monday of the Holy Spirit," also known as Memorial of the Blessed Virgin Mary); Ascension Day (*Hemelvaart/Ascension*, also known as Holy Thursday, or the day Jesus ascended to heaven); and Assumption Day (*Onze Lieve Vrouw hemelvaart/Assomption*, one of the four Marian dogmas of the Catholic Church). *The Pillar*, an American-based online newsletter focusing on the Catholic Church and its role in society, founded by two alumni of the *Catholic News*, posted an article investigating how and why Belgium, a nation that only ranks in twenty-eighth place on the list of countries with the largest Catholic populations, is one that also "drives Catholic news" (Coppen, 2022). Their conclusion? A stunning connection between "good works, small congregations" and an acknowledgment of the fact that while Mass attendance figures are (way) down, the national church's one-hundred-page annual report features many "quirky pictures of young people and pages highlighting charitable works" (Coppen, 2022).

I have seen such "quirky pictures" in real life, but the young people I saw were not in the Food Bank of Brussels (they were, however, in the other two cities I'll describe in subsequent chapters). What I saw across the city was its inhabitants' connection to Catholic ideology playing out in the many soup kitchens and food banks sponsored by Catholic churches in all the city's nineteen communes. It is easy to see the ways in which food is the material agent of "making the stranger welcome in order to better know God," echoing Catholic doctrine that the act of sharing food not only builds communities and brings individuals closer to their spiritual ideal but also proves to them that their God has produced a world where there is always enough, that the deeply held Catholic belief that if there is a problem then God will provide a solution is in fact true (Rudy, 1997, 100).

In this way, activities at all three of the sites I visited in this study are snapshots of the way in which Catholic ethics operate in a secular European capital, although nowhere are they expressed more directly than at the bank. Although plenty of non-Catholic organizations in Brussels offer food to the needy, such as the Salvation Army, the Lutheran and Anglican churches, and various community-based organizations, there is no denying the strong central role played by Catholic churches in the distribution of free food in this city. Of the six hundred organizations that receive food from the bank, more than half are Catholic-based charities, and they serve about 24,429 hungry people each week (Michiels, 2017). In doing so, their provisioning activities reify Catholic ideas about social obligations that have been in social circulation since the advent of the church: People who have enough to eat are required by God to offer hospitality to those in their midst who do not. As Poppendieck notes, "charitable food assistance programs have come to stand in for the state and function as arms of the government" (1999).

It is worth noting that food is not the only form of care that is enmeshed in tensions between church and state and that Belgium is not the only nation in which we can find them. In her ethnographic account of two years of field-work in hospitals and health care facilities in and around Paris, Miriam Ticktin theorizes ways in which time-honored Catholic expressions of charity are deployed in new settings and largely by medical means (2011, 131). In analyzing the operations and politics involved among networks of medical caregivers in France, she, too, explores the tensions and intersections, witting and otherwise, that exist between the church and the state. Ticktin's ultimate claim is that while medical efforts are largely driven by a sense of compassion, compassion itself is a flexible, even contestable concept. "Compassion is not static; its subjects gradually change to fit new contexts and histories even as they appear to be outside of time, outside of history—as universally and timelessly worthy of benevolence. Its signifiers shift," she argues (129). Ticktin's work applies to the efforts I observed in the Food Bank of Brussels, where a literally ancient expression of compassion—in the form of giving food to the needy—both reflects long-standing practices and has shifted to accommodate new contexts (secular food distributions), new materials (the discarded but still edible food also known as food waste), but also new understandings (of food shaming and of the ways in which such distributions promote instead of reduce inequalities in the food system).

For these reasons, the self-identifying progressive food policy experts in Brussels I met with, including those who work for private NGOs as well as for the European Union's sustainability desk and its health minister, all disdained food banks as relics of the past. These policymakers and influencers generally saw food banks as agents that inadvertently enable poverty and hunger and alienate rather than uplift a community's lower classes. Rob Renaerts, the European Union's environmental sustainability consultant, is one of them. In his work on the European Union's sustainability desk, Renaerts says he advocates for models of food waste that involve recirculation based on community participation rather than distribution networks. Renaerts asserts that food distributions do not promote social inclusion because "all people who use them can *do* for themselves is receive." For this reason, he says food banks are a "dead model" (Renaerts, 2017b). "Giving food to poor people does not improve communities. People don't get to participate in local economic life," he said (Renaerts, 2017c). Renaerts predicts that given the European Union's new sustainability goals, food banks are so outmoded that they will become obsolete in the next ten years. (In chapter 4, I will discuss exactly what he thinks will come to replace them.) This is an interesting prediction, but one that does not account for the fact that the lowest levels of poverty are extremely entrenched and that for some community members, economic participation in city life might not ever be possible—for example, for reasons of extreme mental illness and homelessness.

In her analysis of two models of ways in which nongovernmental organizations work with AIDS orphans and children with disabilities in rural Uganda, China Scherz addresses aspects of both Ticktin's critique of the depoliticizing effects of the state's role in humanitarian aid projects and Renaerts's assessment of the unsustainability of food banks (2014, 136–37). The specific question of whether the food bank's expressions of Catholic charity are outmoded and, more damningly, perhaps even embed food recipients in a cycle of poverty rather than extend to them a means by which to become self-sufficient and lift themselves out is one that Scherz addresses in her analysis of Mercy House, a home run by the Franciscan Sisters of Africa: "Do those engaged in charity have a stake in keeping people in poverty so as to maintain a population to whom they can distribute the alms necessary to achieve their own salvations?" she asks (136).

This provocation might be directed toward all entanglements of church-based charities, ethics, and care. In posing it, Scherz effectively probes whether charity and political activism can coexist. To the question, I sought to understand whether charity *specifically in the form of food (waste)* represents an exceptional category of a kind of "charity" best mitigated by both church *and* state. Other anthropologists have considered food as a material mitigator between church and state; an excellent example is Melissa Caldwell's ethnography of welfare recipients in postsocialist Moscow that focuses on the social and economic transactions of poor Muscovites in Christian-based soup kitchens.[2] As in Scherz, Caldwell also notes that some aid environments are "models of assistance that entail a unidirectional flow of aid and power" and "do not allow possibilities for [recipients] to reciprocate for the charity they receive" (2004, 90). Yet she also notes that many of her interlocutors use a vocabulary of "duty and responsibility" to characterize their food-aid distribution efforts. She takes care to explore their concepts of care-as-duty as acts of "mutual rescue or mutual assistance," stressing that the giving of food is an act that is potentially as beneficial to the receivers as it is to the givers (84). This is certainly true at the Food Bank of Brussels, where administrators feel they are doing good deeds in their retirement by serving the poorest among them (Gschwindt, 2017).

That food only moves in one direction has long been true of food banks; it has also long been theorized that volunteers donate labor as a method of spiritual salvation (Lee et al., 2021). What interests me in the specific case of the Food Bank of Brussels and its volunteer-administrators is that the food that's being donated/freely shared is entirely enabled by the state, thanks to the European Union's new policy and Belgium's quick adoption of it. And it's also not just the state. The European Union has compelled private businesses—supermarkets—to enroll in this plan as well, so that now such businesses are virtually required by the state, lest they pay huge fines, to donate to food distribution centers that are largely run by Catholic churches. It's a heady entanglement of interests, resources, and motivations.

Scherz argues that such a private-public-religious three-way partnership cosponsoring the flow of aid in one direction, toward the poor, might not be a bad thing. She notes that many Ugandans view material forms of Catholic charity as deeply intertwined with their own ethics of care and exchange. I saw such feelings expressed by recipients at Site One, at Site Two, and in the bank's own store, in which people who received food seemed willing to accept their own needs as a point of balance between concerns of the church and concerns of the state. What I saw that was novel was the inclusion of supermarket food waste into charitable aid models; this is one way in which, as Ticktin argues, signifiers of care can shift. The edible material in Brussels food distribution hubs that is now being recirculated did not come, as it has for centuries, from community food drives or church collection efforts in which members donate food from their personal stores. It derives, instead, from someplace else: the state's mandate on large-scale supermarkets that, since 2014, are no longer allowed to throw food away. This shift does something interesting in the process: it revalues the food categorized as waste by situating it into a once-private charitable distribution scheme. And it is the state that is driving the efforts, compelling the supermarkets to do so. In this way, what EU policymakers characterize as "innovative food waste policy" is actually a new expression of centuries-old traditions of Catholic Church members' efforts to feed the hungry (Riches, 2018). I think understanding this framing by the state in the context of the nation's religious history is important. First, it reveals the way the state frames seemingly "new" concerns about the environment and the working poor as being solved by its own innovation. Second, history highlights how the state offloaded these familiar problems onto the Catholic Church, whose volunteers were eager to undertake the mission of feeding the poor and connecting to God.

Hard to believe for some as it may be, that last bit about the working poor in Brussels is something that simply did not used to be there. First, there are many more people in Brussels who now need free food than there used to be: "When the food bank opened in 1987, we helped eighteen thousand people a year. Now we help more than twenty-six thousand. The poverty level just keeps increasing just in the Brussels region. Without the supermarket support, we would not be able to survive," Gschwindt said in 2016. Second, there is increasing pressure on Brussels and other EU nations that depend on incinerating waste to stop the practice. Brussels already has some of the worst air pollution in Europe because of it being one of the continent's most congested cities for traffic. Current Capital Region officials, the majority of whom since the spring 2019 elections now come from the local Green Party, have prioritized recycling initiatives designed to promote so-called no burn anti-incineration practices (Keating, 2019; Simon, 2018). The state now supplies surplus food to do two things: provide material care *and* contribute to pollution-reducing agendas.

That the existence of Catholic care networks combined with the steady supply of still-edible food waste can take care of so many state needs may be one reason why Belgium remains one of the few countries in the European Union that does not have a law guaranteeing its citizens the right to an adequate supply of food. As of 2015 when the last such law was proposed, by the national Green Party, the Belgian government vetoed it; legislators on both sides of the political spectrum agreed that the right to food was already sufficiently "addressed by various laws and social measures in the country"

(Riches, 2018, 100). I argue that they are only correct about that because they have such an established Catholic charity network in place, one that is already feeding the hungry such that the government can outsource not only that responsibility to the church but also the new social responsibility of re-circulating food waste—which in a de facto way has now also become the provenance of the church's expressions of hospitality.

To be clear, not one recipient of the Food Bank of Brussels whom I encountered in five years of volunteering expressed a desire to reduce food waste. This fact illustrates findings from urban sociologist Neil Gross, who argues that people struggling to get by every day sometimes see concerns about issues like pollution as classist, perhaps because, as he and other social scientists have posited, environmental activism can be read as a "boutique cause only the well-off can afford to support" (2018). As Gross states, the Yellow Vest demonstrations in Paris provoked working-class residents of the city's outskirts to protest the fact that they could not afford a new tax hike on gas because they did not have the same access to public transportation that their fellow (and much wealthier) urban countrymen did (2018).

Gschwindt said that urban class differences like the ones Gross articulates are exposed in food banks in terms of the distinction between people who are starving, people who are "merely deprived," and people who are volunteering a way of "giving back" (Gschwindt, 2017). Considering the micropolitics of the food (waste) distribution at Site One, at Site Two, and in the food bank's store, there is a spectrum not only between the edible material that is considered food versus waste but also among various kinds of food-related desires, from starvation (the need to eat to survive) to deprivation (the desire to regain lost status) to charity (the voluntary giving of help to other people, in this case by giving them food). As food's worth is determined by factors such as freshness versus spoilage, desires are determined by needs—to survive, to regain lost status, to give to feel closer to God—the latter of which Scherz characterizes as "a desire to reach others less privileged" (2014, 117).

Of course, volunteers must confront the fact that helping others does not always work out how one hopes it will. Anna Peeters can force the recipients at her Site One food distributions to listen to fiery sermons, but she cannot turn them into Christian practitioners; Christina Alonto can staff Site Two's food distribution with security but cannot ensure that people will respect one another. As for Michiels, the bank's director, he can continue to offer free food perks to bank workers if he's willing to endure weeks of a police investigation over stolen goods funneled into a black market and sold illegally. In that case, and in the end, Michiels declined an opportunity to press charges against the offender; he said that it took some effort to persuade the man's social worker to void the state-sponsored contract allowing him to work at the bank, which is all he wanted. "She asked me to give him another chance, can you believe it?" he asked. "I told her, 'He walked out with bags and bags of food, those were the other chances'" (Michiels, 2017). Even still, Michiels said he would not close the bank's "store." "I turn a blind eye to the store because we do so much good, we feed so many hungry people in Brussels," he said (Michiels, 2017).

Perhaps without intending to, Michiels evoked the essence of Catholic hospitality, a mission articulated by Catholic Worker Movement founder and prominent soup kitchen advocate Dorothy Day: "Feed the hungry, house the homeless, visit the sick and the prisoner. You will reap a hundredfold" (Day, 2003, 518). In this, Day articulates the very concept of charity itself, of giving alms to the poor not as a form of sacrificing oneself but as a way of loving, "and in some way caring for" God—fusing the mission to "love thy Lord" with the commandment to "love thy neighbor" (Scherz, 2014, 28).

Even though the Food Bank of Brussels is not affiliated with the church per se, most of its six hundred clients are, and the state uses the fact to its advantage in at least two ways: in relying on church networks to feed the hungry and, since 2014, to reduce food waste to prevent environmental pollution. As the bank's store shows, the people who fall through the cracks are those like Pascal, people who have paid jobs at the bank and yet also do not make enough money to avoid living on the margins. At food bank distributions, I encountered an array of dishonest and/or discreditable behaviors: people prophesizing hatred; people disrespecting others' religious doctrines; people outright stealing food that rightly belonged to those living in poverty. Yet ultimately, I find it difficult to disagree with Michiels. There is simply no question as to the effectiveness of food banks when it comes to providing food to people in need of it. Food banks are complicated by church ethics and state politics, and by those who fall somewhere in the middle of the official labor force and its welfare recipients. Is the food bank model outdated and flawed? Yes. Do the people who work at food banks provide food for a lot of people in addition to providing a tremendous amount of compassion? Yes. As Scherz argues, it is for this reason—what I call compassion, she calls love— that it may be a mistake to draw a hard line between religion and politics. Such a line would foreclose possibilities of helping people cope with poverty. Such a line would misread the acts of Michiels, Gschwindt, Weyckmans, Alonto, and their teams, as enabling rather than as "a form of protest"—as refusals *not* of helping the poor help themselves but instead of turning them over to the neoliberal ideal, which holds that giving social welfare recipients aid hinders them from being able to provide for themselves. Scherz points out that advocating for participation programs over donations has not yet in fact been proven to bring about the so-called end of poverty (Scherz, 2014, 140). I argue that so long as there is poverty, which despite Renaerts's prediction does not seem to be a problem that the next ten years of EU policy can fix, food banks will not become obsolete. And yet, as I will argue in the subsequent chapters, food banks are woefully inadequate when it comes to taking stakeholders' desires into account and giving them a voice in the ways in which hospitality should be offered by those who know what it is like to receive it. And in that case, I would also argue that food banks should be a last line of support, and that other more intersectional, equitable ways of managing food distribution can and should exist.

In chapter 4, I will analyze one model that claims to do just that, by utilizing food waste as a mechanism for converting the working poor of Brussels into productive taxpayers.

CHAPTER FOUR

When Food Waste Goes to Work

Bel Mundo is a Brussels restaurant that looks like many hipster eating places in most European cities. There's IKEA-esque furniture, an open floor plan, and exposed ductwork. But closer examination reveals key differences: a framed statement proclaiming this a "zero food-waste" restaurant, waiters accompanied by trainers who help them converse with customers, and prices that are about 40 percent less than at most local bistros. Bel Mundo happens to be the latest iteration of a thirty-year-old vision among locals in the commune of Molenbeek aimed at social integration and the assimilation of the area's significant (and growing) immigrant populations. Despite its trendy minimalist vibe, this place is redefining the way in which a social welfare state can put capitalism to use for both feeding people and invigorating a labor market.

Context, of course, is key. Brussels is a city with an impressively complex governmental structure, and the key to understanding it in this chapter is that it's the capital of a social welfare state. This distinctly European form of government sprung up in the wake of the great world wars and was designed to mitigate the "profound uncertainties" of the era by protecting the social and economic well-being of citizens (Gosseye & Heynen, 2013). In the case of Brussels, this has meant helping citizens "cope with the problems" that people face in everyday life—such as educating children, accessing health care, and mitigating social injustices—in a particularly decentralized and yet highly governmental way (Goody, 1982). This is because Brussels is a capital city four times over: it is also the capital of the Flanders region; of the nineteen communes that constitute the regional government; and, de facto, of the European Union. In addition, it is the headquarters of the North Atlantic Treaty Organization (NATO) and the principal seat of the European Parliament.

Government intervention in Brussels has been beneficial to the restaurant Bel Mundo. Without it, it would have been much more difficult to acquire ingredients and labor. Remember that since 2014, all four institutions that call Brussels capital—the European Union, the Belgian nation, the Flemish region, and the commune of Brussels—had established food waste reduction goals. To meet these goals, each level of government offered significant funding to organizations explicitly for food waste reduction missions. Bel Mundo qualified for four different levels of funding. This is significant because before 2014,

The furniture and fixtures in Bel Mundo's dining room were built in the on-site workshop, which is run much in the same way as the restaurant itself: interns are paid by government contracts that allow them to learn woodworking skills in order to help them find success on the job market in that trade. All of the light fixtures above the tables are made by those interns and are for sale to visitors. Author photo.

Bel Mundo got its ingredients from a combination of donations and a small budget that was funded by grants and could only afford to pay a handful of workers. In those days it was a much smaller, more modest restaurant, a cafeteria-style spot that was only open for lunch five days a week. But now in the wake of the European Union's new policy in which grocery stores were required to donate surplus edible food they did not wish to or could not sell, Bel Mundo suddenly had a consistent supply of not just low-cost but free ingredients. This allowed its administrators to allocate the money the café took in each day—meals here were never free, just low cost, and all funds were used for operations, on a major upgrade, and the chance to double the workforce. The facelift plans included enlarging the dining room, enhancing the décor, and, most importantly, fueling an on-site labor force for expanded operating hours. The new iteration now has a designated special event room for birthday parties and off-site meetings, and it has the capabilities to cater off-site events. It is now also open three nights a week for dinner and for Sunday brunch.

To understand how Bel Mundo works and how it grew from what was mostly utilized locally as a lunch spot for old people on welfare into a bona fide restaurant with a coffee bar and a local hipster following, it must be situated in terms of Brussels's so-called social restaurants. Such local institutions—forty are scattered among the nineteen communes—have been operational in European cities for hundreds of years and are rooted in the soup kitchens of Catholic churches (Myaux, 2019). Though open to the public, all were designed as state-subsidized eating places for people who receive social assistance—for example, elderly pensioners and single working mothers. They offer clientele the chance to dine out for a fee that welfare administrators characterize as "low enough to defy all competition" (Myaux, 2019). Often this translates to about €3.50 for a generous *plat du jour*, although there is a sliding scale; to pay less, diners must provide proof of state benefit to a cashier.

Social restaurants are funded by communes with assistance from the federal government. Most have a limited menu that includes a single set of options: a starter (almost always soup), a main dish (reliably fish on Fridays), and a small dessert (often a pudding). Other options are available at additional cost: coffee and tea are usually €1 each and local beers €3. A step below social restaurants is "social soup bars," where clients can purchase a bowl of homemade soup for €1. Such places are designed to allow people who have difficulty socializing with other people a welcoming atmosphere, and as such they are often inside community civic centers (Myaux, 2019). There are also institutions called "coffee receptions," which are food carts on street corners that offer only coffee and rolls for a very low price; they do not offer a place for customers to sit, but people often congregate and chat around them. For these reasons social restaurants are associated with poor people, old people, and immigrants, and eating in them has a social stigma (Myaux, 2019).

While the vision of social welfare states like Belgium has always included provisioning food for citizens in need, the climate of European political life is always changing, and presently it is in a moment that many scholars term a "crisis." This crisis is characterized by demographic and economic displacements across the continent (Alexander, 2019). Aspects of heightened senses of nationalism and general unrest have been theorized in terms of global supply chains of "fast fashion" that affect employment throughout Italy (Krause, 2018); the effects of a new cashless banking system on rural inhabitants, retirees, and immigrant populations in Sweden (Peebles, 2019); and drone usage and the regulation of airspace in everyday European life vis-à-vis the Single European Sky initiative (Mentes, 2020). The link between these studies is not only the idea that modern European social life is unstable but also evidence of new arrangements of working and living conditions that reveal Europeans' aspirations and goals for their futures. The events at Bel Mundo offer a glimpse into a kind of sociality that aggregates two aspects of social justice concerns: food waste and disenfranchised labor. This double activation suggests a novel approach not only to European food politics but also to the operation of the social welfare state, linking distinctly capitalist efforts to make a profit to the value of waste and specific forms of care. The forms of care to which I refer are material as well as social. Bel Mundo is an example of the welfare state's support and extension of social benefits beyond the availability of low-cost housing and universal health care. Investing in Bel Mundo means supporting access not only to fresh food for people who otherwise could not afford it but also to the chance for poor citizens and even undocumented newcomers to participate in the social weft and weave of city life by working in and/or patronizing a restaurant. The interns get access to the local job market they would not otherwise have, and the diners get access to a low-cost meal that is a step (far) above a fast-food outlet.

This is an evolution more than an innovation. "Thirty years ago, Bel Mundo was a little like a soup kitchen; once a week, a group of neighbors got together here and made dinner for foreigners and immigrants who were moving in and had nothing," Nena Cornellis explains (2016). "Chef Nena," as she is known among her kitchen interns, is a lifelong *Bruxelloise* and the head trainer of the kitchen interns at Bel Mundo. She notes that the "group of neighbors" had reason for concern. Just west of Brussels's city center, Bel

Mundo's commune of Molenbeek is familiar to consumers of international news for all the wrong reasons. Fourteen of the people tied to the 2016 and 2017 bombings of the Brussels and Paris airports lived in Molenbeek, the second poorest of the city's communes, with 36 percent of people younger than twenty-five unemployed (Cohen, 2016). It, too, is an evolution: when Bel Mundo was founded, the commune was a mostly Flemish and staunchly Socialist paradigm of heterogeneous working-class Brussels.

In fact, Molenbeek was settled at the end of the eighteenth century by migrants from rural Flanders, who named it from the fusion of *molen* (mill) and *beek* (brook). Attracted by the promise of new industrial jobs, so many workers from both Flanders and France settled here that by the nineteenth century the area was referred to as "Little Manchester" (Cendrowicz, 2015). In the wake of local labor shortages after World War II, Molenbeek became the commune most frequented by immigrants from Turkey and North Africa, arriving at the invitation of the Belgian government to build the national railway and work in the coal mines (Reniers, 2000). Over time, those workers became so valuable to the economy that the state naturalized them as citizens to ensure their continued labor (Dupont et al., 2017). Most of the émigrés were men, but two additional waves of immigration allowed for family reunification, and soon there were spouses and children of the new workers in Molenbeek, too.

However, as the number of Muslims moving into the commune grew, so did "white flight" among the Flemish (Conway, 2015). In today's Molenbeek, at least 41 percent of the ninety-five thousand residents identify as Muslim (Cohen, 2016). In fact, it was the grandparents of the Muslim youth of Molenbeek today that Bel Mundo's initial "group of neighbors"—those who choose not to flee it for the Flemish suburbs—pitched in to help. Their original soup kitchen was a place for neighbors to share food and resources. It was so well loved and frequented—perhaps because there were no other attempts at community integration—that eventually the "group of neighbors" incorporated as a nonprofit called Atelier Groot Eiland (the Big Island Workshop). As they won funding grants, they focused on two key efforts: a wood shop to teach newcomers with no marketable job skills how to make furniture and turning the soup kitchen into a café. In developing both, the administrators acquired funding from the Brussels-Capital Region; the Flemish Community Commission; the commune of Molenbeek; and Davisfonds, a Flanders-based Catholic charity that supports the preservation of Flemish culture. From the commune, they were gifted rights to an abandoned office building. By the early 2000s, Atelier Groot Eiland had become one of Brussels's largest social welfare initiatives, so big that in 2010 its board hired a CEO named Tom Dedeurwaerder, a private-sector executive looking to transition to the social welfare world.

Dedeurwaerder had an even bigger vision for the space. In a multiyear process, he spearheaded an effort to expand the dining room and acquire such equipment as a high-end Italian coffeemaker and an industrial ice cream maker (both donated), plus turn a large plot of unused land between the space and some nearby old tenements into a vegetable garden. Dedeurwaerder was subsequently blessed with the new EU policy as of 2014 that mandated the donation of all unsold but edible supermarket food. Now he needed to figure out how to retain staff on a shoestring. Another state solution appeared: the Article 60 programme, a local expression of the European Union's broad "social economy" agenda. This policy stipulates funding for businesses "intended to make profits for people *other than investors or owners*" across member states and includes "cooperatives, mutual aid societies, non-profit associations, foundations, and social enterprises" that "operate a very broad number of commercial activities, provide a wide range of products and services across the European single market, and generate millions of jobs" (Martinos et al., 2020). As of 2016, there were two million such businesses across the European Union (representing about 10 percent of all businesses), employing more than eleven million people, all with the objective "to have a social, societal or environmental impact for the general interest" rather than to retain profit (Martinos et al., 2020). Article 60 provides nine- to eighteen-month work contracts to people living in Belgium who don't have the skills to access the job market but are fit to work; it gives them the chance to acquire experience to put on a résumé and learn a service trade. Dedeurwaerder is currently entitled to twenty people but is constantly working to acquire more.

However, getting an Article 60 contract for people who are not citizens is tricky. The contracts are meant to be reserved for people who already have citizenship, but in practice and because the system is diffuse and has many bureaucratic layers and points of entry, it can and has been a path to citizenship for immigrants. What it requires is the ability of a potential worker to pass a screening for the program with a communal social worker. Who can pass the test? "People who lack training but have potential to learn, people who want to learn to work, that's what they look for," according to Dedeurwaerder (2018a).

Because it is a job-training facility, too, Dedeurwaerder blanches at characterizing it as a social restaurant. "We are a *real* restaurant here, for customers who pay a competitive price, and we make money. And we must do a good job. We are not just a place to sit and have a coffee and stay out of the rain. We train cooks and servers. I am a job-training facility," he says (Dedeurwaerder, 2018a).

As I will show in two ethnographic snapshots that follow, the activities among the staff and the interns at Bel Mundo combine labor training and food waste with social welfare rights and state responsibilities. It is in this amalgam of business objectives and care—of matching cast-off food with cast-off people—that I locate a unique form of morality that connects citizens' efforts to improve access to food, reduce food waste, and provide access to the labor market within the capitalist workings and machinations of the social welfare state. The moral contours to which I refer reveal the state's investment in caring for people who otherwise lack access to benefits provided to the workforce and to some social activities limited to those who can afford them. In funding Bel Mundo, the state supports a program that stimulates the economic life of the city specifically by reusing surplus edible but unsellable supermarket food. Working at Bel Mundo allows welfare recipients and immigrants access to state-funded benefits. For Dedeurwaerder and his staff, these effects constitute doing the most good for the people in Brussels who most need it.

Steak Night

One afternoon in late November, I arrived at Bel Mundo to find my boss Nena Cornelis, chief trainer and kitchen manager, dancing in the kitchen to the song "Fire" by the Pointer Sisters. "Romeo and Juliet ... Samson and Delilah," she belted. She saw me and shrieked: "I have *steaks*, can you believe?"

Steaks? Here? I could not believe it. Brussels's social restaurants typically serve the cheapest foods cooked by means of the least sophisticated techniques: vegetable curries, spaghetti with meatless sauces, roasted chicken thighs (the least expensive cut of the bird). Beef, on the other hand, is popular and expensive and requires skill to prepare well. "The steaks came from Delhaize!" Nena enthused, referring to a supermarket chain's outpost down the block, a store that sends food parcels to Bel Mundo twice a week. Usually, these parcels contain a large array of fresh vegetables on the verge of expiring (and a fair number of them that already have), plus packets of frozen chicken, sausages, and other meats that have been marked down (sometimes two and three times) but never sold and now are a day or two away from their expiration dates. When the food arrives, the staff immediately get to work. Vegetables are pureed into soups and sauces; fruits are cooked into crumbles and cobblers or transformed into ice cream. Bel Mundo has four freezers, and they are entirely full, so full that Nena said she cannot afford to take food from any more groceries.

But there had never been steaks, and here were eighteen New York strips defrosting on the counter, each about ten ounces. "Why didn't they sell?" I asked. I thought to myself: In the height of Western Europe's summer vacation season, even charitable food distribution decreases—so it makes sense that foods that would otherwise be sold are not. Even the very poor might be able to afford a city subway ticket, which could get a person to the North Sea coastal town of Ostend for cheap camping on the beach—maybe that was it. Nena shrugged. She didn't care; these frozen expiring steaks were the best ingredients she'd ever received from any grocery to date.

Now Nena had to figure what to charge for them. This was tricky, because for most of her clientele paying for dinner was already a luxury. According to stickers on the packages, one of these steaks in its prime was about €10; however, it had fallen to €2 by the time it landed here. "I will sell them for €19, all inclusive," Nena decided. This meant that diners would get a bowl of soup, a pan-fried steak with roasted potatoes and sautéed green beans, and a scoop of homemade ice cream for dessert, all for €19. Of course, since Bel Mundo paid nothing for the steaks and nothing for the salaries of the interns, it would make a profit—and in accordance with the EU policy for social economy, all the profits would go toward utilities and salaries for the twenty-four permanent employees.

Next Nena said, "Gather round, I will show you how to cook a steak!" Her cheeks were pink, her voice was high, and her smile was huge. The steaks were no longer frozen but were still cold. Most chefs let steaks come to room temperature before cooking, so I queried. One thing I knew from a lifetime of restaurant work is that an ideal pan-seared steak should have a brown crust and a medium-rare center. To achieve this, cooks must trigger the series of chemical reactions that cause meat to brown quickly; the faster the surface browns, the less likely it is that the interior will overcook. Allowing a steak to come to room temp before it hits the pan is best practice. "It does not have to be perfect. We teach our cooks to make a good steak; that is what matters," Nena said.

First step: "You season it well—well!—on both sides, plenty of salt and pepper," she demonstrated. "Then you get the pan very hot." She turned the flame under her pan until it licked the sides. "In goes a good knob of butter, and you let it sizzle and *just begin, just begin* to brown. And then, in we go with the steak." Nena used tongs to transfer the meat into the pan. A loud sizzle. The gamy scent of meat searing. "Never, ever, flip a steak with a fork. Why?

Because the juices will escape. And you want to save all the juices!" We could hear the scuttling of customers arriving in the dining room. "Touch to see if the steak is done," she said, explaining an old method for testing doneness that can be done without a fancy digital meat thermometer, which she didn't have. Nena slid the steak onto a plate—"Rest it five minutes while you get the rest of the plate together!" she ordered, then demonstrated how to make pan sauce. When that was done, she poured it over the steak. "Voila!"

We took turns sampling. The meat had a lovely golden-brown sear on the outside and an admirably hot-pink center—signs that it had been cooked with expertise—but it lacked the rich flavor and toothsome texture of meat that had never been frozen. Yet it remains one of the most memorable steaks I've ever eaten. In the first hour of dinner service, all eighteen steaks sold.

The Benefits of Being Boss

Pinning down Tom Dedeurwaerder is tough. I scheduled many interviews with him only to be left waiting—once he had to run to the hospital to check on an intern who had overdosed; another time he double-booked me with the mayor of Molenbeek. Yet despite often being late and disorganized, Dedeurwaerder is incredibly popular among his employees. When you finally get his attention, he holds a gaze, asks thoughtful questions, and really listens. To learn what made him transition from work in a Fortune 500 boat-building company to running a social services organization, I proposed to trail him for one workday from beginning to end. It took three years of persistent asking plus a gift of a Duke University Basketball t-shirt, but he relented. He had one condition: as a term of Bel Mundo's generous funding from the Flemish government, Flemish must be spoken whenever possible, so Dedeurwaerder said he did not want my presence to disrupt the language learning of the interns. In my observations, very few of the interns, if any, spoke Flemish on their own—only a handful had managed to learn it before they got here, although some had a few words and phrases mastered—and almost all of them were getting daily lessons in it for free on the premises. This meant that I had to agree not to let anyone pivot from speaking Flemish to speaking English with me.

This stipulation was certainly easy to agree to in theory, but in practice it was a lot more challenging. For one thing, the interns knew I was American, and for them it was infinitely easier to communicate with me in English—they all, with very few exceptions, spoke it, too. For another, my own Flemish is shaky at best, and I wondered if I would be able to understand anyone fully. In the end, it turned out not to matter, because so many languages were spoken in the Bel Mundo kitchen daily that it would have been impossible to regulate. One day I counted French, Flemish, English, Arabic, Urdu, Twi (an Indigenous language of Ghana), and Wolof (an Indigenous language of Senegal). In such a fast-paced and multilingual environment, how could anyone insist on any one language? I later learned that most of the interns attend their language classes off premises anyway.

Another thing I learned was that such an insistence on language on the part of the Flemish government was not unusual. In the years I worked in Brussels, a day didn't go by without spotting the signature bright yellow signs bearing the words "Vlaamse Overheid" ("Flemish government") that are literally plastered all over Brussels—on construction scaffolding, emblazoned on the side of buses. I had to wonder what was behind this intentional branding, inside of the Brussels-Capital Region, on the part of the Flemish government, this desire to let everyone in the city know exactly who was underwriting certain projects and services. Of course, Brussels is also the capital of Flanders, so it makes sense for the Flemish government to be invested in its well-being, but this seemed to be something more than an investment; it seemed like an ongoing flex or assertion of supremacy. Imagine, for example, if the policymakers in the borough of Brooklyn, New York, decided to fund a bunch of projects over the river in Manhattan and put "Paid for by Brooklynites" all over them.

This method of institutional assertion spoke to me of another sort of moral panic, one that has nothing to do with food waste but everything to do with regionalism. It seemed in not only funding certain public services, like free language lessons, but insisting on the ways in which those services must be deployed, the Flemish government also fuels anxiety about the dangers of not being relevant in the eyes of the people who live and work in Brussels. This panic struck me then as unfounded, given the fact that every single piece of official communication in the city, from street signs and subway maps to government documents and product labels, is required to be printed in both languages. This, too, is not entirely unfounded, as 80 percent of people who live in Brussels speak French and only 16 percent speak Flemish, and the Flemish clearly wish to increase their numbers. Appeasing the Flemish government and its conditions was clearly important to Dedeurwaerder, who insisted I know about the language conditions, yet not important enough to amend the real conditions of a multicultural kitchen, either.

On the appointed day, I showed up at 9 A.M., as planned. Dedeurwaerder did not. While waiting, I snooped around his office. There was a well-worn biography of Kofi Annan, the Ghanaian diplomat who served as the seventh secretary-general of the United Nations and won the Nobel Peace Prize.

I recalled that Dedeurwaerder signs his emails with this Annan quote: "Het beste middel tegen armoede is waardig werk" (The best means against poverty is decent work). This motto could stand in for Atelier Groot Eiland's; if ever an organization is motivated by the promise of work—even washing dishes in a restaurant kitchen—it is this one. That food waste is on his mind was also reflected. I found a Dutch cookbook called *Meer Dan de Rest: Eet Beter, Verspil Minder* (*More Than the Rest: Eat Better, Waste Less*), by the founders of an urban farming collective called Eatmosphere. "A third of food production worldwide is wasted. Meanwhile, 15 percent of Belgians live in famine," it began, before offering a selection of vegetarian recipes (Desair et al., 2017). For Dedeurwaerder, food waste connects to Annan and to that idea of the saving grace of work.

Dedeurwaerder finally arrived. He explained that he sought his current job after being "very tired of only working to make money." He took pains to explain that he is not motivated strictly by philanthropy: "I wanted to make a difference, and I looked for ways to do that in the social sector, to work in the social economy. Atelier Groot Eiland is not a charity; we are about finding work for people," he said—once again echoing Annan's sentiments. Where did his desire to "make a difference" come from? "I suppose from my parents," he answered. "They were very active in their church. They had money, they were comfortable, and they were invested in helping people. This is my way." Dedeurwaerder views himself as a 2.0 version of a charitable Catholic, one for whom "charity" is redefined as job training.

I accompanied the boss to the weekly meeting of the organization's twenty-four full-time employees, who include kitchen trainers at Bel Mundo, social workers, and carpentry shop managers. Dedeurwaerder said he knew that all were anxious to talk about the fact that the board had approved a special new benefit: employees could choose between topping up their pension contributions with an additional €250 for each employee annually and receiving €250 in annual discretionary funds expressly to pay for continuing education classes. The catch: all employees had to agree on the same benefit.

A contentious vote unfolded. The thirteen who voted for the pension edged out the eleven who chose the classes. Members of the losing faction began to blame Chef Nena for swaying votes. "If I want to take photography classes, if I want to take Italian lessons, that is for me to pay; our pensions do not cover everything we need, and I should not have to cover the rest myself," she said, her cheeks growing red. Sophie, a longtime Atelier Groot Eiland social worker, fired back: "But you cannot intimidate other people to vote as you do. I would like classes, thank you," she said. Dedeurwaerder jumped in,

Tom Dedeurwaerder is the executive director of Atelier Groot Eiland, and as such he spends a lot of time in the Molenbeek community meeting with local officials and community members, often (and according to them) relentlessly promoting the organization and working to make new partnerships and recruit new interns. Walking down the street with him often involves many shout-outs from locals who stop to chat, which has earned Dedeurwaerder the nickname "the mayor of Molenbeek." Author photo.

Bel Mundo interns learn "front of house" restaurant skills like waiting on tables and managing the bar, which they use to build their résumés. So-called soft skills like friendliness, attentiveness, and politeness are emphasized by the trainers, as well as techniques for honing how to anticipate customers' needs (such as refilling water without having to be asked). Author photo.

saying the matter was decided but that they could take it up again in three years. Chantal, an older woman who works as a kitchen trainer, had been with Atelier Groot Eiland since day one; she did in fact take Italian lessons, and shook her head. Stijn, a young man who is Bel Mundo's restaurant manager, had voted to support the pension top-up; he grinned.

After the meeting, Dedeurwaerder sighed. "What would you have chosen?" he asked me. I admitted that, coming from a country where pensions for workers are not guaranteed, I would have chosen the top-up. "That's just it! We are not American! We have a guaranteed pension, and if you want more—for example, long-term hospital stays, which are not part of our benefits—it is inexpensive and typical for workers to top it up themselves," he said. "That's why I voted for the courses." Those who chose the pension were "old-fashioned," according to him. "It is a modern idea for some people that job satisfaction does not need to be measured in dollars," he added.

There was another logic at play here for Dedeurwaerder: "We are about helping people who are far from the job market to find meaningful work. We want to increase the chances for poor people to find jobs. Should we not take trainings ourselves?" he asked. At Bel Mundo it seems every effort is directed at maximizing *training*. But whether it is interns learning to cook steaks in the dining room or social workers trying to develop photography hobbies, no possibilities would exist without the access to both untapped labor potential and food waste. This not only shows the struggles that this particular social welfare institution faces in terms of its purpose but also reveals the broader tensions at work today in the operations of a modern social welfare state as it must balance its stated purpose of provisioning for its people versus the increasingly dominant forces of late-stage capitalism.

The Flavor of Moral Economy

For the nine months that the kitchen trainees work at Bel Mundo, they are in a liminal state: officially unemployable, yet part of the city's contracted workforce. Whether they are citizens, holders of visas that allow them to be in the country, or obtainers of temporary resident permits, they exist in a "moment in and out of time" in which they participate in activities for the laboring class but are not (yet) members of it (Turner, 1974). In this way, kitchen trainees mirror the ingredients here. This food has been discarded by one set of consumers as waste but is now recirculated in a new context for a new population as food. As liminal entities, both the edible material and the people working to prepare and serve it are "neither here nor there; they are betwixt and between the positions assigned and arrayed by law, custom, convention, and the ceremonial" (Turner, 1974).

Tensions over what it's like to live in liminality were observable on Steak Night. Michel is from Dakar, Senegal, where he worked in construction, then met and married a Belgian missionary and moved to Brussels with her. "I dreamed of Europe," he said, but the dream was short-lived. When he couldn't find a job right away, Michel said the free-spirited missionary he fell in love with grew angry. "But I don't have a college degree! I don't speak Dutch!" he said. After a year, Michel left his wife and moved in with four other Senegalese men; his wife had their marriage annulled, then reported him for deportation. However, a social worker assigned to his case helped Michel fight extradition by applying for Article 60, buying him nine months to find a path to employment. According to Belgian law, if he could somehow get a job and work in it for five years, he could qualify for citizenship (Dedeurwaerder, 2017b). Michel landed at Bel Mundo having never cooked a meal. "In Senegal, my mother and sisters cooked. I didn't even know how to make rice," he said. "But I thought, 'I like to eat, and I need a job, so know what? I'll try it.'" Nena said that Michel impressed her: "He had a gleam in his eye; he wanted to work." Unlike some interns, Michel attended his Dutch lessons without complaint. Eager for cash, he often volunteered for extra shifts. As the end of his contract approached, Nena took the step of advocating to Dedeurwaerder and the board to hire him onto the permanent training staff. "I got lucky; they found money to pay Michel," she said. When I began working at Bel Mundo, Michel was in the process of transitioning into a trainer. "I will become a citizen of Belgium one day, you will see!" he told me.

At fifty-three, Ahmad was the oldest kitchen intern, but he looked older—he was missing some teeth and walked with a pronounced limp. The son of Moroccans who came to Belgium to do railway construction, he was a citizen. Ahmad had even grown up in Molenbeek but had dropped out of school at sixteen to help run his uncle's convenience store. When his uncle sold the shop a few years ago, Ahmad was entitled to collect unemployment and receive health care benefits. However, Ahmad's state-funded benefits include medical but not dental care. When his social worker offered him a contract at Bel Mundo, he didn't want it, but he took it: "I needed a dentist," he said as he shrugged, "but now I like some of the work, especially the dessert station." He also has temporary dental insurance: "The social worker here gave me a voucher so the state will pay the dentist; I'll go next week," he said. "I can go for treatment to get my mouth healthy, but they will not give me new teeth—that you have to pay for yourself," he explained. As I had previously discovered from a volunteer at the food bank who "splurged" on dental implants, even citizens entitled to nearly free dental care are required to pay for procedures deemed cosmetic. Still, Ahmad was excited. "I can take care of my teeth as long as I work here," he said brightly.

Laurent held dual citizenship in Belgium and Togo thanks to family in both places, some of whom had worked in the Brussels government and others of whom reside in Hédzranawoé, where they make textiles. Laurent spoke perfect French but lacked other qualifications: "I don't have a university diploma and I don't speak Dutch, so I got sent here for training," he said. However, another intern told me that Laurent had been arrested twice for shoplifting before being required by his caseworker to take a work contract before he could apply for welfare benefits. "He smiles always, he is pleasant, but he thinks he knows what to do already; meanwhile, he skips steps and is not careful in the kitchen," Nena said. "What will he do when his internship is finished?" I asked Nena, who seemed disinclined to give him a good recommendation. "He will be allowed to collect unemployment for four years before the government will require him to look for work again. He will take advantage of that," she supposed. Laurent described his future to me in different terms: "I don't want to work in a restaurant, of course," he said. "I want to have a business selling designer sunglasses." From his pocket he took a slim black case that held a pair of aviator-style men's sunglasses with a Gucci logo. Whether they were authentic, only he knew. "I have a supplier; I just need to set up a store," he said. This internship would allow him to save to do that.

Finally, there was Chef Nena. Before she came to Bel Mundo five years ago, she had operated her own catering business. The work was inconsistent, and she wanted a more stable income. Her spouse worked in IT, and they had two teenagers. One night in the kitchen we happened to catch a public radio report called "Europe in Crisis." Nena began cursing as the reporter zeroed in on an analysis of the rising costs of college in the European Union. Even though she is a full-time government employee and receives top-notch state-funded benefits, she said that college in Belgium had doubled in cost since she attended—and her son was headed to university in two years. "For my parents, university cost about €3,000, total, for four years, everything included," Nena said. "It will be double for my son, and what's next? We should be rioting in the streets, but we are not!" Although €6,000 for four years of college might seem modest when compared with American college costs, it represents the major way in which Nena values her own work. It was for the stable salary—to pay for college and other expenses—that she abandoned her own business. As a member of Brussels's birthright citizenry, she perceives the rise in college tuition as a shrinking of her rights—the same rights she is trying to help Michel access.

These motivations of the individuals working in Bel Mundo's kitchen reveal connections between food waste, labor, and morality. In not taking in profit and yet offering services "complementary to social security regimes," Bel Mundo fits into the categories of a Brussels social restaurant as well as of the EU social economy (Dedeurwaerder, 2018b). Because of the way in which it combines a business objective with a social purpose, Bel Mundo is governed by internal ethics that combine sociality and belonging with capitalism—because that belonging is only achieved through labor. The people who do the work of transforming food waste into low-cost meals here—from full-timers like Dedeurwaerder and Chef Nena, to displaced refugees who want to become citizens like Michel, to citizens who lack full membership like Ahmad, to dreamers like Laurent who want to fund entrepreneurial visions—are part of the "social economy" in which jobs are oriented toward both profit and social inclusion. In this way, their jobs represent a distinct form of care.

By care, I refer to processes of providing for the well-being of others in the polysemic sense advanced by anthropologists such as Julie Livingston (2012), Elana Buch (2018), and Janelle S. Taylor (2003, 2008). Although these ethnographers conduct fieldwork in clinical settings, I find that their conception of care pertains to this study on a zero–food waste restaurant in Brussels. Here, too, the provisioning of care is "a moral endeavour" as well as an intensely political act" (Muehlebach, 2012, 96). Waste connects to care here if we follow scientists who have sought to understand it as a material capable of remapping the social relationships of belonging and place itself (Douglas, 1966; Reno, 2009).

The analytic of care applies to the way in which food waste is deployed by the Brussels government to both feed and employ the city's immigrant and fragile populations. Care comes from the state, which subsidizes job-training contracts for those it deems capable of working but who are not (yet) capable of landing jobs on the open market. Care comes from the interns, who recuperate, prepare, and serve low-cost meals made from discarded food for people who cannot otherwise afford to dine out. Care comes from the staff, who advocate hiring and benefits for the good of the business, the interns, and each other—as when Nena advocated that the board hire Michel, crafting an argument that helping him would help Bel Mundo improve its efficiency.

In *The Moral Neoliberal* and in the context of the Italian government, Andrea Muehlebach argues that such self-interested expressions of care reveal a form of morality inlaid into what is essentially a capitalist economy. In her investigation of a range of publics in the Lombardy region whose volunteer extrastate efforts express care and love for precarious immigrant populations, she finds that her interlocutors consider it morally good to try to make a profit, just as Dedeurwaerder and his team feel that Bel Mundo should (2012, 26). As Dedeurwaerder says, "We must be a restaurant that makes money; otherwise we will have to rely on government grants that might go away at any time, and then we have done no good at all." As Muehlebach focuses on the role of contracts in processes of enabling care, Dedeurwaerder's efforts, too, highlight the value of the government's Article 60 contracts in enabling

Bel Mundo's kitchen interns—would-be citizens—to gain temporary *paid* employment experience as well as to allow the restaurant to operate with a very low payroll cost (2012, 149).

Is Bel Mundo just another neoliberal enterprise, then? A reasonable question, but I believe that what separates it from this paradigm is food waste. Extending the life of surplus discarded food in a way that generates profit is a key goal, and yet using up surplus food that would otherwise be discarded both benefits the environment and feeds people who have limited access to fresh food. While Muehlebach critiques such arrangements as "tit-for-tat scenarios" in which "the dispossessed ... [scramble] to achieve some sort of place in society ... because ethical citizenship appears to translate the crisis of work into social opportunity," the arrangements between work, food, and care at Bel Mundo reveal something different and perhaps less advantageous to the state (2012, 159). Nena, Michel, Ahmad, and Laurent represent a range of publics intersecting in Brussels, from a full citizen to a person who was on the edge of deportation; working here allows all to access a range of desirable social programs in addition to their salaries. This arrangement is possible because this restaurant is exploiting a resource *besides* labor, besides the surplus value of workers it doesn't have to pay. And that resource is food waste. Because its ingredient costs are next to nothing, Bel Mundo can afford to offer things like free Dutch lessons, free dental care, and extra employee benefits. These are vestiges of the social welfare state's benefits for the public good *and* of a capitalist system's drive toward profit—and this combination of profit-making and care-providing is enabled by the readily accessible supply of food that would otherwise have been discarded.

Muehlebach's theory that capitalism is embedded in the weft and weave of social welfare states is useful in building up to a place where we can see at Bel Mundo the ways that food waste now carries value. Those who run Bel Mundo are moral neoliberal subjects engaging in care work (the desire to "help" others, as Dedeurwaerder states) by using discarded but edible food. Thus, they connect helping others to finding utility in abandoned consumer goods that are sold for a profit. In this way, Bel Mundo's operations are all about finding ways to make good out of what was trash; it is a capitalism made of salvage and called "social economy," and in the end it tastes pretty good.

CHAPTER FIVE

The Affective Abattoir

We work with people from 170 nationalities. Diversity, hyperdiversity, superdiversity: These are terms that we describe as "ordinary." We choose to connect people, regardless of origin or cultural background, through their daily needs: play and food. In the last few years our workplace got a reputation as a NO GO ZONE. Together with the Abattoir, our partners, and the city itself, we turn this place into a MUST GO ZONE! The ten thousand square meters of the Abattoir in Anderlecht welcome one hundred thousand people every week during the various markets. Cultureghem uses the power of this bustling meeting place to form a creative and enterprising zone in the Brussels-Capital Region. Cultureghem is on a quest for a more meaningful shared public space.

This is the mission statement of Cultureghem, an NGO in Brussels's historic meat market, known locally simply as "the Abattoir." The statement itself is nothing if not enthusiastic, complete with exclamation points and ALL CAPS, reflecting the spirit of its founders Eva De Baerdemaeker, a former public school English teacher, and Yannick Roels, an architect and disability rights advocate. The mission does not state that Cultureghem will use food waste to accomplish its goal, nor does it promise its efforts will be well organized. In fact, the statement almost promises that Cultureghem activities will be scrappy, like the wording itself. "Scrappy" is just how Cultureghem's mission looks and feels in practice, as is evident in the three ethnographic snapshots I present in this chapter.

To understand how Cultureghem works, it is crucial to know a few things about the Abattoir itself. As its nickname suggests, the space was conceived of in the late nineteenth century by wealthy city merchants and land developers as a live meat auction house and butchers' quarters. At its heyday at the turn of the twentieth century, the Abattoir's role as Brussels's social and commercial city center rivaled that of La Grande Halle de la Villette, Paris's famed slaughterhouse and public meat market (Borloo, 2014; Zamfira, 2015). This lasted for decades, until the Germans seized the space and used it as their local headquarters during World War II, prompting a steep decline in business that never recovered after the war. There was also a postwar immigration influx of workers invited from Morocco by the Belgian government to help

The Anderlecht Abattoir in Brussels has been described as the last centrally located abattoir in Europe. Built in 1890, it has been an open-air abattoir ever since, although it is now phasing out slaughtering animals in a process that will be completed in 2028. On weekends, the market typically attracts more than 100,000 shoppers, who come for the produce and sundries sold outdoors and the butcher stalls inside. Author photo.

build the city's subway and work in the coal mines on its outskirts; these workers found cheap places to rent in Anderlecht, which prompted subsequent white flight among the mostly Flemish populations, who fled to the suburbs (de Valk & Willaert, 2012; Schoonvaere, 2014). For these reasons and for more than sixty years, the market in the city center sat mostly empty and desolate, 226,000 square feet, including underground storage areas and aboveground industrial meat production facilities composed of 218 tons of cast iron, unoccupied and mostly unused (Borloo, 2014; Zamfira, 2015).

There were still some butchers in Anderlecht, though, who maintained interest in reviving what had once been. Across decades, a couple of attempts to revive the Abattoir failed, until the early 2000s when a loose coalition composed of local real estate investors, city politicians, and urban renewal activists were able to put together funding from city budgets, an EU development grant, and private foundations to mount a comeback. It took more than a decade to get a deal in place. And in the end, the terms of the funding from the European Union stipulated that to revive business in the old marketplace, the developers had to also create social programming to promote local community engagement with it. This is where Cultureghem entered the picture; the consortium hired the group in 2014, when it was then a small urban renewal organization producing arts-inclusion programming around Brussels (Zamfira, 2015; Borloo, 2014).

The history and current demographics of the Abattoir help explain why the European Union felt the need to call for the existence of social inclusion programs in this area, without which there would be no Cultureghem. The first constitution of the city of Brussels was established in 1836; this created a local governmental structure that divides the city into nineteen communes, each of which has its own council and municipal establishments, and each of which is responsible for managing its own public works projects and public spaces (Van Wynsberghe et al., 2009). The commune is the definition of local government in Brussels, and it has quite a bit of autonomy in terms of the management of everyday life of citizens and residents—communes are where citizens vote, where police forces are based, and where social services such as food assistance are administered.

The Abattoir is in the commune of Anderlecht, which of all nineteen communes is both one of the largest and one of the poorest (Diab, 2010). There are twenty-two neighborhoods in Anderlecht. Among them, the most recent census details show tremendous poverty in addition to tremendous diversity: Anderlecht has 120,000 registered residents, 19 percent of whom are from other EU countries (the largest number of whom are from Romania); 13 percent of whom are from countries outside the European Union (the majority of whom come from Morocco, followed by Syria). In total, 7,088 people, 6 percent of people living in Anderlecht, were identified as economically insecure and receive social services including food assistance and unemployment benefits. More than six hundred people in this category were identified as living in conditions of "dangerous poverty." Historians attribute these statistics to "white flight" by the Flemish communities who left when Moroccan immigrants began arriving in the 1960s, taking their businesses and buying power with them (de Valk & Willaert, 2012).

Despite the poverty, Anderlecht never lost the meat trade entirely, and the butchers and meat producers who still work in and around it form a lobbying bloc (De Vries, 2003). These are the folks who formed a consortium of investors connected to the local meat trade and mounted a collective effort to restore the Abattoir and endured round after round of funding rejections and false starts until they lobbied the European Union to invest in Brussels city life. In the end, though, they managed to secure $8 million from the European Union's European Regional Development Fund (ERDF) and the rest from the Brussels-Capital Region, the Flemish federal government, and several of the city's top real estate developers. At first, the newly relaunched Abattoir was just a marketplace, open only on weekends and with only a few meat vendors. The vendors were not aided by the fact that the surrounding customers were generally so poor that the only vendors who succeeded were those who sold secondhand goods; guidebooks warned tourists away from the area altogether, calling it a "no-go zone" (Phillips, 2002). The Abattoir is perhaps best known among locals as place where, as my own landlord put it, "you go to buy cheap alarm clocks and luggage." Here vendors were mostly Moroccan, meat was mostly halal, and produce was obtained from supermarket suppliers after the big buyers have had first pick (Michiels, 2016).

The other problem was that the market was only open on weekends, and for the rest of the week the space was empty. "Getting people excited to come to the new Abattoir was like starting all over again every Monday," De Baerdemaeker said. This was why the European Union had stipulated a social inclusion goal, why the consortium had to make strong efforts to encourage neighborhood stakeholders to use the space, and why Cultureghem was brought on board (De Baerdemaeker, 2017).

When the Abattoir was relaunched in 1992, it once again rejoined a European urban tradition of outdoor food markets dating back to the heyday of the Ancien Régime (Black, 2012). Only this iteration of it was entirely different. In this market's earliest days, when noble families chipped in to erect it so they could stop importing meat from France, its architecture was compared to that of the Eiffel Tower, and its meat markets were considered the very best in the city and among the best in all of Europe. Archival images of the abattoir from the late 1800s reveal an enormous space lined with rows of cattle, and individual family-owned butcher shops in which proud families stand before racks of hanging carcasses. All the people in the photos are white. In today's Abattoir, not only is the meat slaughtering a small part of the activities conducted there today (and there are environmental groups gaining support in the city to stop it altogether)—the weekend produce market dominates most site activity—but the once-staid atmosphere as well as the demographics of the vendors have changed, too.

Now, to visit the Abattoir on weekends is to know sensory overload. Colors, sounds, and smells bounce off the surface of every old iron railing. The air is thick with sweat, by-products of the cattle slaughter that once again happens on site here (but out of sight, in a few of the meat lockers), and the fecundity of rotting plums. It is made heavier by sounds: car horns honking, vendors yelling greetings in French and Arabic, reflecting the languages of the populations who call Anderlecht home, gangs of teens playing soccer on a nearby basketball court, women in hijabs pushing strollers and chatting. Shoppers shove their way to the vendors who they know are the most willing to bargain.

Encore de Menthe

"People with all kinds of backgrounds come here. Jewish, Muslim, and Hindu traders stand side by side here peacefully," said Paul Thielemans, public relations officer for Société Anonyme des Abattoirs et Marchés d'Anderlecht-Cureghem/Slachthuizen en Markten van Anderlecht, the Abattoir's governing organization (Borloo, 2014). That is fair enough, according to my observations, yet it does not go far enough in terms of describing what happens here on Monday mornings at Collectmet.

Every Friday, Saturday, and Sunday from 7 A.M. to 2 P.M., the Abattoir hosts twenty-five produce merchants. As soon as the market closes on Sunday afternoons, Cultureghem sends staff to the vendor stalls with which they have standing arrangements to collect their unsold produce, the items shoppers picked over and did not choose to buy. Then on Monday mornings, Cultureghem's staff and volunteers distribute these foods to anyone who shows up at their meat locker door to collect them. The Abattoir is the only one of the forty outdoor food markets in Brussels to do this; the program is called Collectmet. "Fathers, mothers, grandfathers, and grandmothers who cannot afford to buy fruit and vegetables for their children come for apples, pears, bananas, tomatoes, lettuce, onions, cucumbers, you name it," De Baerdemaeker says.

Market vendors *just give* the unsold food to Cultureghem? I asked her. And then the organization *just gives* the food to whomever shows up at 10 A.M. on Monday morning? It seemed to be too good to be true (and one of those moments when I was made aware of my utter American-ness: blanching upon the discovery that a good or service could be freely given). "Yes, come and see for yourself," De Baerdemaeker said. That is how I ended up at the Abattoir on a day that the Royal Meteorological Institute of Belgium declared one of the hottest in the nation's history: 39.7°C (103.5°F). Air-conditioning hums in some of Abattoir's meat lockers, but not in the one that houses Collectmet.

De Baerdemaeker allowed me to observe under a few conditions: I had to work as a volunteer, distributing the food with the team, and not just observe;

I could not ask "invasive questions" of any recipients; if workers agreed to speak with me, I had to anonymize them as they wished; I could only take photos if given explicit permission from the subjects themselves, and all Cultureghem staff agreed to let me use their first names but not their last names. Photos included here are all used with express permission of the subjects.

Once these terms were set, De Baerdemaeker told me what I was in store for: "People who come to get food from us have a lot of shame. They may not look you in the eye. They may yell at each other, or even at you. Don't take it personally. Most who come to Collectmet are very, very poor. We organize other activities where you can sit at a table and eat a meal for a very small fee; at Collectmet, you see the people who cannot even do that. If you cannot even afford an apple, you will fight like hell to get one," she explained.

Overseeing Collectmet on this day, and on many others, is one of the thirteen diehard Cultureghem volunteers, none of whom are paid but all of whom are given first pick of the vegetables to take home for themselves. Marie-Thérèse is a grandmother of seven who is seventy-five years old; she told me that she has lived in Anderlecht all her life. Her French has the accent of a *Brusselier*, the local term for native speakers of a particular French-Dutch dialect that has been spoken in Brussels since the Spanish Hapsburg rule and that is vanishing, save for a few pockets of speakers (Treffers-Daller, 2002). Marie-Thérèse has a thick ponytail hanging heavy down her back and several missing teeth, and she told me that she gave up wearing a bra a long time ago. Many years ago, she said she went to a high school near the Abattoir before she dropped out as a teen mom. Marie-Thérèse never went back to school; she spent the years of her highest earning potential taking care of children, and now grandchildren. She has neither a high school diploma nor proper writing skills in French or Dutch; as such, Marie-Thérèse exemplifies how women are far less likely to find jobs in Brussels than men, according to one report because of "a desperate shortage of affordable childcare facilities for young children" across the city (Cendrowicz, 2017). Yet despite all this, Marie-Thérèse was, according to De Baerdemaeker, "fierce" and "one of the most dedicated" of Cultureghem's workers. When I saw her, at age seventy-five, lifting a huge crate of cherries taking it outside the locker, I understood.

Marie-Thérèse gave me a bright green apron and introduced me to the other two volunteers. Lina was white, had the *Brusselier* accent, smelled like cigarettes, and wore threadbare jeans. Amira was Moroccan and wore a hijab and a black dress covering her from wrists to ankles. Despite their differences, both met the profile De Baerdemaeker gave of typical Collectmet volunteers: they are women; they live nearby; they are unemployed because they lack credentials like high school diplomas, bilingual language skills, or both; and they want free fresh food. "Fresh" is important, and unique: most who receive social assistance food packages from places like food banks receive prepared and processed foods like canned soups and boxes of pasta (Michiels, 2017). To be able to use almost all those foods, a recipient needs access to things like refrigerators, stoves, and electricity. If you have no food and no way to cook, then you are not out of luck if you are hungry and you come here.

The first task I was assigned: Gather bunches of parsley, some of it visibly on its way to rotting, into bunches. I was confused but did as I was told. Later, I asked De Baerdemaeker, why were we giving parsley to people? It's not food. Her response: "Even if you are poor, food can still taste good, right?" (De Baerdemaeker, 2017).

Next up: Cut whole watermelons into single-serving chunks and wrap them in plastic. As I did this, I thought of my work as a prep chef in fancy restaurant kitchens, places where the fruits were pristine, like museum pieces. Unlike in those days, when I was trained by a sous chef to produce fruit garnishes for the purpose of aesthetic perfection on the plate, this mission felt more hurried and haphazard (and certainly less well appointed—I thought of the sharp chefs' knives in that kitchen with longing as I worked with a rather dull cleaver here), but it was no less urgent and no less supervised—Marie-Thérèse watched me carefully, holding up chunks I cut to make sure they were sized so everyone could get an equal share.

At 11 A.M., we opened the door to the forty-five people who were lined up outside waiting. They were 98 percent women, almost all wearing hijabs. The fact that this population is who show up for the lowest still-edible quality of food is some proof of Belgium's failure to integrate its waves of Moroccan immigrants (Blainey, 2016). Marie-Thérèse told me that visitors know to line up upon arrival, as entry is first come, first served. She admits people a few at a time. Lina, Amira, and I stood behind fold-out tables handing out the produce. Each recipient got four whole tomatoes, two bunches of parsley, two large hunks of watermelon, a couple of carrots, and as many cherries and zucchinis as each could carry. After all those in line had been through the locker, Marie-Thérèse let those who still lingered, about half of the original crowd, come through a second time. After that, about a dozen people were still milling around outside. I wondered what they were waiting for, and then I got an answer.

At this point, Marie-Thérèse produced, from a crate stored in the back of the locker that I had not seen before, bundles of mint and called out to those who were left, telling them they could come in. Up until this moment, distribution had run smoothly, with a couple of exceptions. For example, I handed a bunch of parsley to one woman who, upon inspecting it, shook it at me. She indicated that she wanted a better-looking bunch. Since not everyone in line has parsley yet, I ignored her and handed parsley to the next person. She persisted, and then yelled out: "Persil!" Marie-Thérèse, who at that point was handing out tomatoes next to me, turned to face the woman. "Hssssss!" Marie-Thérèse warned, then picked up a tomato as if to throw it at the woman. The woman backed down, eyes lowered, and headed to the next table.

That was nothing compared to the mint distribution. No one had warned me about this Collectmet ritual, a version of which I later learned took place every week and was the reason some people lingered. As a nation, Morocco consumes the largest amount of mint in the world; there it is customary to begin and end not only each day but also each meal with a cup of mint tea (Wolfert, 1973). Moroccans constitute most Middle Eastern immigrants in Brussels and in Anderlecht, and so mint is a popular item around here (De Baerdemaeker, 2017). While De Baerdemaeker said she reserves the unsold mint that the market vendors give her for Barratoir, the zero–food waste pop-up restaurants on Wednesdays, there are often bunches of it that will spoil before that time. These Marie-Thérèse can distribute on Mondays at Collectmet.

As Marie-Thérèse warily invited those who remained to come get a bunch, they were almost already inside the locker, elbowing each other out of the way. All the mint was gone in a moment, and the women wanted more. "Encore de menthe! Encore de menthe! Encore de menthe!" they began saying, at first quietly, and then more loudly when none was immediately forthcoming. It was as if they knew that there was some more, somewhere, that was being held—which, in fact, there was, per De Baerdemaeker's instructions. After two hours of offering "mercis" for watermelons, carrots, and tomatoes, the women had clearly had enough. Those who had previously been pushing one another were now bound by a desire for an herb that connected them to their culture. "Encore de menthe!" they persisted.

I imagined being unable to afford regular access to the ingredients in the foods that connect me to my own heritage—matzoh ball soup, challah, latkes. In that moment, I would have given the pleading women who were standing in front of me all the mint in the world. Luckily for Cultureghem's other programs, I didn't know where any more of it was. Marie-Thérèse held up her hand. "Assez!" she shouted. Enough. She, Lina, and Amira, clearly having done this before, moved in front of the tables, spreading their arms wide and walking forward, causing the women to fall back, and back, and back, until Marie-Thérèse pulled the locker door closed. Amira handed me a broom and I began to sweep the floor, now littered with smushed tomatoes, discarded rubber bands, and carrot leaves. "*Encore de menthe! Encore de menthe!*" I could hear the small band outside the locker, still chanting. After a few minutes, their cries subsided. Locked inside the storage room, we finished cleaning until Marie-Thérèse released us, opening the door. Sunshine flooded in. At the compost bin, a woman and a child were picking through a crate of moldy cherries.

Encore de Soupe

Making soup with refugees in a public park during a heat wave is not easy. By mid-July, though, we had it down. Our team included Cultureghem staff plus volunteers from an organization founded by an environmental activist whom I'll call Emma and funded by the Brussels-Capital Region. Emma designed her storytelling-for-justice organization for the purpose of drawing refugees living in Parc Maximilian near the Gare de Bruxelles–Nord train station into conversation with citizens, hopefully producing friendly relations in the process. The idea: "We share the stories and experiences that matter to us, in our lives. From these experiences, we can inspire each other for a better living-together." City officials estimate that six hundred to seven hundred refugees (whom the Belgian government considers undocumented immigrants) live in this park, without regular access to food, water, or shelter (Schlee, 2018). Earlier that spring, Emma had invited Cultureghem to bring in mobile soup kitchens and staff to help her with the story sharing, and that's how we ended up here.

When it went well, it went like this: At 9:30, we meet at the Abattoir to load the mobile soup kitchen truck with ingredients. We drive four kilometers to the park, where volunteers gather. We unpack the truck. Note that this was no ordinary truck: the truck *was* the soup kitchen. Its panels, floorboards, and walls ingeniously unfolded to reveal burners, pots, cutting boards, knives, and even benches. However, the truck lacked two things: electricity and water. But both were available at the park: Electricity from a truck that sells pricy crêpes with gourmet fillings to nearby office workers. The water we brought with us from Cultureghem offices, giant jugs full used to fill a makeshift sink, which we will empty and refill as necessary.

Emma explained that women hid in remote areas of the park; living among so many men make them vulnerable to assault, so she said that they tended to stick with each other, brothers, cousins, and, if they have them, husbands. We peeled and chopped veggies salvaged from the Abattoir weekend market: zucchinis, carrots, tomatoes, eggplants. Our activities were designed to attract attention, and they did. Young men approached: Did we have coffee? Water? We responded: No coffee, yes water, and would you like to join us making soup? Some did; some liked to talk while others did not; some enjoyed hanging out but not participating. Emma gave us rules for engaging with refugees. We should not ask where a person is from or how he got to Brussels (potentially traumatizing); we should ask what a person likes to eat (potentially normalizing). Whether or not people talked, soup got made. Almost always it was a thick puree, the orange-brown of health food cuisine. At first only five or so pitch in to cook, then by the end about twenty, but more than one hundred come to eat. Ana walked deep into the park to look for women to escort to the truck. We served until the pots were empty. We washed dishes and many refugees helped, we packed up the truck, and we drove to the Abattoir and unpacked. One week later, we repeated the whole process.

In practice, I found Emma's rules useless; the refugees *wanted* to talk about how they had gotten to Brussels, despite the fact that their journeys were hard and sad. That is how I met a man whom I'll call Bilal, from Darfur. He walked up to the truck, grabbed a peeler and a carrot from my pile, and got to work. After a bit, he said this out of the blue: "Of course many people died on the boat to Naples. We had to throw them overboard and the bodies were heavy." Not knowing what else to do, I put a hand on his shoulder. "It's ok," he said, gently removing it.

One day in the middle of July, everything that could go wrong did. First, Ximena and I realized we had only one ladle instead of two. Then Bilal came over, in bad shape. "I need help finding a shower," he asked. Though I wanted to help him, I would need permission from my landlords to bring a refugee into their home. I told him I would do what I could. (In the end, my landlords said that they would prefer it if I did not bring a refugee into their home. I called four friends on Bilal's behalf, including a foodbank worker, but none offered him a place to shower. I wish I had just done it.)

Next, we noticed that the truck that let us use their plugs for our mixer was not there. Another volunteer and I went to a nearby office building to ask to use an electrical outlet. The closest one was the headquarters of Engie, a French multinational electric and gas company. There are two ironies here. First, the nearest source of electricity was an electric company. Second, Engie is involved in "downstream" utility services—meaning they fund waste management programs. Yet their guards nearly denied us, a zero–food waste operation, the chance to make soup from discarded vegetables, when we asked them if we could plug in our mixer to puree soup for refugees in the park. Finally, one agreed: yes, we could, but we had to be fast and use the service entrance. Two men and I then carried two hot stockpots of soup plus an industrial mixer across a busy street, then into the Engie building, in view of the refugees, the Engie executives, and everyone on the street. As we hurried back, soup splattered our jeans and the people in the park grew anxious. The longer we took, the more people showed up, the louder their chatter. Then the cops arrived.

"Every few months, the police just raid the park," Yannick said. Upon later research, I learned that he wasn't exaggerating: indeed, every few months, Brussels-Capital Region police kick refugees out of the park. A few are arrested and a small number get deported, but most make it to the train station and wait it out there.[1] Three vans pulled up about one hundred feet from our truck. Out poured officers, all in helmets with faceguards, all carrying shields. There were at least two dozen. Each held a gun and together they formed a horizontal line across the park. They yelled, "Bougez-vous!" (Move!) Every two minutes, the officers advanced their line forward a few feet. The refugees were scurrying, picking up bedrolls and backpacks, running out of the park. But where did they go? Some fled through the streets, but most congregated on the park's edge, next to our soup truck. The police ignored us; their unspoken message was that volunteer groups were not their problem. Once gathered on the curb, the cops left the refugees alone. When the park looked empty, the cops left. Within five minutes, it seemed that all the refugees had come back and that there were somehow more of them. And they were hungry. Some began shoving. I sensed people standing behind me, felt breath on the back of my neck. I heard whispers—"Soup, soup, soup"—over and over. More than one hundred hungry men.

There was a fidgety, restless vibe. The air was tense. I felt hot and sweaty. My hands were shaking. I filled jar after jar, one at a time. When he saw the crowd amass, Yannick had come over to us from the dishwashing station he had been manning; now he was standing tall in the truck bed, overseeing soup distribution. He called out, over and over: "Everyone will eat; stay calm." He directed women to come to the front of my line to get soup right away. Some men saw this and tried to take the soup from the women. Yannick yelled, "Leave them alone!" and they stopped. One man came to me: "I have a pregnant wife," he said, thrusting an empty jar in my face. "Bring her to me and I'll give her soup," I said. "But she's just right there," he countered. No one stood where he pointed. "No," I told him. He disappeared into the park.

We ran out of jars and had to wait until the dishwashers could bring clean ones. Many people asked for salt, which we had in two round cartons—until they were both empty. "Soup without salt is like life without love!" Ana pronounced. Then we ran out of soup. "C'est fini!" Yannick shouted. People went back to lying on their bedrolls in the shade, or else sat on benches by the truck,

More than one hundred people are living in Parc Maximilien, a nearly twenty-two-acre space in the northern part of Brussels near one of its three main train stations. They are mostly refugees camping out and trying to use Brussels as a stop on the journey to European belonging and not as a destination but are unsure exactly how to make that happen for themselves. Cultureghem volunteers arrived with a food truck designed to make soup on the spot using the Abattoir's unsold decomposing vegetables, for which the refugees eagerly queued. Author photo.

smoking cigarettes if they had them. I heard some people singing as they washed dishes. I stood next to Yannick while he smoked. He told me that before he created Cultureghem, he ran a soccer league for homeless people that held tournaments in public parks. He found corporations to sponsor the twelve teams. Was that police raid a waste of time? I asked. Yannick said yes, but that it was not the fault of the police; the police were just doing their jobs. "They're told to clear the park, and they do it," he said of the city officials who are periodically required by the city to dispatch officers into the park and make a handful of arrests. "But for only five minutes!" I responded. "Tell the politicians," Yannick responded. "All of this," he was waving his hand in a wide-sweeping gesture that took in the whole park, "is the fault of politicians."

Encore de Courgette

"Barattoir" is Cultureghem's name for its weekly zero–food waste pop-up restaurant at the Abattoir. The restaurant consists of picnic tables set up next to a buffet-style hot line of vegetarian dishes, all made from unsold Abattoir produce. Beginning at 9 A.M., volunteers show up to cook with Cultureghem staffers. There is also a station for washing dishes as well as a compost bin—all out in the open, in the market space. Sometimes singers and dancers perform during the meal (unpaid, but they pass a hat). Customers pay €5 for a big plate of food; if they cannot afford this, they can have a free bowl of soup. Each time I volunteered, more than twenty occasions over three summers, at least ten people got free soup. Sometimes homeless people showed up at 9:30 A.M., willing to cook the lunch and serve it in exchange for a full meal.

The effort feels amateur, like throwing up a theater in a barn for a puppet show, and yet, when Barattoir began in 2017, it fed about forty visitors each week. By 2018, it was up to one hundred, with a record high of 206 (De Baerdemaeker, 2018b). None of it happens without Kofi Mensah. He is a dynamo at rallying troops and pumping up those around him—and his spinach "burgers," a frequent lunch offering I had the chance to taste many times while volunteering, are good, too. Kofi holds a team meeting at 9:30 A.M. on Barattoir mornings, always once a week on Wednesdays, during which he assigns tasks to volunteers and ensures that lunch will be ready at noon. Each Wednesday, he starts fresh: he has no idea of how many volunteers will show up to cook or how many diners will show up to eat. He also has only two days to plan menus, because they must be based on the previous weekend's unsold market produce. These conditions require unflappable determination and the ability to think on one's feet. "I love my job!" he says.

Kofi is thirty years old, is Ghanaian, and had been in Brussels for five years. He tells me that he ended up here from his native Ghana because he followed the path of romance. When he met a Belgian missionary while in college at home, he said he believed that God had sent him a sign to follow the woman back to Brussels. He did, learning the Flemish language in the process—but the romance fizzled. What lingered was Kofi's desire to stay in Brussels. While waiting for a visa and squatting in an apartment in Anderlecht, he saw a bunch of Cultureghem volunteers working with kids on the playground one day and signed up to volunteer on the spot. Kofi was such an outstanding volunteer that De Baerdemaeker says she offered him a job after his first day. Kofi says that ultimately he aims to go back to school to become a social worker or a minister, but for now he is one of Cultureghem's few paid staffers. He will keep this job until his new partner, a Ghanaian woman in college in Antwerp, finishes her degree. Kofi's official title is "Coach of the People and Master of the Food."

I arrived early one morning in the summer of 2018 just as other volunteers were showing up. Kofi was taking in the crew, assigning tasks. There was Ximena, a regular volunteer. Ximena explained to me that her husband was a French mycologist who was hired by the Abattoir's investors to cultivate mushrooms in the facility's dank underground tunnels (in hopes that they could be sold in the market). She said that even though he had a permit to work in Belgium, she did not. She said she came to Cultureghem because she wanted to do something with her days. "When I got here two years ago, I was lonely. The Belgians are all tall, I am short; they like plain food, I like spicy food; they speak Dutch, I don't," she said, describing her initial experience in the country. "My husband works in the mushroom lab all day, and I had nothing to do. One day I came with him, saw Cultureghem in the Abattoir, and introduced myself to Eva and told her, 'I can cook, and I can volunteer'" (Heuzé, 2018).

Ximena is often Kofi's right hand at Barratoir because she shows up every week without fail and she can cook (De Baerdemaeker, 2018b). We were also joined by four women "from the neighborhood," Ximena said—older women she recognized who volunteered from time to time, all with short white hair who showed up, cooked lunch, and got to eat for free. "They're pensioners," she said. De Baerdemaeker often encouraged me to bring friends to volunteer, and on this day, I did: my twelve-year-old son, Dylan, whom I pressed into volunteering to fulfill his school community service hours. I learned that Cultureghem often uses social media to invite local students my son's age to fulfill their volunteer hours at Barratoir; another volunteer, Fiona, an expat from Scotland whose husband works at the European Union, had brought her similarly aged son, too. Kofi gave us all the details on the menu du jour: squash soup; zucchini fritters; sautéed mushrooms; a salad of tomatoes, cucumbers, and onions; rice; and, for an additional €1, a crêpe filled with sautéed peaches.

Dylan and I were assigned to peel and grate about fifty zucchinis. Our "station" was a fold-out table, and we had about ninety minutes to get through as many of them as possible. The zucchinis were waterlogged—these were ones that had been passed over by market vendors, and I could see why, as some didn't look like they would last the day without turning to rot. In the Abattoir, the heat was sweltering, the peelers were dull, and the compost bins stank. "Why are you making us do this?" Dylan asked. Near us, a young woman named Martine chopped tomatoes so ripe that their juices bled down her cutting board onto the street; she was a friend of Roels's from art school. "I'm a starving graphic designer," she said with a smile. Dylan wore a basketball t-shirt, and before long he, Martine, and Kofi were talking sports as we all peeled and chopped and did our assigned tasks. "Our national women's team, the Belgian Cats, have heard of them? No? We just won the EuroBasket," Martine told Dylan. By now, zucchini residue stained both of our hands: sticky, itchy, tough to wash off. We didn't have time to anyway, because it was 11:30. At 11:30, workers on Cultureghem's other projects leave their desks and help the Barratoir team prepare for guests. They unfold the tables for eating and dress them with colorful floral plastic tablecloths. One worker each week is assigned to set up and man a beverage station, offering free coffee and tea (and local beers for sale for €3 each, which I noticed that few guests ever buy). Kofi plugged in portable speakers—donated—and played reggae from his iPod. We volunteers assembled the buffet.

Dylan and I mixed our grated zucchini with flour and egg and shaped this into fritters. We had to fry about two hundred fritters in only thirty minutes. Too many for one cook and one pan. Kofi said Dylan could manage a pan himself so we could double the turnout. "He is only twelve! He can't fry food by himself!" I exclaimed of a child who at home can barely pour a bowl of cereal. "When we work with children, we teach them to cook for themselves! How else can he learn? Relax, Mom," Kofi said. I was reluctant but did not want to mess up lunch for anyone. And sure enough, as I looked around, I saw other kids—who came with parents, like Dylan and some much younger, wielding knives to chop, operating blenders with sharp metal blades, and ferrying hot pans to the dishwashing station. What might look dangerous in another context, or even like child labor, was acceptable, even encouraged here, perhaps because the mothers were nearby, perhaps because the kids seemed purposeful and happy, perhaps because this is a "community-sponsored" restaurant and not a "real" one. Allowing children to take part in a quasi-professional cooking environment with real dangers—knives, flames— clearly reflected Cultureghem's goals of bringing people together on equal terms and trusting that there was enough well-intentioned support for all.

We transferred the fritters, miraculously having made the right amount, into the buffet table as the clock struck noon. "Welcome to Barratoir!" Kofi said, then allowed the line of hungry people who had been waiting—I counted more than eighty, who looked to be from all walks of life—to come through with their plates. The Abattoir was quiet when we arrived; now people chatted, bobbed to reggae, and settled down to lunch at the communal tables.

Coming through the food line near the end was a disabled teenager with her caretaker. She wanted more rice, but when her caretaker tried to give it to her, she shooed the caretaker's hand away. She pointed instead to Dylan, who scooped some rice onto her plate. His smile was huge.

A Recipe for Equity?

The Cultureghem activities that I have explored here move beyond existent and widely suggested paradigms for food waste reduction that include such activities as consumer reeducation or changes in consumer food-shopping patterns (Bryce, 2013). Instead, they provide models for the ways in which messy assemblages of people and food in an urban marketplace can create community, and even models of the kinds of sociality that shared meals can produce.

The two Cultureghem programs in which I regularly volunteered over four years—Collectmet and Barratoir—are quite different and yet can be characterized by messy intersections of food and people, sometimes even dangerous ones. For example, even though the meat locker and the market itself are required to have inspections from communal sanitation officers, Cultureghem programs face problems inherent to these surroundings. As Rachel Black points out in her ethnography of the social life of an historic food market in Turin, Italy, many traditional European open-air markets in which food is sold feature conditions such as persistent vermin not only that are difficult to regulate but that oppose the values of commerce, that a place selling food be "orderly, efficient, and hygienic" (2012). The Abattoir is no exception, as I saw vermin lurking in corners and under tables as well as dirt and debris blowing up from the ground onto the mobile cooking carts and into the food. When I observed these things, I also saw Cultureghem's staff and volunteers stomping out the invaders, brushing off the dirt, and carrying on cooking. These actions are exactly what I mean by carrying out food-related sharing by means of scrappy collaboration. Then there were messy encounters of a more human variety: Marie-Thérèse threatened to hurl a tomato; I balked at my kid cooking over boiling oil. Given how tense these types of interactions and activities were, could they still be considered commensal, and even illustrative of the ways in which food can unify and bring people together in common cause? Is "commensal" a vast enough experiential category to include instances of risk, shame, and even bodily harm? I began to think that sharing a meal at a table with other people entails the possibilities for these kinds of unharmonious exchanges, too.

Cultureghem's programs, united as they are by repurposing food that would otherwise be wasted, pose the question of exactly what flavor, if you will, of sociality that scrappy collaborations around food can generate. I sought to discover whether they promote social inclusion, as Cultureghem was funded for the purpose of doing, in this formerly abandoned and fraught urban space. The space matters: it was vibrant on weekends and desolate the rest of the time, a condition of who felt welcome there, and when. What I have come to believe is that in the diverse and often literally messy collaborations featuring people from wildly different backgrounds gathering to obtain, cook, and/or eat together at Collectmet and Barratoir, there is a new and edgier kind of commensality that is fueled by food waste. This commensality promotes relations of impermanent intermittence that creates lasting but often more temporary social bonds as well as allows for the existence of simmering social tensions. This is in part because no program at Cultureghem is ever the same twice. The "who" here is always shifting, both in terms of food preparers and consumers. The menu is also always shifting; the same foods that did not sell at last week's market are not always the ones that are rescued from the waste bins the following week. This constant impermanence matters because it affects the perceived regularity and rituality of the commensal meal. Cultureghem events are the opposites of, say, typical liturgical and calendrical feast days in which all participants are members of a certain group who meet routinely (annually, seasonally, etc.) and enjoy the same foods together on each occasion.

This vision of an alternate commensality aligns with one described by the cultural anthropologist David Sutton. In his studies of the "taste memories" of Greek cooks before and during that nation's financial crises, he tracks "the use of food both as metaphor and practice to understand and combat the effects of neoliberal policies" (2021, 141). Sutton argues that commensal meals do much more than bring people together because they have political relevance and are especially useful in understanding contemporary European contestations over immigration and belonging (2021). Sutton urges us to consider commensal meals not as occasions in which social relations are always affirmed and cemented, but instead as patchy occasions in which the sensory intensity inspired by eating something familiar and tasty promotes the ability of those gathered to, for a time, see beyond their "assumed differences." He says that there may even be, in these new kinds of commensal meals, ecological implications. Such a framing speaks to the theory of "cosmopolitan sociality" advanced by anthropologist and scholar of the social effects of migration

Nina Glick-Schiler, which Sutton also cites: "The welcome that some Europeans gave the refugees in the fall of 2015 was not an expression of tolerance to strangers, but an acknowledgement that we are all facing the consequences of a global warring, and the depredations and displacements of capital accumulation. In that sense, we are all refugees" (2021, 7).

Cultureghem certainly engages refugees in a sense of temporary togetherness fueled by cooking and eating together. And there are ecological implications: without originally intending to, the Cultureghem programs have reduced the Abattoir's food waste by 40 percent, a fact that has enabled its organizers to seek funding from designated environmental organizations and thus broaden their community ties. This, too, is the kind of commensality theorized by the Dutch visual artist and anthropologist Yvonne le Grand in her investigation of a temporary vegan zone in Lisbon, Portugal (2015). Le Grand found that vegans and vegetarians who live and work in countries where eating meat is the norm offer a lens into how community can be built through shared meals and activism. If an alternative diet can be a political strategy not only to create fellow feeling but also to attempt to counter the global corporate food system, I believe that Cultureghem's programs show us that food waste can count as "food" and that fellow feeling can be complicated by intense political differences.

This reconsideration of sharing food prompts a (re)consideration of incidences of commensality as expressions of politics, particularly as acts of resistance. In the kinetic and hodgepodge nature of Cultureghem activities, I found people from wildly diverse backgrounds sharing in efforts to repurpose edible but unsold and discarded food. Many of the people who do this work as well as who benefit from it, such as Marie-Thérèse, Ximena, Martine, and Amira, are united by a politics of survival, of a willingness to make do with the refuse that others throw away. As the American studies scholar Psyche Williams-Forson highlights in her work on ways in which Black people (broadly defined) engage their material worlds, especially with food and food cultures, understanding commensality as resistance troubles anthropological accounts of food that primarily treat it as embodying cultural identity (Lévi-Strauss, 1964, 26; Goody, 1982, 219; Williams-Forson, 2006). As these actors find value in food waste—by which I mean unsold market produce that would otherwise be discarded—they use it to remap social relations in a major European city's once-thriving marketplace.

In recognizing the efforts at Cultureghem as an alternate and political form of commensality, this study takes inspiration from those conducted by scholars of American studies who have long recognized the value of using leftover, so-called undesirable foods from traditional marketplace settings to sustain communities. The most innovative argument about this I've seen is in Williams-Forson's *Eating While Black*, which discusses the perceived viability of dollar stores as legitimate shops for food, a reconsideration she argues can broaden a topic that is polarizing—for example, whether or not any "good" food exists at dollar stores—because revaluing such put-down places "can challenge how we think about accessing food and also can allow people to exercise food choices without making them feel bad about their decisions" (2022, 143).

Such analyses attend precisely to the "scrappiness" of making do with food that was beneath another consumer's radar, making them consonant with my own efforts to theorize the significance of Cultureghem's efforts in Brussels today. In my engagement with Cultureghem, I attended to volunteers' efforts as "creating something from the scraps" of edible materials that others have regarded as useless (Williams-Forson, 2006, 189). While I still argue that Mintz had it right when he argued, in *Sweetness and Power*, for food's (particularly sugar's) role in producing class distinctions, what we see in these scrappy collaborations is that even its devalued forms (as opposed to its overvalued ones, by which I mean its commodities) can collapse them.

In fact, depending on the context of who is doing the cooking and who is doing the eating—and, crucially, where those events of cooking and eating take place—food can collapse or reify borders between people, food, and culture. While Cultureghem's founders do not advocate for overthrowing capitalism, they also do not operate against its extractive logics. In fact, it is the industrialized food system, which thrives on producing ever more food even as ever more of it winds up in incinerators and landfills, upon which its existence depends. Cultureghem relies on rather than resists market; without excess unsold food, there wouldn't be weekly zero–food waste pop-ups or free-food distribution sessions. These activities operate in addition to the fact that the organization itself still charges a per-plate fee for those who can afford it, and so it, too, is involved in the exchange of funds. Also, the organization still applies for federal funding and uses it to pay some of its staff members; and the Abattoir itself, while conceptualized by the organization as a "public" space, is run by a private consortium who use the space to drive a profit, including renting private vendors space to sell food. The fact that an NGO whose mission is to revitalize a mostly abandoned urban space partners with government and private institutions to fund food waste recirculation activities exemplifies the concept of gastropolitics. A social movement is entangled with the state in a way that involves culinary practices. In this case, in the economic and social configuration of life in the Anderlecht commune of Brussels near the Abattoir, gastropolitics necessarily involves racial and economic tensions over who gets to eat what, and which forms of edible discard matter in the everyday lives of those in the neighborhood and beyond. While cooking or buying lunch at a zero–food waste pop-up café is not as straightforward as obtaining food in a grocery store, it is a form of exchange that sometimes involves currency and always involves spontaneity, creativity, and a level of disorganization.

In this way, it aligns with what the anthropologist Anna Tsing describes in her book *The Mushroom at the End of the World* as a site that operates "both inside and outside of capitalism" (2015, 63). Through her analysis of the proliferation of the matsutake mushroom in abandoned lumber towns and deserted forests and those who harvest and sell them, she explores the precarious labor and subtle hope of mushroom pickers. I see a similar set of variables and vibes at Cultureghem.[2] Instead of exotic and valuable mushrooms and the tensions around them over value, the "units" of currency, if you will, at Cultureghem are foods that have been rejected by market consumers and yet, by means of creative measures of transformation and a precarious labor force, provide sustenance that is both material and social.

CONCLUSION

A Spectrum of Edibility

While working in the kitchen of one of the world's only truffle restaurants, I saw chefs throw away a tremendous amount of delicious-looking food in accordance with that high-end establishment's mission of making and selling aesthetically perfect meals. Curiosity about what became of all the "good trash" when it left those premises drove me to abandon research on the elusive and expensive woody spore in favor of conducting this study on discarded edible food instead. In a short time, I went from hand-forming truffle raviolis, a meditative process involving carefully measuring and handling pristine ingredients, to peeling waterlogged zucchinis in a public park and chopping them with a red plastic IKEA knife. The years of additional fieldwork took me into the offices of EU policymakers, of various social workers and welfare services coordinators across the nineteen communes of the city of Brussels, and into too many kitchens to count, from those in restaurants to makeshift ones in a city market to private ones in residents' and citizens' homes.

"Why don't we have this?" That is the number one question I receive when I present this material and my findings, from audiences as different as my colleagues in American studies at UNC–Chapel Hill to the students in my food studies courses to the people who sign up for the adult-ed food workshops I occasionally lead at my synagogue. What they mean is, why don't we, in the United States, have programs like those you describe in Belgium—for example, social restaurants, or subsidized employment contract for food bank workers, or the funding to collect unsold produce in farmers' markets and repurpose it? This is the very same question I asked when I began this project. It also handily answers the question of why chapter 2, "Why Belgium?," was necessary. The short answer is that people in Brussels—citizens and residents alike—have more options for food sovereignty, via policies, partnerships, and grassroots networks than "we" do.

The "Why don't we have this?" question gives me the chance to share important takeaways from my study. First among them: If a government wishes to create opportunities and programs designed to reduce food waste, starting with consumer food waste reeducation messages like television commercials and public service campaigns does a lot less toward the goal than funding an organization that collects unsold produce in an urban market and giving it away does. My evidence: A little NGO housed in an urban market like Cultureghem has singlehandedly reduced food waste in one of the city's largest markets by 40 percent—so imagine what the model could do with more funding, such as material support for workers. Similarly, public service campaigns like billboards urging people to throw away less food are far less effective than a policy that requires supermarkets to donate surplus edible unsellable food does: the social restaurant Bel Mundo alone uses up all the unsold food from just four supermarket locations. These are small examples—one social restaurant and four grocery stores—but they reveal possibilities for improving food sovereignty beyond consumer scolding, with state involvement, and by addressing structural problems in the food system instead of consumer decision-making.

On a more theoretical level, the "Why don't we have this?" question also reveals both the possibilities and the limitations of a social welfare state when compared directly with a more laissez faire capitalist economy. For example, the ways in which the social welfare states of the European Union have traditionally prioritized social problems all but guarantee that when a big policy happening occurs—like when the European Union made it compulsory for all large-scale groceries to donate edible but unsellable food—there are already channels in place to direct goods and services to people who can use them. In Belgium, these channels even predate the social welfare state, extending to the Catholic Church's efforts starting in the Middle Ages, which shows how the state has been able to mobilize them all along. On the other hand, a modern social welfare state in a global economy like Belgium—and Belgium is by no means the only state in the European Union currently facing the complexities of extending social welfare benefits amid a growing population and a sclerotic economic forecast—has become taxed by all sorts of challenges, including intense population growth, internal rural-to-urban migration, global human rights crises that fuel external immigration, and an aging group of Baby Boomers who rely on more social welfare resources than originally planned. That a once-robust social welfare state now struggles to meet all of its provisioning promises has enabled many of the programs I studied to exist. In my fieldwork, I have observed that in an overtaxed social welfare state, the state consistently offloaded provisioning responsibilities to activist organizations and efforts. That said, it did so while also offering varying degrees of funding opportunities and social networking support. The most impactful of all is the Article 60 program, which serves newcomers to the state as well as others who have trouble accessing the job market and the state at the same time. This program is what makes social restaurants work.

In addition to economic questions, "Why don't we have this?" also speaks to issues involving social and political organizing. Anthropologists increasingly confront issues of activism and address questions of how, when, and by what means it is ethical to become involved in the struggles we see on the ground during our fieldwork. To be honest, this was a no-brainer for me. It doesn't feel like an epic leap into partisan territory to say that in collecting data for more than five years among stakeholders recirculating food in Brussels, I have developed a suite of ideas that now allow me, and in fact qualify me based on all my participation in those activities, to propose policy interventions for a more equitable system of food distribution. If one thing has become clear to me over the course of conducting this research, it is that certain food waste redistribution activities can allow for both a new and expansive remapping of food politics as well as for a reexamination of the sociality of communal eating experiences. I have seen a variety of ways in which a social welfare state—even one struggling with too many people to provide its typical benefits to like Belgium—can efficiently manage its food system. Some of their methods include allowing for the state to pressure policymakers into working with private businesses. In the case of reducing food waste, the state's decision to compel large supermarkets to donate food they don't wish to sell (or think is no longer worth trying to sell, for a variety of reasons) has benefited food banks, but I found those are only most useful to people who are living on the margins of poverty and not as much for Brussels's new class of the working poor. On the other hand, social restaurants and urban space planners have been able to take state and private funding and create meaningful activities that use up what a supermarket or outdoor market would otherwise discard, in the process producing new forms of urban sociality.

I often ask my students to imagine the US government regulating, say, their local Kroger, Harris Teeter, Publix, or Piggly Wiggly. "What if the government said: 'You can't throw away food that is about to exceed its sell by date. If you don't sell all those roasted chickens, and if you have boxes of cereal whose advertised contents have expired, you *must* give them away from now on or pay a huge fine'—what do you think would happen?" I will never forget one student's stunned reaction: "That's Un-American!" he said. And in many ways, he's right, at least in terms of how many Americans would view such a policy as the government getting in the way of private enterprise and as an example of overregulation. It is, however, a really good way to reduce food waste—by making sure the food stays in the system and gets to people who use it before it becomes trash.

The fact is that in countries across the global north where accumulations of excessive amounts of food waste are a far bigger problem than in the global south, the perceived need to reduce food waste has achieved a level of angst-ridden discourse that could be described as a moral panic (Gustavsson et al., 2011). Moral panics sometimes mobilize people in the wrong direction—for example, toward regulating issues that do not require it (like the music teenagers listen to) and restricting freedoms. In the contemporary discourse on food waste, it is always depicted as a problem that needs solving. And yet there are two separate reasons as to why (to "solve" hunger and to "fix" the environment). More befuddling still, and, of chief concern to me, is the fact that both justifications, problematic as each one is, manage to cast all consumers as shamefully wasteful (Gunders, 2015). The most popular solution that I have seen to address both problems has been deployed by government and policy institutions and expressed through mass media messaging—such as government-funded television commercials, public service campaigns, and advertisements on billboards, on subways, and in free pamphlets in groceries. The message is uniform and encourages individual consumer habits such as better food storage, more efficient and thoughtful purchasing ("smarter planning"), and learning how to cook with leftovers ("give leftover scraps a second life with new recipes") (Gunders, 2015). Such messages frame the problem of food waste as a moral and practical failure on the part of consumers who shop and use food in ways that let other people go hungry, in the process harming the environment and depriving hungry people of food. These messages are often funded by states themselves—through government health and education agencies, for example—and although they might suggest good ideas for consumers to follow, they also succeed in turning consumer attention away from the massive structural problems in First World food systems that virtually guarantee the continued existence of tremendous amounts of food waste in the first place.

An example of one of the most popular solutions to the problem of food waste currently offered in public scholarship comes from the author and journalist Michael Pollan, whose well-intentioned and popular writing offers a social history of the excesses of industrial agriculture. Pollan's main contention is that people should learn to opt out of capitalist food systems and to do so by growing more of their own food or by doing things like taking part in activities like community gardening endeavors (Pollan, 2004, 2006). Pollan's logic is that if people were confronted with the reality of how much time and effort it takes to grow food, they would waste less of it. According to this position, even if one does not professionally grow food (i.e., by becoming a farmer), she could still participate in occasional acts of gardening that would increase her sensitivity to not overbuying and then not having the time to consume food before it spoils. While a meritorious idea, the focus here is on amending individual consumer behaviors toward the idea that deeper knowledge about food systems could address the global problem of food waste; it does not address the structural problems of unequal food distribution. Nevertheless, Pollan presents community gardening not only as a solution to environmental distress but also as a political act. He argues that growing your own food is a great a way to protest the industrial food system, processes of food commodification, and the production of excessive food waste: a meal made with food one grows for oneself, he stresses, is "a meal at the end of the shortest food chain of all" (Pollan, 2007, 277). Pollan characterizes growing food as constitutive of the production of a "radically self-made meal" made of "mutualism" between nature and culture: "Everything you sense in the garden—the colors and patterns, the flavors and scents—is not only comprehensible but answers to your desires. . . . And we are in some sense an extension of a garden's plants, unwitting means to their ends" (277).

As a lifelong cook and one who has done so at a professional level, I agree that growing one's own food can be a form of (re)education good for acquainting eaters with food production literally from the ground up. I agree that observing such processes can feel magical, and I am not immune to the romanticism. When I shelled buckets of fresh spring peas destined to become a rich lemongrass-spiked puree at La Truffe Noire, I marveled at the beautiful bright-green casing protecting the tender legumes—the drudgery of cooking prep became the chance for an epiphany. However, I also find Pollan's advocations exclusionary. For example, he does not acknowledge that gardening almost always requires landownership and complicated terms of property relations to access. I think of Williams-Forson's assertions about the value of "dollar stores" in offering high-quality foods at low prices to consumers whose lives require them to focus first not on the conditions of food production but on its cost to their households. Williams-Forson is concerned with families struggling to get by and with not passing judgment on consumers for where they obtain food and what criteria drive their choices. She's not promoting capitalist excess; she's promoting the idea that it should not be shameful to be a price-conscious consumer, and that shaming people who are devalues all of humanity: "What would it mean for food freedom and liberation if we encouraged people to access food how and from where they are able? We seem to herald foragers, back-to-the-landers, and dumpster divers for their ingenuity, but we are willing to look down upon people who access food from the dollar store because we define it as 'cheap' and somehow unwholesome" (Williams-Forson, 147).

I might extend Williams-Forson's logic here to include surplus discarded but still edible food, for which there seems to be no glory in admitting you eat (let alone seek out). Such attitudes prove the pervasive logic in high-income countries, that you are not only what you eat but also where you shop for it. What if we are in fact not defined by where we obtain our food? Attentive to this question, in *Black Food Geographies* (2019), anthropologist Ashanté Reese analyzes the structural forces that determine food access among African American residents of neighborhoods in Washington, D.C. Reese is explicitly concerned with the way local forces can work against large structural inequalities in the food system, specifically by applying "self-reliance as a strategy for coalition and institution building" (2019, 137). Such a strategy is essential, she argues, because food access is never "solely about individual consumption" but must be understood as an avenue by which communities can make their own survival and become independent of state assistance. Reese's interlocutors characterize growing their own food and running their own local groceries in areas largely devoid of traditional farmland and where there are no groceries for many miles around as a way of resisting the structural forces that seek to shame and devalue them, and as means of political protest (139). I saw evidence of precisely her theory in two of my sites, in the ways that food waste was being deployed by various publics to circumvent power structures. Citizens and residents of Brussels have taken it upon themselves to intervene in traditional modes of food distribution (i.e., grocery shopping) by recirculating food waste to invigorate the local labor force with more skilled workers (Bel Mundo) and revitalizing a desolate urban landscape and engage residents in a socioeconomically depressed neighborhood (Cultureghem). This shows that efforts not to *reduce* but to recirculate food waste can go beyond resisting the industrial food systems—can be revalued and reused to feed people—even as the very existence of such waste depends on the industrial food system. The recirculation efforts do more than just feed people, though; the point of this study is that they also produce new social landscapes in the process.

I have framed food waste as a potential that exists along what I have called a spectrum of edibility, in which various forms of food and waste can be situated alongside actions, ethics, and forms of social belonging that are produced when we recirculate food that some consumers overlooked for other people eager to revalue it. Along this spectrum, food waste exists not as the opposite of food but something that spans a gradation of materials and affects.

And, as such, it offers an array of uses and meanings depending on who is doing the provisioning and what their aims are—for example, it can be used to enact different kinds of care, as well as different forms of power.

The spectrum of edibility is based on a general conception—explicitly articulated by those I worked with in this study—that food waste is not a problem to eradicate or reduce but rather an opportunity, one that people working in each site imagines differently. At the Food Bank of Brussels, food waste expresses hospitality. At Bel Mundo, food waste extends the Brussels labor market. At Cultureghem, food waste invigorates abandoned urban cityscapes. In the process, food waste becomes an agent of care for communities whose members lack adequate and/or affordable food access. Accordingly, I read food waste as an embodiment of what political theorist and philosopher Jane Bennett calls "vibrant matter." Bennett asks readers to reconsider the commonly held assumption of matter as passive, as a set of substances and materials that can only be acted upon by humans but contain no actual enlivening agency. She makes a case that physical substances and materials that occupy space and possess mass do more than just sit there; she argues that they have agency and can make things happen, too. She asserts a belief in "the capacity of things—edibles, commodities, storms, metals—not only to impede or block the will and designs of humans but also to act as quasi agents or forces with trajectories, propensities, or tendencies of their own" (2010, viii). One case study she presents is potato chips, which Bennett argues exhibit the ability to challenge human agency because the "powerful dietary fats" they contain "call forth" the instinct to consume, and keep consuming, them: "That food can make people larger is a fact so ordinary and obvious that it is difficult to perceive it as an example of a nonhuman agency at work" (41).

This is heady stuff, and to apprehend it requires a degree of imagination. Even if you don't believe that the fats in potato chips are calling to you on an affective level, Bennett is certainly right about one key point, which is that too little writing about food in the social sciences "attends to the force of materiality" that acknowledges food as an "ontologically real and active, lively presence" (2010, 43). So, taking up Bennett's challenge, if we imagine recirculated food waste as an actant, what can it do in the world? According to the examples in my work at the Food Bank of Brussels, the social restaurant Bel Mundo, and the NGO activities of Cultureghem, the answer is: expand opportunities for social belonging for those who otherwise struggle to afford the privilege of it. Following Bennett's theory, food and food waste are both alive—they are examples of matter that, among various publics and to various ends in Brussels, contain the potential to enable social membership. As the food in the three sites that I have studied is continually judged by workers and volunteers as worthy of recirculation or not, the people who ultimately make use of the recirculated foods are judged, too—both by people on the inside of the operations and by people on the outside of them. And just as some foods are "rescued" from fates in incinerators or landfills, some people are elevated to new levels of social belonging.

This argument troubles certain anthropological accounts of food that treat it not as an actant like Bennett does but instead as the embodiment of identity itself (Lévi-Strauss, 1969; Goody, 1982, 219). The "you are what you eat" school of thought is as compelling as it is age-old and is hardly unexplored. As Sidney Mintz put it in one section of his exhaustive annual review of the anthropology of food, "Like all culturally defined material substances used in the creation and maintenance of social relationships, food serves to both solidify group membership and to set groups apart" (Mintz & DuBois, 2002, 109). Mintz describes the ways in which the "imagined" categories of ethnicity and nationhood support the fact that "associated cuisines may be imagined, too"— often for the purposes of concretizing solidarity among group members. He gives as an example a study conducted by the sociologists Gaye Tuchman and Harry Gene Levine, which analyzes "the urban Jewish love affair with Chinese food, throwing light on both groups." Indeed, Tuchman and Levine focus on the ways in which the children and grandchildren of Jewish people who immigrated from Eastern Europe to New York City after 1930 incorporated Chinese restaurant food into their new Jewish American culture. In so doing, the authors succeed in proving that, at least for the many New York Jewish people they interviewed, Chinese food was "a flexible open-ended symbol, a kind of blank screen on which they have projected a series of themes relating to their identity as modern Jews and as New Yorkers" (1993, 385). Mintz notes studies aligning food and identity tend to focus on issues of "intrafamilial food allocation, familial division of labor, obesity, ethnicity, fasting, and sexual identity" in addition to food's role in solidifying divisions of race, class, and social position—all of which, and across cultures, demonstrate the close connection between what people eat and who they perceive themselves to be.

What I have found in my research allows me to approach food waste in terms of the ways it enables three different yet overlapping expressions of care provisioning: hospitality, neoliberal ethics, and scrappy collaborations. In comparing them, I find similarities in the ways organizers and workers in all three models conceive of recirculated food not only as necessary for the survival of many fragile populations but also as constitutive of spiritual and social connection. This type of connection is what the feminist anthropologist Donna Haraway describes as "making oddkin," a theory that she uses to describe new ways that she thinks humans can interact with objects in the natural environment for the purpose of survival but, more importantly, for producing new forms of sociality (2016). If we extend Haraway's logic to recirculated food, we can read food waste—edible food that was once someone else's overlooked surplus or even trash—as a form of potential. We can see it as a material that resonates with hope, and with the power to transform social worlds. Thus, recirculated food has the capacity to create (and signify) value in two senses: if it is a material worthy of "decent consumption," then its consumers must be worthy of "decent treatment" in society. That recirculated food can "do things" in the world, can confer meaning and open opportunities for people instead of just rot in landfills or burn up in incinerators, shows that it can remap urban social relations even as it is being reconfigured—into soups, restaurant meals, and care packages.

Outside of food studies and anthropology, there are some scholars whose works have already moved in this direction, and these works informed the ways I thought about my work as I was doing it. I often thought of the American studies and Southern studies scholars who have long recognized the value of using leftover, undesirable food from traditional marketplace settings to sustain communities. Some researchers critique and downright dismiss work in Southern studies as "nostalgic" accounts of "moonlight and magnolias and mint juleps," and some even for good reason. For example, Pulitzer Prize–winning African American journalist Isabel Wilkerson denounces the valorization of "the mammy" stereotype and argues against Southern historians who imply that enslaved people were always superb cooks and that cooking ability was somehow in their DNA (2020).

However, I find it relevant in illuminating ideas about the liveliness and utility of food waste. Some work in Southern studies attends precisely to the "scrappiness" of making do with food that was someone else's trash, and it would be impossible not to find them consonant with my own efforts here to attend to the recirculation of food and waste in Brussels today. In fact, to leave Southern-and-soul-food scholars out of this work as well as out of considerations of equitable food policy is to neglect the complicated history, acts of resistance, and lived legacies of both oppression and care as they are expressed in the (re)circulation of food (Taylor, 1982; Joyner, 1984; Egerton et al., 1987; Engelhardt, 2003; Williams-Forson, 2006; Harris, 2011; Ferris, 2014). These accounts not only attend to racist institutional food policies but also rely on archival materials from Southern communities—diaries, letters, maps, almanacs, community cookbooks and recipe collections, and travelogues—to connect food to the formative class politics of a region. In some ways they could not pertain more to my work at Cultureghem, for example, in which volunteers push back against logics of "creating something from the scraps" of what other people regard as useless and find beauty, dignity, and sociality in the process instead (Williams-Forson, 2006, 189). I, too, have come to understand profound ways in which communities use food waste to both produce and collapse class distinctions.

Such studies also attend to the gender disparities in the production, consumption, and distribution of food. Although this project has not been explicitly informed by arguments in gender studies, in conducting it I have taken inspiration from feminist anthropologists who have argued against "ideological doctrines of disembodied scientific objectivity" and in favor of privileging "situated knowledges" of community members and local stakeholders (Haraway, 1988, 576). And this is important because when we think of food waste as being invigorating, it illuminates ideas about what food can be and do in the world *beyond* help humans survive. For example, Marianne Lien's *Becoming Salmon: Aquaculture and the Domestication of a Fish* (2015) is a classic food ethnography in the sense that its subject is the politics of salmon farming in Norway. However, and in as far as situated knowledge goes, its innovation is in its attempt to theorize the experience of fish farming from the perspective of the *salmon*. Lien's aim is to "expand and explore the idea of what a human ethnographer can be and do as a situated and embodied sentient being" as she seeks to apprehend a process of domestication through observing the salmon's own expressions of its wants and needs (165). In making the salmon her guide for gathering data, Lien pushes the concept of standpoint to a new level. Similarly, while much attention in anthropologist Heather Paxson's *Life of Cheese* (2012) is devoted to the efforts of dairy farmers and artisanal craftsmen who produce the titular foodstuff, equal attention is paid to the conception of American artisanal cheeses as "unfinished commodities" (2016, 13–15, 59): "What is it that cheese microbes are imagined to do? In breaking enzymes in milk, releasing odors and flavors, that originated in the fodder digested by ruminants, microbes connect place and taste in a very material way" (198). In both cases, the authors link the very human activity of food production with the natural world that produces it. Discarded food is certainly a part of that natural world, and catching it before it becomes fertilizer seems to be the single most effective way to "reduce" the harms that occur to people and the environment when food is wasted.

Finally, I return to the "Why don't we have this?" question. I would like to point out that in the United States we do have some glimmers of programs that offer services and activities, if not exactly like what I saw in Brussels, then certainly in keeping with them—and of course I believe these are worth supporting. Along the course of this research, I learned about many initiatives that do some of the things that some of the institutions I studied in Brussels do—for example, there are many well-run food banks throughout the United States, there are "food waste" grocery stores in Denmark, there are versions of social restaurants springing up around Europe, and there are online apps that sell "misfit" unsold "ugly" produce via subscription service. All worthy endeavors to note. But my favorite US-based food waste reduction initiative is The People's Kitchen (TPK) in Philadelphia.

When the COVID-19 pandemic hit, chef Christina Martinez, a James Beard restaurant award winner for her Mexican restaurant South Philly Barbacoa, took the work she had already been doing feeding fellow undocumented Philadelphians to the next level. With her partner Ben Miller, she began offering nightly pay-what-you-can vegetarian dinners, all open to the public with no reservations. By the end of the year, the couple was approached by Aziza Young, a local private chef and activist who had been working to provide low-income North Philadelphians, many elderly and nonambulatory, with low-cost meals, to work together. Miller contacted chef Jose Andres, whose World Central Kitchen NGO provides meals in the wake of natural disasters, and successfully secured some funding to scale up the operation. Martinez and Miller made use of an old taco storefront that had been part of Martinez's empire, and El Compadre: TPK, a space dedicated to preparing and distributing entirely free meals to anyone in the city who needs them, was born. What makes the place unique is its all-volunteer workforce, which consists of many local cooks and chefs, and the fact that its ingredients come entirely from donations—from some supermarkets but also from the nearby historic Italian Market's many, many vendors and from street produce sellers, who drop off their extra unsold food, no questions asked. As of April 2021, TPK has given away more than fifty thousand free meals to Philadelphians, who need only walk past the storefront during lunch and/or dinnertime to pick up a neatly wrapped hot meal. Should they walk by after TPK's official operational hours, they'll find a community refrigerator storing more meals that they can take for free—all of the food on the table and in the fridge is free for the taking, and the "instructions" on the fridge involve leaving no trash and encouraging sharing.

I learned about TPK and all its projects from a dear friend who happens to be an accomplished pastry chef and food writer, April McGreger. She serves as TPK's "Lead Fermenter," a self-chosen title that means she's often leading preserving and pickling workshops for the TPK staff and volunteers as well as

The People's Kitchen of Philadelphia is an organization dedicated to feeding the hungry and poor in that city; it was founded during the pandemic by chefs and restaurateurs Cristina Martinez and Ben Miller in conjunction with chef Aziza Young. It sources surplus food from supermarkets and the nearby historic Italian market to provide more than 200 free meals a day to anyone who needs one, no questions asked, which are arrayed outside the organization's front door. Author photo.

for the local schoolchildren who visit on school field trips and the homeschooling groups who come by, and for any other community organizations that are looking for good ways to make the most of produce before it spoils and rots. It's a mission that requires advanced knowledge not only of recipes but of the processes required to safely sanitize and store food—the kind of knowledge McGreger, a Mississippi native who grew up on her family's sweet potato farm, knows more than a thing or two about. McGreger says that growing up on a farm means ingredients are either feast or famine, and so she learned quickly about how to stretch the life of an ingredient; and today she clearly enjoys sharing that knowledge with Philadelphians.

One frigid day in early December of 2022, I went with McGreger to TPK to see what a typical workday was like, and what it might have in common

The People's Kitchen makes use of a "community refrigerator" to help ensure that there is always something a visitor to the organization can find to eat, day or night. The fridge often contains a selection of fresh produce plus any meals that were not picked up at lunchtime but are still fresh. April McGreger, the organization's designated fermentation expert, leads free community workshops in fermentation techniques, and her sauces, salsas, and preserves are often on offer in the fridge as well. Author photo.

with some of the sites in this study. At 8 A.M. we arrived there, both of us looking not unlike the fictional Rocky Balboa when he went to work at the meatpacking plant in this same city. We were layered up in hoodies and knit caps, and when got inside it wasn't a whole lot warmer—one thing TPK doesn't need to worry about, since it's not a restaurant, is heating the place for guests. When we showed up, we were greeted by a few people rummaging through the boxes of produce from vendors at the nearby Italian Market. Usually, these vendors bring their unsold and unusable produce to TPK's doorstep, and today's assemblage including more than twenty boxes—stuffed with fresh asparagus (going limp), cantaloupes (mostly dented, fragrantly ripe, and a little oversweet smelling), poblano peppers, heads of collards and kale, and much more.

April's job was to figure out a dish to make using up some of that produce plus whatever else might be in the freezer, and simultaneously sort through what was in those boxes and determine what could be saved and stored for future uses. The two of us set to work alongside a couple of other regular volunteers who showed up—both members of the local Philadelphia area chapter of Les Dames d'Escoffier International, an organization founded in 1976 by Carol Brock, the Sunday food editor of the *New York Daily News*, for the purpose of supporting women working in the hospitality industry (Les Dames d'Escoffier, n.d.). Today there are forty-four chapters across the United States, Canada, Mexico, the United Kingdom, and France, consisting of more than 2,600 members working across the food, restaurant, and beverage businesses. I had long known about the organization, but my impression was that it was designed as a kind of "chamber of commerce" for women working in restaurants. While that may have been how it was when I was working for food magazines in New York City in the late 1990s, today's "Dames," as they refer to themselves, include altruism as their top priority: "We are committed to creating lasting change in our communities through focused philanthropy" (Les Dames d'Escoffier International, n.d.).

April directed us to prepare the meal she'd quickly been able to devise. In the kitchen's enormous freezers, stuffed with foods with last-minute "special" stickers just like the ones I saw in Bel Mundo's freezers, McGreger found boxes of unsold frozen breakfast sausages. They had been donated from a nearby grocery chain. We opened their packages and began reheating them in vast restaurant-sized, beaten-up cauldrons. After that process was coming along, we roasted the poblanos that the other two volunteers had prepared and seeded (some were too slimy to eat, others perfect—it reminded me of sorting exactly such produce in the kitchens at Bel Mundo and in the Abattoir at Cultureghem). We peeled and diced onions; we steamed rice. It was a busy morning. McGreger was blasting Shania Twain from her cellphone. I ran a mission to a corner coffee shop for sustenance; I was right at home in this kind of place, doing this kind of work. Once the sausages were browned and filled the air with the scent of woodsy sage, we had the makings of a hearty dish: rice with sausage, poblanos, onions, and greens. This we began portioning out in TPK's array of standard restaurant take-out containers—also donated by area restaurants. Once we had about thirty portions and had taped take-out-style plastic-wrapped cutlery sets to them, we unfolded a picnic table outside on the sidewalk, stacked them there next to a big chalkboard that listed ingredients and said "FREE!" on it, and went inside to clean up and see what kinds of other food in the produce boxes needed prepping, sorting, and freezing for other uses.

We found a lot to do—peeling garlic; roasting tons of the grapes that a produce vendor had left for us that could be used in yogurt parfaits; sorting through overripe berries to make some jams. While we did them, I had a chance to observe South Philadelphians walking by the window, picking up the lunches we'd set out—some appeared tired, cold and worn down, or precisely what you'd expect at an urban food kitchen, but more often I saw other kinds of people who use this service—people who rode up on city bicycles, packed the food in their backpacks, and rode away, smiling and waving at us; and people who looked like neighborhood regulars strolling up, chatting with one another and other people on the street, taking a meal or two and walking along. There was an incredible array of diversity: old women speaking Chinese sorting through the boxes of greens we hadn't managed to bring in yet (which is allowed and even encouraged); young construction workers clearly on the job and swinging by in their paint-stained overalls speaking Spanish with one another; two bike messengers reminding me that such a courier service still existed in the cyber age.

Equally amazing to me was how well thought-out the distribution at TPK was. For example, the food was served hot in disposable containers, which means that nothing needed to be reheated or prepared in any way— having a stove or a fridge or was not a barrier to a meal. Also, the meals were exceptionally tasty, far from the garden-variety vegetable soups I had so often encountered. These volunteer cooks were chefs, which was Miller's idea from the beginning. "We're making chef-prepared, very high-quality hot meals, and I think that's unique in and of itself. This is not a soup kitchen. It's very good food. We want to feed people good food, and make them feel happy and dignified about that" (Duchene, 2020).

I asked McGreger, if chefs and activists can make this happen here in Philly, wouldn't it theoretically be possible to have "People's Kitchens" all over the country, in big cities? McGreger paused before agreeing. She noted that it was important that something like this started in Philly, that it had to do with the character of the city. Indeed, the extreme poverty that the pandemic exposed is keenly felt here. About one in five Philadelphians—more than 330,000 people—suffer from food insecurity (Lejeune, 2022). That's almost the same number—268,000—of food-insecure people in Brussels today, who report that they skip meals daily because they cannot afford them (Jong, 2022). Philadelphia is also subject to the same kind of conservative political scrutiny that Brussels has been. When Trump referred to Brussels as a "hell hole" in 2016, Fox News columnist David Marcus attacked Philadelphia—in an outstanding example of an attempt at creating moral panic—as being beneath American standards: "There is perhaps no city on earth more associated with corruption than Philadelphia, where kickbacks are a hobby and graft is nearly perfected. Such has it always been" (Marcus, 2023). The link between cities facing real crises—Trump was talking about Muslim immigration, Marcus about opioid addiction—and innovative food recirculation could not seem more apt.

Yet if we who are concerned about both environmental crises and hunger are waiting for cooks and activists in all the world's cities facing poverty crises to solve food waste issues, we might be waiting a long time. The support for such programs remains unique. In the case of Brussels, it exists only because of a policy that explicitly pressures supermarkets. In Philly, it exists only because a canny chef in a once-in-a-lifetime pandemic found enough willing partners in a historic food marketplace to cowboy some programming. I conclude this study, then, by pointing out the reasons why "we" don't have such programs. That's not to say I'm without hope. In fact, I hope that rather than convincing consumers to change how they shop—a losing proposition, given a capitalist food system that values nothing so much as the overproduction of choice, and thus continues to reward the production of more and more food—we might be able to encourage if not food waste reduction than massive efforts at recirculation. Encouraging programs and people not to eat more or buy less (or buy less and eat more) and instead to redistribute food from areas where there is too much to areas where it can be used up seems to do the most good for both hungry people and for ecological conditions of the planet. These are not programs operated on million-dollar budgets, either.

Even though the policy forcing groceries to donate unsold but edible food may come from the highest level of the European Union, the institutions don't run the programs; they solicit grants and project plans from local groups to do that, allowing them the autonomy to put their local community knowledge to work. Bel Mundo, Cultureghem, and TPK are not funded by massive governmental agencies, and they are entirely built on knowledge about local food producers and consumers. They were organized from the ground up, and not from the top down.

The advantage of uniting ideas about highly localized knowledge when it comes to food and political power, as Reese, Williams-Forson, and others do, with findings that advocate for food as a material not *only* "alive with meaning," as Paxson puts it, but also with capabilities to produce new relationships, as Lien does, proves that food has the capacity to do things—like realign issues of unequal distribution. In aligning these studies, and in fact in theorizing food waste as having the capacity to "do" things, I enact Haraway's "making oddkin" process: braiding strands of ideas that do not neatly fit together for the express purpose of imagining a different and less threatening kind of future on a damaged planet. This is the kind of ingenuity that Haraway advocates for in describing the processes of thinking through the problems of environmental pollution, of "giving and receiving patterns, dropping threads and failing but sometimes finding something that works, something consequential and maybe even beautiful that wasn't there before, of relaying connections that matter, of telling stories in hand upon hand, digit upon digit, attachment site upon attachment site, to craft conditions for finite flourishing on terra, on earth" (Haraway, 2016, 4).

My framework describes the efforts and affects involved in redistributing, repurposing, and reallocating surplus food among the communities who work for and are served by both Bel Mundo and Cultureghem. While neither one of those institutions circumvents capitalist modes of labor extraction and commodification, both manage to do more than recuperate discarded food that would otherwise have been discarded—in the process recirculating it to people who in some cases need it (as in the case of refugees in the park and of people surviving on social welfare at Collectmet) or else to want it (as in the case of people who dine at Bel Mundo and the Abattoir, because they want to belong to city life but otherwise cannot afford to do so).

The activities at Cultureghem and Bel Mundo move beyond existent and widely suggested paradigms for food waste reduction. They provide excellent models for the ways in which messy assemblages of living beings, materials, and circumstances that do not traditionally "belong" together mark a stand against environmental devastation and climate change. While food banks will likely always exist as a social safety net to provide food for people living on the margins in conditions of bare life, social restaurants and social inclusion programs offer efforts to feed people that are ultimately more inclusive of local shareholders' desires—for work, for places to play, and for good meals to eat.

Finally, I acknowledge that none of programs described in this study do much to overthrow the unjust industrialized global food supply chain. Such a system, with its focus on agribusiness and market-induced insistence on abundant low-cost foods, all but ensures "massive waste, overconsumption, poorer nutrition, and a reliance on fewer, more concentrated farms to feed the world" (Little, 2019, 6). What can research on a small and scrappy network of people working to recirculate food waste in a small and scrappy city do to inform us, then? The stakes of reshaping the understanding of food in general, not to mention food waste, are high. This is a planet with a growing population and shrinking resources, and although there is enough food on it to feed all the people, humanity is doing a poor job of organizing the distribution of it so that the people who need it have access to it. This suggests that food is the same as any other commodity and can be generalized by an industrial system as the equivalent of, for example, shoes, or heating oil. I believe that food is in fact an exceptional commodity. The problem, in fact, with the global food system—which leads to so much food waste—is the fact that food *is* largely treated the same way as other commodities—and so, to successfully reduce it, it must be understood in terms beyond others. I believe that it needs to be understood in terms of its exceptionalities as a material expression of hope and care.

In concluding this study, I encourage the acknowledgment of food as an exceptional material that cannot be treated in the same way as other commodities, which in turn allows us to utilize locally situated knowledges about the best and most workable recirculation practices for food waste. Depending on how it is eaten and who is doing the eating, food can collapse or reify borders—as in the case of the Moroccan women demanding mint at the Abattoir. None of the people in the programs I analyze here advocate for overthrowing capitalism, or for operating against its extractive logics and its industrialized food system that thrives on producing more and more and more food even as more and more and more of that food winds up in incinerators and landfills. What they have discovered, though, is that there are creative measures of recirculating food from people who have overlooked and even trashed it to people who will, if not treasure it, desire it, and use it. Until there is a revolution, this may be the best we can do.

Acknowledgments

I'm a foodie. I do not like the term, but I don't deny it, either. The happiest memories of my childhood were spent in my Mema's kitchen making mandelbrot. As a kid when I ate breakfast, I dreamt about what we might be having for dinner (wishing for brisket, always), and as I grew up, I became increasingly curious about what my friends were having. What kind of child enjoys grocery shopping? Me. I have made a lifetime hobby out of scouring the supermarket—any supermarket in any size city or town where I find myself—combing the aisles to spy new-to-me flavors and products. When I had a baby, I strapped him into his carrier and walked the aisles, which soothed us both (likely for different reasons). This is all to say that I could not have done this fieldwork without frontloading the so-called ethnographic I. My methods and my sense of self are entwined.

When I imagined what I wanted to do for a living, I saw myself cooking and baking as well as growing food and procuring it, but not *just* that. I longed to talk to people about food, observe them cooking, baking, growing, and procuring, and think about what these activities mean for our lives here on earth, together. For this reason, I have found homes in more than one academic discipline: I have an undergraduate degree in journalism and a PhD in cultural anthropology, and now work in American studies. The distinctions between them are less interesting to me than the aspects they have in common, particularly the focus on participant-observation, which is the essential (though not the only) method of food studies.

In my careers in food, I have discovered that life's big rituals and feasts are often less interesting than the quotidian, everyday encounters. I have come to care a lot about how people toss together concoctions on busy weeknights, or piece together bits and bites they find when they fend for themselves, than I do about, say, a birthday party. The gift that anthropology has given me is the chance to spend a lot longer than most journalists can investigating the value of food in people's everyday lives, and in a place that I have come to love dearly—the vastly underrated city of Brussels—and in a time when the calculus of what counts as "food" versus "waste" is shifting.

This project is enriched by all those who have invited me into their food worlds. This especially includes the anthropologist Filip De Boeck, who showed me the charms of his native city and connected me to many of the interlocutors in these pages; Rob Renaerts, a Brussels-based sustainability expert who answered every single question I had about modern life in Brussels, no matter how dumb, without complaint and often while offering me strong coffee and tremendous good humor; and the administrators at the three sites where I did most of my fieldwork—the kind and compassionate Tony Michiels at the Food Bank of Brussels; the engaging and energetic Tom Dedeurwaerder at Atelier Groot Eiland; and the righteous and spirited duo of Eva De Baerdemaeker and Yannick Roels at Cultureghem. I have learned so much from you all about why it matters to recirculate food and the ways in which food might be a conduit for peace and justice.

To the foodies of Brussels: Thank you to the incomparable restaurateur Luigi Ciciriello and his team at La Truffe Noire, especially Chefs Aziz Ur-Rehman Bhatti and Erik Lindelauf. There is no better restaurant in the world, and none will ever be closer to my heart. I am forever changed by the experiences, culinary and otherwise, I had in your kitchen.

To the journos, food and otherwise: I have learned everything about how to tell a good story from my mentors: Charles Whitaker at Northwestern University, a teacher and friend; Patrick Clinton, once at Northwestern University and forever a friend; and Tina Ujlaki at *Food & Wine*, who taught me how to think expansively about a meal while enjoying it. Colman Andrews is the best writer on food in the world, and he has my special thanks; it was the luckiest break of my life when he hired me, long before it was a cool thing to do, at *Saveur*. Many other excellent journalists and food writers have inspired me directly and indirectly, and I will not name them all here except to note that I could not have come this far without the friendship and support of the five-time World Champion barbecue pitmaster Myron Mixon and the all-around excellent literary agent and devoted friend Superagent Michael Psaltis.

To the academics, thank you to: my dissertation adviser and friend Anne Allison, a soulful writer and theorist who shaped this project from its inception and helped me confront its toughest questions; Orin Starn, an incomparably loyal friend and confidant, a good cook, and a gifted writer; Wesley Hogan, a friend, mentor, and graduate committee member whose creativity and energy buoyed me through the long haul of graduate school and beyond; Fatma Derya Mentes, my sharp-witted writing partner and most favorite co-conspirator; Sharon Patricia Holland, a brilliant thinker, fierce ally, and formidable cook; Seth Kotch, a tough mensch and the best colleague; Margaret "Lou" "Downtown" Brown, fellow anthropologist, excellent editor, and true friend; Josh Reno, font of friendship and support, whose work on waste theory is thrilling to read and who routinely helps me out for no good reason; Daniel Pomp, who has generously advised me in many ways of the Academy; Harris Solomon, an early guide and consummate close reader; Gabriel Rosenberg, who provided meaningful insight especially in the Cultureghem chapter. Thank you to Psyche Williams-Forson for the spark of her scholarship and kindness of her guidance. Thank you to Marcie Cohen Ferris and Bill Ferris for their enduring friendship, support, and respective scholarship.

Thank you to the Cultural Anthropology department at Duke for making exceptions, especially Engseng Ho, Ralph Litzinger, Charlie Piot, Rebecca L. Stein, supportive friends Anne-Maria Makhulu and Katya Wesolowski, and the great Diane Nelson (in memory).

Thank you to my colleagues in the American Studies Department at UNC, who have welcomed and nourished me (and had to start doing those things during a pandemic): Gabrielle Berlinger, Daniel Cobb, Kita Douglas, Elizabeth Engelhardt, Bernie Herman, Glenn Hinson, Tim Marr, Michelle Robinson, Patricia Sawin, Rachel Willis, and Jennifer Camelle Washington. Thank you especially to Antonia Randolph for the friendship and solidarity. Thank you to two special UNC graduate students who have shared my classrooms, inspired me with their projects, and allowed me into their hearts and minds: Claire Bunschoten and Khari Chanel Johnson. Thank you to the team at the UNC Press, especially Elaine Maisner, a great friend, an exceptional baker, and an editor who can see both the forest and the trees; and to María Isela García, who picked up this project and, with tremendous thoughtfulness, carried it to the finish line. Thank you to the two anonymous readers who improved this book with their gentle guidance and firm direction, and who I always felt were cheering me on from the sidelines.

Thank you to my comrade April McGreger, who shepherded me through The People's Kitchen and is simply the best cook I know.

Thank you to the Kehillah Synagogue Loving Kindness Committee for showing me the joy of sharing food so freely, so often, and with such a fighting spirit—the essence of community—especially Nancy Curtis, Rabbi Jen Feldman, and the incomparably patient and cool Jill Kuhlberg.

Thank you to these most beloved friends and family, for holding me as I worked on this project: Kevin Arnovitz, Brooke Balick and Peter Van Pelt, Julie Bender Cevallos, Bob Bennett (in memory), Laura Bennett and Chris Dolan and Claire Dolan, Briton Bieze and Jon Herstein, Paul Bogas, Elaine and Wayne Byrd, Ashley Cassell Carson, Maggie Dietz, Andrea Eisen and Daniel Pomp, Patricia Gammon, Francois Huet and Odile Repolt, Maya Parson and Grant Ramsay, Joanna Simoni and Dmitri Mitin, and Chris Sims.

There are not enough thanks to offer Louis and Dylan Davidson, my most beguiling interlocutors, who delight me even when they don't and whom I love beyond measure. Thank you, Andrew Davidson, who does not stop believing.

I had astounding support and so fear that I have forgotten someone important; any omissions are unintentional and regrettable.

Finally, to anyone who reads this book, thank you. Writing it has been a recipe combining the difficult with the astonishing. I offer it to you as evidence that making a big change can be worth a shot; that moving in the direction of a dream, even at a snail's pace, even when everyone around you thinks you're nuts, can still get you there. One last word: It's fine to throw away a strawberry sometimes; you won't go to hell for it. Sharing food is love.

Appendix
Works Consulted on the History of the Occupations of Belgium

Barnard, Benno, ed. 2005. *How Can One Not Be Interested in Belgian History: War, Language and Consensus in Belgium since 1830*. Dublin: Trinity College.

Conway, Martin. 2012. *The Sorrows of Belgium: Liberation and Political Reconstruction, 1944–1947*. Oxford: Oxford University Press.

Cook, Bernard A. 2005. *Belgium: A History*. Studies in Modern European History 50. New York: Lang.

De Vries, André. 2003. *Brussels: A Cultural and Literary History*. Cities of the Imagination. New York: Interlink Books.

Humes, Samuel, and Wilfried Martens. 2014. *Belgium: Long United, Long Divided*. London: Hurst & Company.

Prevenier, Walter, Wim Blockmans, and An Blockmans-Delva. 1986. *The Burgundian Netherlands*. Cambridge: Cambridge University Press.

Reybrouck, David van. 2015. *Congo: The Epic History of a People*. Translated by Sam Garrett. First Ecco paperback edition. The International Bestseller. New York: Ecco.

Vanthemsche, Guy. 2012. *Belgium and the Congo, 1885–1980*. Cambridge University Press.

Vanthemsche, Guy, and Roger de Peuter. 2023. *A Concise History of Belgium*. Cambridge Concise Histories. Cambridge: Cambridge University Press.

Witte, Els, Jan Craeybeckx, and Alain Meynen. 2000. *Political History of Belgium from 1830 Onwards*. Antwerp: Standaard.

Notes

Introduction

1. Garcia (2020). A brief history of the "How It Started . . . How It's Going" meme craze of 2020 was described in a *New York Times* "Explainer" column: "The basic concept is to show the passage of time through oppositional bookends. The more surprising the second photo, the better."

2. Wilk (1999, 244–55). Two of my personal favorite anthropologists who have written on food have also brilliantly explored and extended Bourdieu's work on distinction. The first is Richard Wilk in his article "Real Belizean Food," in which he defines Bourdieu's concept of distinction as when "class tastes are bound together into systems, with internal logic and structure, by sentiments and dispositions and rooted in childhood and a lifetime of learning" to prove that the established hierarchy of taste in Belize was disrupted by the Belizean independence in 1981, which brought in "new flows of information and goods" (1999, 252). Wilks argues that "a stable regime of taste" is now a thing of the past in Belize, as "foreign goods create local identity on a global stage." This matters because "Belizean cuisine is a concept invented almost entirely outside of Belize. Under a national label it submerges ethnic distinctions between what Belizeans call 'Spanish' food (tamales, garnachas, chirmole), and Garifuna dishes like cassava bread and fish stew (sere), and Creole foods like boil-up and rice-and-beans" (253).

The second is Brad Weiss in *Real Pigs*, in which he argues for readers to consider ways "in which class dispositions are embodied and do not simply reflect dominant structures of political economy, but rather constitute the often unconscious—or taken-for-granted— values of a hierarchical order by means of the practical acidity of subjects." He acknowledged that this is a "heavy ideological load" not just for readers but, and perhaps especially, for food service industry professionals across fields who "work to challenge corporate models of production and consumption" yet sometimes, as Weiss astutely points out, end up stuck in a process by which they "reproduce many of the features of the social order that are burdened with a longer legacy of inequality and exclusion" (2016, 36).

Chapter One

1. Across disciplines, scholars have of course also studied food practices in Europe for decades. One of the most notable of these in the context of this study is Braudel's deep analysis of food as an agent of social transformation of the Mediterranean region, which attended to the idea that the poor are relegated to the leftover foods of the rich: "When a food that has been rare and long desired finally arrives within reach of the masses, consumption rises sharply, as if a long-repressed appetite has exploded. Once popularized [in both senses of the word—becoming less exclusive and more widespread] the food quickly loses its attraction. . . . The appetite becomes sated. The rich are thus doomed to prepare

the future life of the poor. It is, after all, their justification; they try out the pleasures that the masses will sooner or later grasp" (Braudel, 1982,184).

2. For Lien, domestication is not a binarized nature/culture divide; it is a process of mutuality between human and animal that is indefinite, a biosocial becoming. "If we ever look back at a time when Atlantic salmon underwent dramatic changes, it would be right now," Lien writes, "and the hot spot would be the fjords of western and northern Norway" (2015, 166). The new "salmon domus" being formed there, Lien concludes, is an organic expression of salmon and people "making space for one another" (165). Most moving to me: Lien describes her emotional response to an unexpected, large-scale die-off of fish ("an excellent cohort scheduled to be smolts in the spring") because of unexpected ice formation on the surface of the tanks. "I accept the vet's claim that [the salmon] probably don't feel pain," she writes, but that knowledge did not stop workers at the site from feeling devastation, bearing out her theory of mutual aid between salmon and people (137).

3. Douglas (1974, 61–83). Douglas's study is structural because she seeks to code foods as acceptable or unacceptable and to understand how that process works among different categories of eaters. She not only invokes Lévi-Strauss in *The Raw and the Cooked* (1964), but also argues that he didn't go far enough in his symbolic analysis of a binary world of food that establishes social contexts. To her, he doesn't pay enough attention to the particulars, only to the generalizable. In her own essay, Douglas gives many charts, abbreviations, and diagrams, literally illustrating her attempt to prove that food is a language and that meals are its grammar, and that decoding a meal is not only possible but also an important part of understanding human social life: "Food categories therefore encode social events" (44). It makes perfect sense to Douglas, if not to all of her readers, that the act of eating can be broken down into units (menus, meals) and that these units can be broken down into components; the smallest of all is the "gastronomic morpheme, 'the mouthful'" (48). Regardless, I enjoy this article because I agree that a home is a great place to start to think about systems of eating—as Douglas asserts, it is a bounded universe. And as she points out, homes that are bound by more vast contexts (like the ancient dietary customs of the Jewish religion, to which she devotes considerable attention) are harder to decode. What I find key to her work are her explorations of food's messages and meanings in terms that while not universal are nevertheless inclusive of their particular social contexts (52). Douglas concludes that a meal is like a poem, in that it has rules and rhythms that offer "the assurance to the reader [or eater] and to the poet [or cook] himself that the poet [or cook] is in control of the disorder both outside him and within his own mind" (53).

4. Millar (2014). Millar differentiates and probes the categories of "precarious work" and "precarious life" among workers in a garbage dump in Rio de Janeiro, Brazil. *Catadores* is Portuguese for "collectors," a term that itself provides a clue into the way these people perceive mining refuse at Jardim Gramacho, at one time the largest garbage dump in Latin America and still an important one today. Millar explains that *catadores* are neither dumpster divers nor dispossessed people combing the dump for the purpose of accumulating resources that they aren't otherwise able to access (because they don't make enough money, for example). Rather, their work as collectors involves them navigating deeply unpleasant conditions in order to obtain recyclable materials (paper, scrap metal, aluminum, cardboard, plastics) that are then sorted, bundled, and sold to larger scrap dealers in Rio or to recycling plants in the south of Brazil, where they are further refined and resold to pack-

aging, construction, automotive, and textile industries whose reaches extend to the United States, Europe, and China. Millar argues for the way in which *catadores*' work is both a modification of neoliberal values—"public" garbage has been privatized in this case—and a rebellion against it, since *catadores* work for themselves and operate outside the official state system of recognized employment.

5. Headey and Alderman (2019). As a recent study funded by the International Comparison Program of the World Bank proved, manipulating food prices for the goal of reducing hunger and improving health outcomes depends on the economic situation of the country that's maintaining the low food prices: "As countries develop, their food systems get better at providing healthier foods cheaply, but they also get better at providing unhealthier foods cheaply" (Headey & Alderman, 2019). What this means is that in poorer countries, nutrient-dense foods tend to be more expensive (for example, with eggs and milk more costly than rice and beans), while in wealthier nations, of which Belgium certainly is one and which are the focus of this study, since these produce far more food waste, foods that are less nutrient dense (for example, soda) cost just about the same as more nutritious ones and require less preparation time. This disparity shows that food prices are often driven by market logics rather than focused on nutrition and equity, and that food waste is not factored into the equation. It also doesn't explain how there can be too much food so that much is wasted in some places but there is not enough to eat in others.

6. Following the logic in *Ordinary Affects* (Stewart, 2007), the affects of a food's production have the potential to become *something*. What Stewart describes as the surges, contact zones, surfaces, resonances, and "currents of feeling" that are "scratching the surface" of life in late-stage capitalism produce "a flash of agency" (99). For example, when brushing the dirt off mushrooms at La Truffe Noire, I felt a kind of slow peace. At La Truffe Noire, I also witnessed diners seeming to experience phenomenological excitement-attachment to what they ate—you could see it in how they sighed after taking bites of food, or sometimes closed their eyes to savor a bite, or even sometimes groaned audibly in enjoyment. And of course, you could see this attachment, however fleeting it may have been, in their pervasive desire to snap photos of their food with their phones before, during, and after consuming it.

7. The term "gastropolitics" was originally coined by Arjun Appadurai to theorize the ways in which food aligns with social rank in Tamil Brahmin life, where communal meals are "crucial determinants of future status and reputation" (Appadurai, 1981, 494–95). In the forty-one subsequent years since the term was coined, it has been adapted by countless scholars interested in the politics of food, many of whom now use it to refer to general contestation between access to food and policies of the state and to describe the ways in which citizens in the developed world manipulate food to both include and exclude various populations.

One of my favorite instances of the term comes from the food reporter Hanna Raskin, who deployed the term to describe feedback from minor league baseball fans in Asheville, North Carolina, on their ballpark hotdog offerings: "Americans have become increasingly concerned about their food's origins, but Western North Carolinian eaters are apparently among the few baseball fans who don't check their gastropolitics at the turnstile. Let followers of the Savannah Sand Gnats busy themselves with dizzy bat races and bobblehead giveaways: The Tourists' faithful care deeply about who made their hot dogs. How many other ballparks can boast of selling meat products from a family farm just 16.1 miles from the pitcher's mound?" (Raskin, 2009).

Perhaps one of the most prominent and important analyses of gastropolitics in recent years comes in sociologist Michaela Desoucey's *Contested Tastes: Foie Gras and the Politics of Food* (2016). In investigating the production and consumption of the liver of geese and/or ducks fattened by force-feeding practices in France and the United States, Desoucey analyzes state regulations according to the social, ethical, and moral debates that undergird not only meat consumption and luxury food consumption but also traditional so-called artisanal methods of food production versus more modern and updated techniques. In arguing that the French National Assembly and the French Senate took actions to legally protect foie gras production as part of the gastronomic heritage of the French nation in 2005 for the purpose of preempting European legislation by the European Union against certain aspects of foie gras production because of animal rights concerns, Desoucey extends Appadurai's concept. She uses the term "gastronationalism" to demonstrate ways in which food is deployed to define a collective state identity and secure the future economic welfare of a nation: some 80 to 90 percent of the world's foie gras is produced in France. According to Desoucey, since foie gras produced in these ways accounts for a multibillion-dollar industry, the value of these methods of production to French people was not only sentimental but actual.

8. Harris Solomon analyzes the ways in which a street food typical of Mumbai called the vada pav was politicized by a local party, and then was made with mechanized processes promoted as "clean" and safe by corporate franchises. In so doing, he flips the usual script, noting that "studies of street food tend to cast the street as the bit part, with food as the charismatic lead," in which he wishes to investigate the politics of the street in terms of its transformative potential and its role in food processing (2015). Finally, Heather Paxson uses the term to discuss the uneven ways food safety is enacted at US ports of entry, where state regulators perceive in certain foods danger of contamination, while importers and producers experience threat to their typical practices of provisioning and commerce (2019).

Chapter Two

1. Blainey explains his realization that "anthropologists have largely neglected Belgium as an opportunity to understand the sociopolitical culture of the European continent as a whole" came when his work on Santo Daime, a new spirituality from Brazil attracting devotees in the West, led him to "this small but crucial section of Europe" (2016, 479). Blainey argues that as much as Europe is "a concept" for many anthropologists, Belgium should be understood as a "process" of European history, one with a "fraught sense of nationhood" observable in a "microcosm of social processes" (480).

2. In probing "the anthropology of the everyday" in the context of some cruddy—for lack of a better term—sites of surplus food recirculation, I have been inspired and guided by the work in Kathleen Stewart's ethnography *Ordinary Affects* (2007). Stewart's admittedly experimental attempt at apprehending the "tangle" of feelings—high and low, mundane, and exciting—on the surface of everyday life in present-day American culture absolutely impacted how I went about this study. The "present-day" is described by Stewart as "a United States caught in a present that began some time ago" and that defies the oft-used indexical terms like "neoliberalism, advanced capitalism, and globalization . . . and the five

or seven or ten characteristics used to summarize and defend it shorthand" and that "do not in themselves begin to describe the situation we find ourselves in" (1). Instead, Stewart would like to frame the present "as a scene of immanent force" composed of a "shifting assemblage of practices and practical knowledges, a scene of both liveliness and exhaustion, a dream of escape or of the simple life" (1). This moment, however difficult and messy, has promise, in other words, or potential, but that potential can be small and vague and only involve the task of keeping on, and that sense of things is certainly what I've sought to describe in many instances here.

3. Michael Birnbaum referred to the Belgian government as "particularly molasses-slow" in the *Washington Post* article "Without a Government for a Year, Belgium Shows What Happens to Politics without Politicians" (2019). Journalist Tim King went a step further than Birnbaum in a column in *Politico*, describing the Belgian state as one of "deep dysfunction" haunted by "patronage and parochialism" (2015).

4. Anne Allison's "Home and Hope" chapter in *Precarious Japan* is about the effect of home for Japanese youth who face economically precarious times. If you have no hope of having a job, then you have no future. What is your homelife like? Front and center is a theory, following Bachelard, about home as a real place with virtual significance; the house is "a tool for analyzing the soul" (2013, 77). In the case of Allison's subjects, the cultural and social alienation they feel is a product of their political economy—but it has moved into their homes, like a dark cloud from which they cannot emerge. The question Allison has is how they're learning (or not) to live with the cloud. But Allison does not find these times hopeless—for those who hang on in cruel times, there is a "radical" hope, a "queer" way of making and having a home, in which different arrangements, different social potentials, and different kinds of relations are possible (examples are sprinkled throughout the chapter: cat cafes, robot care, self-help groups led by former hikikomori [adolescents and young adults experiencing a distinct form of social withdrawal characterized by becoming recluses in their parents' homes, unable to work or go to school for months or years]: "And this, in itself, is something" (121). This research on food waste recirculation in Brussels has been inspired by Allison's queering of both the home and the everyday associations of it. I follow this logic to discuss surplus discarded food as, still, a way of having a meal, a way of sharing a feast, of still eating and of being "in itself, something"—in this case, something to eat, to feel full both physically and spiritually.

Chapter Three

1. Reno's ethnography is his attempt to study what happens to our garbage and to whom it happens after we throw it away. His basic premise is making the familiar strange, to "reconnect waste producers to our landfills" (2014, 1): the United States is collective home of the most wasteful people in the history of the world, yet very few of us know what becomes of our waste. Based on fieldwork as a laborer at a transnational landfill on the outskirts of Detroit, Reno describes a certain kind of consumption as "reproducible sameness" (2014, 11) This refers to a desire in consumers for their commodities to be exactly the same as previous versions that they have already bought as well as future ones they may want to buy. Reno theorizes that the rise in intricate, elaborate packaging on electronic goods and toys is

a result of this commitment to sameness. The logic is that such involved forms of packaging ensure that goods do not get damaged en route from factory to retailer to consumer, yet in the end consumers waste all of that additional packaging. The irony, Reno points out, is that there might be a perfectly good commodity—a can of Coke, for example—that would satisfy a consumer ideal of "Coke," except for a small dent or a smudge on its label. This observation allows him to conclude that a lot of waste in landfills preserves not only consumer ideals but also corporate brands.

2. Melissa Caldwell's ethnography of poverty and social welfare in postsocialist Russia focuses on the everyday life and social and economic transactions of poor Muscovites attending Christian Church of Moscow soup kitchens. The concept of "making do" is a kind of politics for Caldwell and refers to the Muscovites' survival techniques as an alternative form of security developed when the liberalizing official economy stopped offering sufficient aid. Of special interest for my work is the third chapter's discussion of an alternative economy in which in the absence of "the socially disruptive force" of money, mutual assistance and altruistic/reciprocal exchange replace the market (2004, 69). This makes me think strongly of the Brussels Federation of Food Banks. In these alternative economies, social networks offer the chance to obtain goods that the market no longer delivers.

Chapter Five

1. Hervey (2018). One of the most noteworthy of such routine raids on Parc Maximilien: A dramatic citizen-led protest took place on January 21, 2018, when the local League of Human Rights arranged for 2,500 Brussels citizens to form a human chain around the park's refugees to keep them from being arrested. It made international news.

The protest was also at least partly in response to the deportation of Sudanese refugees several weeks before. As ordered by the Belgian secretary of state for asylum and migration Theo Francken, nine Sudanese men who were seeking refuge in Brussels were deported and then tortured by members of the Khartoum government upon their return as retribution (Schreuer, 2018).

2. By "similar variables and vibes" in Tsing (2015), I refer specifically to the chapter "Open Ticket," which is for me the most powerful section. In a logged-over portion of a national forest in Oregon, which Tsing calls "Open Ticket" after a way of setting a market value between pickers and buyers (it is Tsing's own nickname for a selling technique), she presents a notion of what mushroom foragers mean by "freedom" (making a living, sometimes just barely, outside the capitalist system of traditional nine-to-five employment— except the matsutake is a link in a vast global supply chain whether or not they want it to be). Nevertheless, "open ticket" describes a practice that gives pickers agency and power, mostly because the space and place in which they work are the antithesis of a factory. It is like Cultureghem in that the conditions are different every day, as are the terms of negotiating; there is conviviality and sociality; and there is "salvage capitalism" presenting a different way of making money whose goal is self-sustenance rather than accumulation. One of Tsing's overarching points is that out of destruction (global warming, ecological crisis, and in the case of Cultureghem, abandoned urban life), there are ways of thinking about an(other) type of life—such as the life of the "companion species" of a mushroom—that can exist amid geological and/or biological ruins. The pickers are "haunted" by ghosts of

the Hmong, but there are other ghosts and hauntings here, too. The city haunts the forest; the work of pickers is haunted by images and notions of traditional labor; people who have been traumatized go to the forest to relieve themselves of their ghosts. In "Open Ticket," Tsing describes the processes and series of translations that make "salvage capitalism" work. In her description of the relations between the pickers and the buyers, we see a different way of being in the world: the pickers aren't "workers" but "searchers"—they're not laboring for bosses or for the state or for set wages, they have to be savvy and avoid being caught foraging on lands in which that practice is prohibited, and although their work is not a traditional "job," they have to trade and negotiate in order to survive (77).

Bibliography

Abdelfatah, Rund, Ramtin Arablouei, Jamie York, Julie Caine, Laine Kaplan-Levenson, Lawrence Wu, Darius Rafieyan, Victor Yvellez, and Julia Carney. 2021. "Capitalism: What Makes Us Free?" Throughline. www.npr.org/2021/06/28/1011062075/capitalism-what-makes-us-free.
Abélès, Marc. 1991. *Quiet Days in Burgundy: A Study of Local Politics*. Cambridge Studies in Social and Cultural Anthropology 79. Cambridge: Cambridge University Press.
Albala, Ken. 2007. *The Banquet: Dining in the Great Courts of Late Renaissance Europe*. The Food Series. Urbana: University of Illinois Press.
Alderman, Liz. 2012. "Ranks of Working Poor Grow in Europe." *New York Times*, April 2, 2012. www.nytimes.com/2012/04/02/world/europe/in-rich-europe-growing-ranks-of-working-poor.html.
Alexander, Kelly. 2019. "The Cast-Off Kitchens of Brussels." Hot Spots, *Fieldsights*, October 22. https://culanth.org/fieldsights/the-cast-off-kitchens-of-brussels.
Allison, Anne. 1994. *Nightwork: Sexuality, Pleasure, and Corporate Masculinity in a Tokyo Hostess Club*. Chicago: University of Chicago Press.
———. 2013. *Precarious Japan*. Durham, NC: Duke University Press.
Alonto, Christina. 2018. History of [Site Two]. In person, on site at [Site Two], one-on-one, July 5, 2018.
Anderson, E. N. 2005. *Everyone Eats: Understanding Food and Culture*. New York: New York University Press.
Anderson, Jon. 2015. "Belgium's Crisis of Faith." *Catholic Herald Magazine*, October 15, 2015.
Anigbo, Osmund A. C. 1987. *Commensality and Human Relationship among the Igbo: An Ethnographic Study of Ibagwa Aka, Igboeze L.G.A. Anambra State, Nigeria*. Nsukka: University of Nigeria Press.
Appadurai, Arjun. 1981. "Gastro-Politics in Hindu South Asia." *American Ethnologist* 8, no. 3 (August): 494–511. https://doi.org/10.1525/ae.1981.8.3.02a00050.
Appleby, Joyce. 2010. *The Relentless Revolution: A History of Capitalism*. New York: W. W. Norton & Company.
Apuzzo, Matt, and Milan Schreuer. 2018. "Belgium's Prime Minister Resigns after Revolt over Migration." *New York Times*, December 19, 2018, sec. A.
Arel, Stephanie N. 2016. "Savoring Taste as Religious Praxis: Where Individual and Social Intimacy Converge." In *Sensing Sacred: Exploring the Human Senses in Practical Theology and Pastoral Care*, edited by Jennifer Baldwin, 57–70. Lanham, MD: Rowman & Littlefield.
Bacchi, Umberto. 2017. "'Halve Food Waste by 2030': EU Lawmakers Urge Member States." https://www.reuters.com/article/idUSKBN15825C.

Bailey, Anthony. 1972. *The Horizon Concise History of the Low Countries*. New York: American Heritage.

BBC. 2018. "Belgium's Charles Michel Submits Resignation Amid Migration Row." December 18, 2018. https://www.bbc.com/news/world-europe-46611320.

Beardsley, Eleanor. 2018. "French Food Waste Law Changing How Grocery Stores Approach Food Waste." *NPR: All Things Considered*. February 24, 2018. https://www.npr.org/sections/thesalt/2018/02/24/586579455/french-food-waste-law-changing-how-grocery-stores-approach-excess-food

Belasco, Warren James. 2006. *Meals to Come: A History of the Future of Food*. California Studies in Food and Culture 16. Berkeley: University of California Press.

Belgian Federal Government Informational Website. n.d. "The Role of the Monarchy." Belgian Federal Government. www.belgium.be/en/about_belgium/government/federal_authorities/king/role_monarchy.

Belien, Paul. 2005. *A Throne in Brussels: Britain, the Saxe-Coburgs and the Belgianisation of Europe*. Exeter, UK: Imprint Academic.

Belin, Hughes. 2019. "Profit, Consumption and Value Chains: Following the Trail of Brussels' Food Waste." *Brussels Times Magazine*, July 5, 2019. www.brusselstimes.com/60118/profit-consumption-and-value-chains-following-the-trail-of-brussels-food-waste.

Bennett, Jane. 2010. *Vibrant Matter: A Political Ecology of Things*. Durham: Duke University Press.

Bentley, Amy. 1998. *Eating for Victory: Food Rationing and the Politics of Domesticity*. Urbana: University of Illinois Press.

Beriss, David. 2019. "Food: Location, Location, Location." *Annual Review of Anthropology* 48, no. 1 (October 21, 2019): 61–75. https://doi.org/10.1146/annurev-anthro-102317-050249.

Berlant, Lauren Gail. 2011. "Slow Death (Sovereignty, Obesity, Lateral Agency)." In *Cruel Optimism*, 95–121. Durham, NC: Duke University Press.

Bertulot, Florence. 2019. "True or False: 4 Belgian Stereotypes." IHECS co-founded by the European Union, January 7, 2019. https://www.ihecsperience.com/discover-belgium/true-or-false-4-belgian-stereotypes-2/.

Bestor, Theodore C. 2004. *Tsukiji: The Fish Market at the Center of the World*. California Studies in Food and Culture 11. Berkeley: University of California Press.

Birnbaum, Michael. 2019. "Without a Government for a Year, Belgium Shows What Happens to Politics without Politicians." *Washington Post*, December 20, 2019.

Black, Rachel. 2012. *Porta Palazzo: The Anthropology of an Italian Market*. Contemporary Ethnography. Philadelphia: University of Pennsylvania Press.

Blainey, Marc G. 2016. "Groundwork for the Anthropology of Belgium: An Overlooked Microcosm of Europe." *Ethnos* 81, no. 3 (May 26): 478–507. https://doi.org/10.1080/00141844.2014.968180.

Bloch, Maurice. 1985. "Almost Eating the Ancestors." *Man* 20, no. 4 (December): 631. https://doi.org/10.2307/2802754.

———. 1999. "Commensality and Poisoning." *Social Research*, Food: Nature and Culture, 66, no. 1 (Spring): 133–49.

Boas, Franz. 1925. *Contributions to the Ethnology of the Kwakiutl*. New York: Columbia University Press. https://doi.org/10.7312/boas90748.

Boffey, Daniel. 2018. "Belgian PM Charles Michel Resigns after No-Confidence Motion." *The Guardian*, December 18, 2018, sec. Europe. www.theguardian.com/world/2018/dec/18/belgian-pm-charles-michel-resigns-no-confidence-motion.

Borloo, Jean-Pierre. 2014. "The Abattoir: A Market Tailored to the City." Canal.Brussels: The website of the Canal Plan and the Canal Area. be.brussels: The Brussels Capital Region, November 25, 2014. https://canal.brussels/en/content/abattoir-market-tailored-city.

Bourdieu, Pierre. 1977. *Outline of a Theory of Practice*. Translated by Richard Nice. Cambridge Studies in Social Anthropology 16. Cambridge: Cambridge University Press.

———. 1984. *Distinction: A Social Critique of the Judgement of Taste*. Translated by Richard Nice. London: Routledge & Kegan Paul.

Bourgeois, Delphine. 2018. "Brussels: Multicultural Hub throughout History." Brussels Express, February 12, 2018. https://brussels-express.eu/brussels-a-multicultural-hub-throughout-history/.

Braudel, Fernand. 1982. *Civilization and Capitalism, Fifteenth–Eighteenth Century*. Berkeley: University of California Press.

———. 1995. *The Mediterranean and the Mediterranean World in the Age of Philip II*. Berkeley: University of California Press.

Brunsden, Jim. 2018. "Belgium's Migrant Crisis Exposes the EU Asylum Gap." *Financial Times*, February 11, 2018, sec. World. www.ft.com/content/4848628a-0831-11e8-9650-9c0ad2d7c5b5.

Brussels Environment. 2010. *Plan dechets, Plan de prévention et de gestion des déchets*, May, Brussels Environment, Brussels, https://document.environnement.brussels/opac_css/elecfile/Plandechets_2010_FR.

Brussels Times. 2015. "Almost One in Three Brussels Residents' Earnings below Poverty Threshold." October 14, 2015. https://www.brusselstimes.com/brussels/35127/almost-one-in-3-brussels-residents-earnings-below-poverty-threshold.

———. 2019. "Belgium's Socialist Trade Union Fights for €14." December 14, 2019. https://www.brusselstimes.com/83856/belgiums-socialist-trade-union-fights-for-e14-minimum-wage.

Bryce, Emma. 2013. "The Conundrum of Food Waste." *New York Times*, January 25, 2013, sec. Green: Energy, the Environment and the Bottom Line. https://archive.nytimes.com/green.blogs.nytimes.com/2013/01/25/the-conundrum-of-food-waste/.

Buch, Elana D. 2018. *Inequalities of Aging: Paradoxes of Independence in American Home Care*. Anthropologies of American Medicine: Culture, Power, and Practice. New York: New York University Press.

Buyck, Cathy, Laurens Cerulus, and Cynthia Kroet. 2017. "A Year after Brussels Attacks: What's Fixed and What's Still Broken." *Politico*, March 21, 2017. www.politico.eu/article/a-year-after-brussels-attacks-whats-fixed-and-still-broken/.

Caldwell, Melissa L. 2004. *Not by Bread Alone: Social Support in the New Russia*. Berkeley: University of California Press.

Caldwell, Melissa L., Elizabeth C. Dunn, and Marion Nestle, eds. 2009. *Food and Everyday Life in the Postsocialist World*. Bloomington: Indiana University Press.

Campos, Paul F. 2004. *The Obesity Myth: Why America's Obsession with Weight Is Hazardous to Your Health*. New York: Gotham Books.

Caplan, Patricia, ed. 1997. *Food, Health, and Identity*. London: Routledge.
Carter, Dylan. 2022. "Record Number of Food Bank Users in 2021." *Brussels Times*, May 19, 2022. www.brusselstimes.com/226015/record-number-of-food-bank-users-in-2021.
Cendrowicz, Leo. 2015. "Paris Attacks: Visiting Molenbeek, the Police No-Go Zone That Was Home to Two of the Gunmen." *The Independent*, November 15, 2015, sec. Europe. www.independent.co.uk/news/world/europe/paris-terror-attacks-visiting-molenbeek-the-police-nogo-zone-that-was-home-to-two-of-the-gunmen-a6735551.html.
———. 2017. "So Rich, yet So Poor: How Brussels Became a City Divided." *Brussels Times*, June 14, 2017. www.brusselstimes.com/belgium-education/42906/so-rich-yet-so-poor-how-brussels-became-a-city-divided.
Chakrabarty, Dipesh. 2007. *Provincializing Europe: Postcolonial Thought and Historical Difference*. Princeton Studies in Culture / Power / History. Princeton, NJ: Princeton University Press.
Ciciriello, Luigi. 2015. The History of La Truffe Noire Restaurant in Brussels. In person, on site at La Truffe Noire, one-on-one, June 8, 2015.
———. 2016. Truffle Acquisition and Procurement for La Truffe Noire. In person, on site at La Truffe Noire, one-on-one, July 7, 2016.
———. 2017. Kitchen Operations and the Future of La Truffe Noire on Its 30th Anniversary. In person, on site at La Truffe Noire, one-on-one, July 28, 2017.
———. 2018. The Value of the Michelin Guide in a Changing World of Brussels Fine Dining. In person, on site at La Truffe Noire, one-on-one, July 27, 2018.
———. 2019. How EU Policies and Politics Affect (or Don't) Fine Dining in Brussels. In person, on site at La Truffe Noire, one-on-one, July 31, 2019.
Ciciriello, Luigi, and George Renoy. 1999. *Truffles from the Heart*. Brussels: Les Editions de La Truffe Noire.
Cohen, Roger. 2016. "Europe is Struck at its Heart." *New York Times*, March 22, 2016, sec. A: 23.
Cohen, Stanley. 1972. *Folk Devils and Moral Panics: The Creation of the Mods and Rockers*. Routledge Classics. Abingdon, Oxon: Routledge.
Conway, Martin. 2015. "What Is It about Molenbeek? The Bit of Belgium That Was a Base for Paris Terror Attacks." *The Conversation*, November 20, 2015. https://theconversation.com/what-is-it-about-molenbeek-the-bit-of-belgium-that-was-a-base-for-paris-terror-attacks-51007.
Coppen, Luke. 2022. "Belgium's Catholic Church: Shrinking but Still Influential." *The Pillar*, September 22, 2022. www.pillarcatholic.com/p/belgiums-catholic-church-shrinking-but-still-influential.
Cornellis, Nina. 2016. "Social Restaurants in Brussels." In person, on site at Bel Mundo, one-on-one, February 16, 2016.
———. 2017. "The History of Atelier Grote Eiland." In person, on site at Bel Mundo, one-on-one, August 1, 2017.
Counihan, Carole. 2005. "Food, Feelings and Film: Women's Power in *Like Water for Chocolate*." *Food, Culture & Society* 8, no. 2 (September): 201–14.
Counihan, Carole, and Penny Van Esterik, eds. 2013. *Food and Culture: A Reader*, 3rd ed. New York: Routledge.
Crapanzano, Vincent. 2003. "Reflections on Hope as a Category of Social and Psychological Analysis." *Cultural Anthropology* 18, no. 1 (February): 3–32. https://doi.org/10.1525/can.2003.18.1.3.

Crate, Susan A. 2011. "Climate and Culture: Anthropology in the Era of Contemporary Climate Change." *Annual Review of Anthropology* 40, no. 1 (October 21): 175–94. https://doi.org/10.1146/annurev.anthro.012809.104925.

Crutzen, Paul, and E. F. Stoermer. 2000. "The 'Anthropocene.'" *IGBP Global Change Newsletter*, May 2000.

Curran, Patricia. 1989. *Grace before Meals: Food Ritual and Body Discipline in Convent Culture*. Urbana: University of Illinois Press.

Davis, Deborah S., and Sara L. Friedman, eds. 2014. *Wives, Husbands, and Lovers: Marriage and Sexuality in Hong Kong, Taiwan, and Urban China*. Stanford, CA: Stanford University Press. https://doi.org/10.1515/9780804791854.

Day, Dorothy. 1963. *Loaves and Fishes: The Inspiring Story of the Catholic Worker Movement*. Second reprint. Maryknoll, NY: Orbis Books.

De Baerdemaeker, Eva. 2017. Barratoir and Collectmet Operations. In person, on site, one-on-one, July 25, 2017.

———. 2018a. Cultureghem Community Partners and Growth Plans. In person, on site, one-on-one, December 12, 2018.

———. 2018b. Evolution of Cultureghem/Cultivating Urban Space in Brussels. In person, on site, one-on-one, June 1, 2018.

———. 2019. NGOs in Brussels. In person, on site, one-on-one, December 13, 2019.

———. 2020. Urban Planning Policy in Brussels and the EU. In person, home of De Baerdemaeker, one-on-one, July 17, 2020.

De Baerdemaeker, Eva, and Yannick Roels. 2017. Cultureghem's Founding, Funding, and Operations. In person, on site, one-on-one, June 27, 2017.

De Boeck, Filip. 2017. The Social Life of Brussels. In person, one-on-on, September 19, 2017.

———. 2018. Brussels City Culture Questions and Research Progress. In person, one-on-one, June 20, 2018.

Dedeurwaerder, Tom. 2017a. "The History of Atelier Grote Eiland." In person, on site at Belmundo, one-on-one, February 14, 2017.

———. 2017b. History and Operations of Atelier Groot Eiland, Heksenketel, Bel Mundo. In person, on site, one-on-one, August 2, 2017.

———. 2017c. "Social Welfare Provisioning in Brussels vis-à-vis Social Restaurants." In person, on site at Bel Mundo, one-on-one, August 1, 2017.

De Lorenzo, Daniela. 2018a. Artikel 60/Finer points of the social assistance program vis-à-vis Bel Mundo. In person, on site, one-on-one, December 2, 2018.

———. 2018b. Day in the Life of a Social Welfare Administrator in Brussels. In person, on site, one-on-one, December 12, 2018.

———. 2019. Staff Meeting Atelier Groot Eiland Benefits Discussion. In-person observation of staff meeting with short interview, June 26, 2019.

———. 2020a. "Belgium's Congolese Mark 60 Years since DRC's Independence." *Al Jazeera*, June 30, 2020. www.aljazeera.com/features/2020/6/30/belgiums-congolese-mark-60-years-since-drcs-independence.

———. 2020b. "Congolese Diaspora in Belgium Wants Action, Not Words." *Deutsche Welle*. https://www.dw.com/en/dark-past-brighter-future-the-congolese-diaspora-in-belgium/a-53936898.

DePaepe, Marc. 2010. "Sous Le Signe Du Paternalisme: Les Politiques Educatives Des Belges Au Congo (1908–1960)." In *L'ecole et la Nation: Actes du Séminaire Scientifique*

International, edited by B. Falaize, C. Heimberg, and O. Loubes, 435–42. Lyon: Ens Lyon.

Desair, Steven, Joris Lens, and Mathias Dirckx. 2017. *Meer Dan de Rest: Eet Better, Verspil Minder*. Belgium: Lanoo: Tielt.

Desoucey, Michaela. 2016. *Contested Tastes: Foie Gras and the Politics of Food*. Princeton Studies in Cultural Sociology. Princeton, NJ: Princeton University Press.

De Souza, Rebecca. 2019. *Feeding the Other: Whiteness, Privilege, and Neoliberal Stigma in Food Pantries*. Cambridge, MA: MIT Press.

Destatte, Philippe. 1997. *L'identité Wallonne: Essai Sur l'affirmation Politique de la Wallonie Aux XIX et XXèmes Siècles*. Collection "Notre Histoire." Charleroi, Wallonie: Institut Jules Destrée.

De Valk, Helga, and Didier Willaert. 2012. "Internal Mobility of International Migrants: The Case of Belgium." In *Minority Internal Migration in Europe*, edited by Nissa Finney and Gemma Catney, 13–28. London: Routledge.

De Vries, André. 2003. *Brussels: A Cultural and Literary History*. Cities of the Imagination. Oxford: Signal Books.

De Winter, Lieven, and Kris Deschouwer. 1989. "La Corruption Politique et Le Clientelisme: Le Spectre Italien?" In *Où va la Belgique: Les Soubresauts d'une Petite Démocratie Européenne?*, edited by M. Swyngedouw and M. Martiniello, 139–52. Paris: L'Harmattan.

Diab, Khaled. 2010. "The Real No-Go Area in Brussels." *The Guardian*, February 8, 2010. www.theguardian.com/commentisfree/2010/feb/08/brussels-crime-police-unemployment.

Douglas, Mary. 1966. *Purity and Danger: An Analysis of Concepts of Pollution and Taboo*. London: Routledge & Paul.

———. 1974. "Deciphering a Meal." In *Myth, Symbol, and Culture*, edited by Clifford Geertz, 61–83. New York: W. W. Norton.

Duchene, Courtney. 2020. "The People's Kitchen: Local Chefs Are Serving Food to Those in Need, while Fueling Awareness and Action around Social Justice." *Philadelphia Citizen*, November 23, 2020. https://thephiladelphiacitizen.org/peoples-kitchen-philadelphia/.

Dunaway, Finis. 2017. "The 'Crying Indian' Ad That Fooled the Environmental Movement." *Chicago Tribune*, November 21, 2017. www.chicagotribune.com/opinion/commentary/ct-perspec-indian-crying-environment-ads-pollution-1123-20171113-story.html.

Dupont, E., B. Van de Putte, J. Lievens, and F. Caestecker. 2017. "Partner Migration in the Moroccan Community: A Focus on Time and Contextual Evolutions." In *Moroccan Migration in Belgium: More Than 50 Years of Settlement*, edited by C. Timmerman, N. Fadil, I. Goddeeris, N. Clycq, and K. Ettourki, 105–24. Leuven: Leuven University Press.

Durkheim, Émile, and Joseph Ward Swain. 2008. *The Elementary Forms of the Religious Life*. Mineola, NY: Dover.

Dzhambazova, Boryana. 2019. "Bulgarian Orthodox Prelate Rebuffs Pope and Condemns Efforts to Unify Churches." *New York Times*, May 6, 2019, sec. A: 8.

Egerton, John, Ann Bleidt Egerton, and Al Clayton. 1987. *Southern Food: At Home, on the Road, in History*. New York: Knopf, distributed by Random House.

Eisenberg, Ron. 2004. *The JPS Guide to Jewish Traditions*. Philadelphia: Jewish Publication Society.

Engelhardt, Elizabeth Sanders Delwiche. 2003. *The Tangled Roots of Feminism, Environmentalism, and Appalachian Literature*. Ohio University Press Series in Ethnicity and Gender in Appalachia. Athens: Ohio University Press.

Engelhardt, Elizabeth S. D., and Lora E. Smith, eds. 2019. *The Food We Eat, the Stories We Tell: Contemporary Appalachian Tables*. New Approaches to Appalachian Studies. Athens: Ohio University Press.

European Commission Special Report. 2019. Commission Delegated Decision (EU) of 3.5.2019 supplementing Directive 2008/98/EC of the European Parliament and of the Council as regards a common methodology and minimum quality requirements for the uniform measurement of levels of food waste. C(2019)3211.

Ferns, George, and Kenneth Amaeshi. 2019. "Struggles at the Summits: Discourse Coalitions, Field Boundaries, and the Shifting Role of Business in Sustainable Development." *Business & Society* 58, no. 8 (November): 1533–71. https://doi.org/10.1177/0007650317701884.

Ferris, Marcie Cohen. 2010. *Matzoh Ball Gumbo: Culinary Tales of the Jewish South*. Chapel Hill: University of North Carolina Press.

———. 2014. *The Edible South: The Power of Food and the Making of an American Region*. Chapel Hill: University of North Carolina Press.

Figurska, Jolanta. 2022. "Retail Operators in Poland Implement Value Added Tax Reductions." Office of Agricultural Affairs, Warsaw. PL2022-0003. https://fas.usda.gov/data/poland-retail-operators-poland-implement-value-added-tax-reductions.

Fimister, Alan. 2008. *Robert Schuman: Neo-Scholastic Humanism and the Reunification of Europe*. Philosophy & Politics, no. 15. Brussels, Belgium: P.I.E. Peter Lang.

Firth, Raymond. 1937. "Anthropology Looks at Economics." *Science and Society: A Journal of Human Progress* 1: 48–55.

Fisher, Andrew. 2017. *Big Hunger: The Unholy Alliance between Corporate America and Anti-Hunger Groups*. Food, Health, and the Environment. Cambridge, MA: MIT Press.

Fleming, Sam. 2020. "Brussels Faces Fight over Minimum Wage Pledge for EU." *Financial Times*, January 2, 2020. www.ft.com/content/48a97ab4-231b-11ea-b8a1-584213ee7b2b.

Food and Agriculture Organization of the United Nations. 2018. FAO+Belgium. A report on partnership. Rome. https://www.fao.org/3/CA2369EN/ca2369en.pdf.

Foucault, Michel. 1998. *The Will to Knowledge: The History of Sexuality, Vol. 1*. London: Penguin.

Fox, Renée C. 1978. "Why Belgium?" *European Journal of Sociology* 19, no. 2 (November): 205–28.

———. 1994. *In the Belgian Château: The Spirit and Culture of a European Society in an Age of Change*. Chicago: I. R. Dee.

FPS Economy—Statistics Belgium (Quality report Belgian SILC 2015) via HSO (2016 Social Barometer).

"French Food Waste Law Changing How Grocery Stores Approach Excess Food." 2018. *All Things Considered*. Washington, DC: National Public Radio, February 14, 2018. www

.npr.org/sections/thesalt/2018/02/24/586579455/french-food-waste-law-changing-how-grocery-stores-approach-excess-food.

Frow, John. 2003. "Invidious Distinction: Waste, Difference, and Classy Stuff." In *Culture and Waste: The Creation and Destruction of Value*, edited by Gay Hawkins and Stephen Muecke, 25–38. Lanham, MD: Rowman & Littlefield.

Galbraith, Kate. 2012. "The Battle Against Food Waste." *New York Times*, January 5, 2012. https://www.nytimes.com/2012/01/16/business/global/the-battle-against-food-waste.html.

Garcia, Angela. 2010. *The Pastoral Clinic: Addiction and Dispossession along the Rio Grande*. Berkeley: University of California Press.

García, María Elena. 2021. *Gastropolitics and the Specter of Race: Stories of Capital, Culture, and Coloniality in Peru*. Oakland: University of California Press.

Garcia, Sandra. 2020. "How It Started . . . How It's Going, Explained." *New York Times*, October 15, 2020. www.nytimes.com/interactive/2020/10/15/style/how-it-started-meme.html.

Geertz, Clifford, ed. 1974. *Myth, Symbol, and Culture*. New York: W. W. Norton.

Giles, David Boarder. 2016. "Distributions of Wealth, Distributions of Waste: Abject Capital and Accumulation by Disposal," 198–218. London: Deakin University. https://dro.deakin.edu.au/articles/chapter/Distributions_of_wealth_distributions_of_waste_abject_capital_and_accumulation_by_disposal/20867749.

———. 2021. *A Mass Conspiracy to Feed People: Food Not Bombs and the World-Class Waste of Global Cities*. Durham, NC: Duke University Press.

Gille, Zsusza. 2007. *From the Cult of the Waste to the Trash Heap of History: The Politics of Waste in Socialist and Post-Socialist Hungary*. Bloomington: Indiana University Press.

Goody, Jack. 1982. *Cooking, Cuisine, and Class: A Study in Comparative Sociology*. Themes in the Social Sciences. Cambridge: Cambridge University Press.

Gosseye, Janina, and Hilde Heynen. 2013. "Architecture for Leisure in Post-War Europe, 1945–1989: Between Experimentation, Liberation and Patronization." *Journal of Architecture* 18, no. 5: 623–31.

Gross, Neil. 2018. "Is Environmentalism Just for Rich People?" *New York Times*, December 14, 2018. www.nytimes.com/2018/12/14/opinion/sunday/yellow-vest-protests-climate.html.

Gschwindt, Harry. 2016. "The History of Food Banks in Brussels." In person, on site at the Food Bank of Brussels, one-on-one, February 19, 2016.

———. 2017. "The European FEAD Program." In person, on site the Food Bank of Brussels, one-on-one, July 25, 2017.

Gunders, Dana. 2015. *Waste Free Kitchen Handbook: A Guide to Eating Well and Saving Money by Wasting Less Food*. San Francisco: Chronicle Books.

Gustavsson, Jenny, Cristel Cederberg, Ulf Sonesson, R. Otterdijk, and Alexandre Meybeck. 2011. *Global Food Losses and Food Waste: Extent, Causes, and Prevention*. Rome: Food and Agriculture Organisation.

Guthman, Julie. 2004. *Agrarian Dreams: The Paradox of Organic Farming in California*. California Studies in Critical Human Geography. Berkeley: University of California Press.

Guyer, Jane I., ed. 1987. *Feeding African Cities: Studies in Regional Social History*. International African Library. Bloomington: Indiana University Press in association with the International African Institute, London.

Hackworth, Jason R. 2007. *The Neoliberal City: Governance, Ideology, and Development in American Urbanism*. Cornell Paperbacks. Ithaca, NY: Cornell University Press.

Hall, Stuart, ed. 1978. *Policing the Crisis: Mugging, the State, and Law and Order*. Critical Social Studies. London: Macmillan.

Hamilton, Shane. 2003. "Cold Capitalism: The Political Ecology of Frozen Concentrated Orange Juice." *Agricultural History* 77, no. 4 (October 1): 557–81. https://doi.org/10.1215/00021482-77.4.557.

Han, Clara. 2011. "Symptoms of Another Life: Time, Possibility, and Domestic Relations in Chile's Credit Economy." *Cultural Anthropology* 26, no. 1 (February): 7–32. https://doi.org/10.1111/j.1548-1360.2010.01078.x.

———. 2012. *Life in Debt: Times of Care and Violence in Neoliberal Chile*. Berkeley: University of California Press.

Haraway, Donna Jeanne. 1988. "Situated Knowledges: The Science Question in Feminism and the Privilege of Partial Perspective." *Feminist Studies* 14, no. 3: 575. https://doi.org/10.2307/3178066.

———. 2016. *Staying with the Trouble: Making Kin in the Chthulucene*. Experimental Futures: Technological Lives, Scientific Arts, Anthropological Voices. Durham, NC: Duke University Press.

Haspel, Tamar. 2017. "Junk Food Is Cheap and Healthful Food Is Expensive, but Don't Blame the Farm Bill." *Washington Post*, December 4, 2017. https://www.washingtonpost.com/lifestyle/food/im-a-fan-of-michael-pollan-but-on-one-food-policy-argument-hes-wrong/2017/12/04/c71881ca-d6cd-11e7-b62d-d9345ced896d_story.html.

Harrabin, Roger. 2007. "China Building More Power Plants." BBC.co.uk, June 19, 2007. http://news.bbc.co.uk/2/hi/6769743.stm.

Harris, Jessica B. 1999. *Iron Pots and Wooden Spoons: Africa's Gifts to New World Cooking*. 1st Fireside ed. New York: Simon & Schuster.

———. 2011. *High on the Hog: A Culinary Journey from Africa to America*. 1st US ed. New York: Bloomsbury.

Harris, Marvin. 1998. *Good to Eat: Riddles of Food and Culture*. Long Grove, IL: Waveland.

Harvey, David. 2012. *Rebel Cities: From the Right to the City to the Urban Revolution*. New York: Verso.

Haskin, Jeanne M. 2005. *The Tragic State of the Congo: From Decolonization to Dictatorship*. New York: Algora.

Hawkins, Gay. 2005. *The Ethics of Waste: How We Relate to Rubbish*. Lanham: Rowman & Littlefield.

Hawkins, Gay, and Stephen Muecke, eds. 2003. *Culture and Waste: The Creation and Destruction of Value*. Lanham, MD: Rowman & Littlefield.

Headey, Derek, and Harold Alderman. 2019. "The High Price of Healthy Food . . . and the Low Price of Unhealthy Food." *World Food Bank Blogs* (blog), July 23, 2019. https://blogs.worldbank.org/opendata/high-price-healthy-food-and-low-price-unhealthy-food.

Headland, Thomas N. 1997. "Revisionism in Ecological Anthropology." *Current Anthropology* 38, no. 4 (August): 605–30. https://doi.org/10.1086/204648.

Heath, Deborah, and Anne Meneley. 2007. "Techne, Technoscience, and the Circulation of Comestible Commodities: An Introduction." *American Anthropologist* 109, no. 4 (December): 593–602. https://doi.org/10.1525/aa.2007.109.4.593.

Heath, Ryan. 2017. "Brussels Is Blind to Diversity." *Politico*, December 11, 2017. www.politico.eu/article/brussels-blind-to-diversity-whiteout-european-parliament/.

Hervey, Ginger. 2018. "Belgian Government Faces Backlash over Migration Policy." *Politico*, January 22, 2018. www.politico.eu/article/theo-francken-belgian-government-faces-backlash-over-migration-policy/.

Heuzé, Etna Torres. 2018. Cultureghem Insider's View. In person, on site, one-on-one, June 27, 2018.

Hird, Myra J. 2012. "Knowing Waste: Towards an Inhuman Epistemology." *Social Epistemology* 26, no. 3–4 (October): 453–69. https://doi.org/10.1080/02691728.2012.727195.

Hochschild, Adam. 1998. *King Leopold's Ghost: A Story of Greed, Terror, and Heroism in Colonial Africa*. 1st Mariner Books ed. Boston: Houghton Mifflin.

Hoffmeyer, Jesper. 1996. *Signs of Meaning in the Universe*. Advances in Semiotics. Bloomington: Indiana University Press.

Holtzman, Jon D. 2006. "Food and Memory." *Annual Review of Anthropology* 35 (June 14): 361–78. www.annualreviews.org/doi/10.1146/annurev.anthro.35.081705.123220.

Jacobs, Ryan. 2014. "The Dark Side of the Truffle Trade." *Atlantic Monthly*, January 15, 2014. www.theatlantic.com/international/archive/2014/01/the-dark-side-of-the-truffle-trade/283073/.

Janisse, Kier-La, and Paul Corupe, eds. 2016. *Satanic Panic: Pop-Cultural Paranoia in the 1980s*. Surrey: FAB.

Jong, Belle de. 2022. "More Than Half of Brussels Residents Struggle to Make Ends Meet." *Brussels Times*, June 21, 2022. www.brusselstimes.com/242224/more-than-half-of-brussels-residents-struggle-to-make-ends-meet.

Jordan, Jillian, Paul Bloom, Moshe Hoffman, and David Rand. 2016. "What's the Point of Moral Outrage?" *New York Times*, February 26, 2016, New York edition, sec. SR.

Joyner, Charles. 1984. *Down by the Riverside: A South Carolina Slave Community*. Champaign: University of Illinois Press.

Keating, Dave. 2019. "EU Plans to Transfer Energy Powers from Capitals to Brussels." *Forbes*, April 9, 2019. www.forbes.com/sites/davekeating/2019/04/09/eu-plans-to-transfer-energy-powers-from-member-states-to-brussels/?sh=714f50511189.

Kim, S., and B. M. Popkin. 2006. "Commentary: Understanding the Epidemiology of Overweight and Obesity—A Real Global Public Health Concern." *International Journal of Epidemiology* 35, no. 1 (February): 60–67.

King, Tim. 2015. "Belgium Is a Failed State." *Politico*, December 2, 2015, sec. Brussels Sketch. www.politico.eu/article/belgium-failed-state-security-services-molenbeek-terrorism/.

Klein, Matthew C. 2015. "What's the Deal with Belgium?" *Financial Times*, August 20, 2015. www.ft.com/content/f60117b0-2dbb-3c84-a1df-f982c07ba97b.

Kolnai, Aurel. 2004. *On Disgust*. Edited and with an introduction by Barry Smith and Carolyn Korsmeyer. Chicago: Open Court.

Krause, Elizabeth L. 2018. *Tight Knit: Global Families and the Social Life of Fast Fashion*. Chicago: University of Chicago Press.

Kummer, Corby. 2016. "The Good, the Bad, and the Ugly: How to Think about the Food We Waste." *New Republic*, March 14, 2016. https://newrepublic.com/article/130812/good-bad-ugly.

Lakhani, Nina, Aliya Uteuova, and Alvin Chang. 2021. "Revealed: The True Extent of America's Food Monopolies, and Who Pays the Price." *The Guardian*, July 14, 2021. https://www.theguardian.com/environment/ng-interactive/2021/jul/14/food-monopoly-meals-profits-data-investigation#:~:text=A%20joint%20investigation%20by%20the,fridges%20brimming%20with%20different%20brands.

Laporte, Dominique. 2000. *History of Shit*. Translated by Rodolphe El-Khoury and Nadia Benabi. Cambridge, MA: MIT Press.

Larmer, Brook. 2018. "E-Waste Offers an Economic Opportunity as Well as Toxicity." *New York Times Magazine*, July 5, 2018. www.nytimes.com/2018/07/05/magazine/e-waste-offers-an-economic-opportunity-as-well-as-toxicity.html.

Latour, Bruno. 2010. "An Attempt at a 'Compositionist Manifesto.'" *New Literary History* 41, no. 3 (Summer): 471–90.

Lee, Richard Philip, C. Coulson, and K. Hackett. 2021. "The Social Practices of Food Bank Volunteer Work." *Social Policy and Society* 22, no. 3: 408–25.

Le Grand, Yvonne. 2015. "Activism through Commensality: Food and Politics in a Temporary Vegan Zone." In *Commensality: From Everyday Food to Feast*, edited by Susanne Kerner, Cynthia Chou, and Morten Warmind, 51–64. Oxford: Bloomsbury.

Lejeune, Christine Speer. 2022. "How to Fight Food Insecurity in Philly." *Philadelphia Citizen*, July 19, 2022. https://thephiladelphiacitizen.org/how-to-fight-philadelphia-food-insecurity/.

Les Dames d'Escoffier International. n.d. "About Les Dames d'Escoffier International: Our History." Professional Organization. LDEI.org. Les Dames d'Escoffier International. https://ldei.org/about/.

Lévi-Strauss, Claude. 1964. *The Raw and the Cooked*. Translated by John Weightman and Doreen Weightman. New York: Harper & Row.

Lien, Marianne E. 2015. *Becoming Salmon: Aquaculture and the Domestication of a Fish*. Oakland: University of California Press.

Little, Amanda. 2019. "Climate Change, Food, and You." Radio Cherry Bombe. Accessed September 12, 2019. https://cherrybombe.com/radio-cherry-bombe/climate-change-food-and-you.

Livingston, Julie. 2012. *Improvising Medicine: An African Oncology Ward in an Emerging Cancer Epidemic*. Durham: Duke University Press.

Lleshi, Bleri. 2014. "Brussels on Strike: Rich City, Poor Citizens." *EUobserver*, December 15, 2014. https://euobserver.com/opinion/126904.

Loobuyck, Patrick, and Leni Franken. 2011. "Towards Integrative Religious Education in Belgium and Flanders: Challenges and Opportunities." *British Journal of Religious Education* 33, no. 1: 17–30.

Marcus, David. 2023. "The Tragedy of Philadelphia Reveals a Sad Truth about Our Government." FoxNews.com, July 3, 2023. www.foxnews.com/opinion/tragedy-philadelphia-reveals-sad-truth-about-our-government.

Martens, John, and Andrew Clapham. 2012. "Belgian Budget Goal Challenged as 2011 Deficit Misses Target." *Bloomberg Business*, January 13, 2012.

Martinos, Haris, et al. 2020. "The Impact of Social Economy at the Local and Regional Level." Commission for Social Policy, Education, Employment, Research, and Culture.

Brussels: European Union. https://cor.europa.eu/en/engage/studies/Documents/Impact-of-social-economy.pdf.

Marx, Karl, and Frederick Engels. 1970 [1846]. *The German Ideology*. London: Lawrence & Wishart.

Mentes, Fatma Derya. 2020. "Governing the Air: Regulation of the Commercial Aviation in the Middle East." PhD diss., Duke University.

Michiels, Tony. 2016. Discussion of Brussels Food Bank Operations. In person, one-on-one interview at the Brussels Food Bank, June 30, 2016.

———. 2017. Discussion of Site One and Site Two Operational Schemes. In person, one-on-one interview at the Brussels Food Bank, August 1, 2017.

Millar, Kathleen. 2014. "The Precarious Present: Wageless Labor and Disrupted Life in Rio De Janeiro, Brazil." *Cultural Anthropology* 29, no. 1: 32–53. https://doi.org/10.14506/ca29.1.04.

Miller, Daniel. 1998. *A Theory of Shopping*. Ithaca: Cornell University Press

Mintz, Sidney W. 1985. *Sweetness and Power: The Place of Sugar in Modern History*. New York: Viking.

———. 1996. *Tasting Food, Tasting Freedom: Excursions into Eating, Culture, and the Past*. Boston: Beacon.

Mintz, Sidney W., and Christine M. DuBois. 2002. "The Anthropology of Food and Eating." *Annual Review of Anthropology* 31, no. 1: 99–119.

Muehlebach, Andrea Karin. 2012. *The Moral Neoliberal: Welfare and Citizenship in Italy*. Chicago: University of Chicago Press.

Myaux, Déborah. 2019. "*Aide alimentaire. Les protections sociales en jeu*." Louvain-la-Neuve: Éditions Academia.

National Research Council. 2000. *Waste Incineration and Public Health*. Washington, DC: The National Academies Press. https://nap.nationalacademies.org/catalog/5803/waste-incineration-and-public-health.

Nestle, Marion. 2002. *Food Politics: How the Food Industry Influences Nutrition and Health*. Oakland: University of California Press.

———. 2015. "Sidney Mintz: 1922–2015: Some Personal Memories." *Food Politics* (blog), December 29, 2015. https://www.foodpolitics.com/tag/sidney-mintz/.

Numbeo. n.d. "Cost of Living Comparison Between Brussels and Lima." Accessed April 24, 2024. https://www.numbeo.com/cost-of-living/compare_cities.jsp?country1=Peru&country2=Belgium&city1=Lima&city2=Brussels&tracking=getDispatchComparison.

Nuttin, Joseph. 1976. "Stereotypes of Flemish and Walloon Ethnic Groups in Belgium." *Mededelingen van de Koninklijke Academie voor Wetenschappen* 38, no. 2: 3–86. https://psycnet.apa.org/record/1979-05804-001.

Obinger, Herbert, et al. 2022. "Mass Warfare and the Development of the Modern Welfare State: An Analysis of the Western World: 1941–1950." In *International Impacts on Social Policy: Short Histories on Global Perspective*, edited by Frank Nullmeier, Delia González de Reufels, and Herbert Obinger, 21–34. London: Palgrave Macmillan.

O'Brien, Martin. 2008. *A Crisis of Waste? Understanding the Rubbish Society*. London: Routledge.

OECD. 2019. *OECD Economic Surveys: Belgium 2019*. Paris: OECD Publishing.
Ortiz, Diego Arguedas. 2019. "Food Waste: How to Stop Throwing Away Good Food." The BBC in Association with Corteva Agriscience. https://www.bbc.com/future/bespoke/follow-the-food/the-wasteful-fate-of-a-third-of-food/.
Owusu, Bruno. 2017. Working Life at the Brussels Food Bank. In person, on site at the Food Bank in Brussels, one-on-one, June 25, 2017.
"Paul Bloom: Why Do We Create Stereotypes." 2014. Audio. *The TED Radio Hour: Playing with Perceptions*. NPR, November 14, 2014. www.npr.org/2014/11/14/362373052/why-do-we-create-stereotypes.
Paxson, Heather. 2012. *The Life of Cheese: Crafting Food and Value in America*. California Studies in Food and Culture 41. Berkeley: University of California Press.
———. 2019. "'Don't Pack a Pest': Parts, Wholes, and the Porosity of Food Borders." *Food, Culture & Society* 22, no. 5 (October 20): 657–73. https://doi.org/10.1080/15528014.2019.1638136.
Peebles, Gustav. 2019. *The Euro and Its Rivals: Currency and the Construction of a Transnational City*. Bloomington: Indiana University Press, 2019.
Phillips, Laurence. 2002. *Paris—Lille—Brussels: The Bradt Guide to Eurostar Cities*. Buckinghamshire: Bradt Travel Guides.
Pollan, Michael. 2004. "Our National Eating Disorder." *New York Times*, October 17, 2004. National ed., sec. 6.
———. 2006. *The Omnivore's Dilemma: A Natural History of Four Meals*. New York: Penguin Press.
Poppendieck, Janet. 1999. *Sweet Charity?: Emergency Food and the End of Entitlement*. New York: Penguin Books.
Raskin, Hannah Rachel. 2009. "Get Yer Locally Grown Hotdogs Here." *Mountain Express*, April 8, 2009, sec. Food News. https://mountainx.com/food/food-news/040809get_yer_locally_grown_hot_dogs_here/.
Reed-Danahay, Deborah. 2017. "Bourdieu and Critical Autoethnography: Implications for Research, Writing, and Teaching." *International Journal of Multicultural Education* 19, no. 1 (February 28): 144. https://doi.org/10.18251/ijme.v19i1.1368.
Reese, Ashanté M. 2019. *Black Food Geographies: Race, Self-Reliance, and Food Access in Washington, D.C.* Chapel Hill: University of North Carolina Press.
Renaerts, Rob. 2017a. Food Waste Recuperation and Recirculation Programs in Brussels. In person, on site at Coduco, one-on-one, August 29, 2017.
———. 2017b. The History of EU Food Waste Policy. In person, on site at Coduco, one-on-one, August 2, 2017.
———. 2017c. Soup, Ice Cream, Bread Recuperation/Brussels Beer Project/Food Recuperation Programs in Brussels. In person, Vismet restaurant, one-on-one, December 6, 2017.
———. 2018. EU Sustainability Programs. In person, on site at Turn und Taxis/EU Sustainability Office, one-on-one, February 2, 2018.
Reniers, G. 2000. "On the Selectivity and Internal Dynamics of Labour Migration Processes: An Analysis of Turkish and Moroccan Migration to Belgium." In *Communities and Generations: Turkish and Moroccan Populations in Belgium*, edited by R. Lesthaeghe, 59–93. The Hague/Brussels: NIDI/CBGS.

Reno, Joshua. 2009. "Your Trash Is Someone's Treasure: The Politics of Value at a Michigan Landfill." *Journal of Material Culture* 14, no. 1 (March): 29–46. https://doi.org/10.1177/1359183508100007.

———. 2014. "Toward a New Theory of Waste: From 'Matter out of Place' to Signs of Life." *Theory, Culture & Society* 31, no. 6 (November): 3–27. https://doi.org/10.1177/0263276413500999.

———. 2016. *Waste Away: Working and Living with a North American Landfill*. Oakland: University of California Press.

Richards, Audrey I. 1995. *Land, Labour, and Diet in Northern Rhodesia: An Economic Study of the Bemba Tribe*. Repr. Classics in African Anthropology. Münster Hamburg: Lit.

Richardson, Seth. 2016. "Obedient Bellies: Hunger and Food Security in Ancient Mesopotamia." *Journal of the Economic and Social History of the Orient* 59, no. 5 (November 7): 750–92. https://doi.org/10.1163/15685209-12341413.

Riches, Graham. 1986. *Food Banks and the Welfare Crisis*. Ottawa: Canadian Council on Social Development.

———. 2018. *Food Bank Nations: Poverty, Corporate Charity and the Right to Food*. Routledge Studies in Food, Society and the Environment. London: Routledge.

Riches, Graham, and Tiina Silvasti. 2014. *First World Hunger Revisited*. London: Palgrave Macmillan.

Robinson, Francis. 2010. "Belgian Debt and Contagion." *Wall Street Journal*, November 26, 2010.

Rodriguez, Gregory. 2007. "Belgium's Identity Crisis." *Los Angeles Times*, September 17, 2007. www.latimes.com/archives/la-xpm-2007-sep-17-oe-rodriguez17-story.html.

Rogers, Heather. 2005. *Gone Tomorrow: The Hidden Life of Garbage*. New York: New Press.

Rosenberg, Daniel, et al. 2021. "Burned: Why Waste Incineration Is Harmful." *National Resources Defense Council: Expert Blog* (blog), July 19, 2021. www.nrdc.org/bio/daniel-rosenberg/burned-why-waste-incineration-harmful.

Rudy, Kathy. 1997. *Sex and the Church: Gender, Homosexuality, and the Transformation of Christian Ethics*. Boston: Beacon.

———. 2011. *Loving Animals: Toward a New Animal Advocacy*. Minneapolis: University of Minnesota Press.

Scherz, China. 2014. *Having People, Having Heart: Charity, Sustainable Development, and Problems of Dependence in Central Uganda*. Chicago: University of Chicago Press.

Schlee, Maxime. 2018. "Theo Francken: Brussels 'Pampering' NGOs and Asylum Seekers." *Politico*, August 10, 2018. www.politico.eu/article/theo-francken-brussels-park-maximilien-pampering-ngos-and-asylum-seekers/.

Schlosser, Eric. 2012. *Fast Food Nation: The Dark Side of the All-American Meal*. 1st Mariner Books ed. Boston: Mariner Books/Houghton Mifflin Harcourt.

Scholliers, Peter. 2009. *Food Culture in Belgium*. Food Culture around the World. Westport, CT: Greenwood.

Schoonvaere, Quentin. 2010. "Studie over de Congolese Migratie En de Impact Ervan Op de Congolese Aanwezigheid in België. Analyse van de Voornaamste Demografische Gegevens." *Studiegroep Toegepaste Demografie UCL and Centrum Voor Gelijkheid van Kansen En Voor Racismebestrijding*.

———. 2014. *België-Marokko 50 Jaar Migratie: Demografische Studie over de Populatie van Marokkaanse Herkomst in België*. Federaal migratiecentrum.

Schreuer, Milan. 2018. "Belgium in Uproar over Torture of Sudanese It Deported." *New York Times*, January 10, 2018. www.nytimes.com/2018/01/10/world/europe/belgium-sudan-theo-francken.html.

Schuetze, Christopher F. 2018. "German Food Bank Reopens Doors to New Foreign Applicants." *New York Times*, April 4, 2018. www.nytimes.com/2018/04/04/world/europe/germany-food-bank-foreigners.html.

Schuman, Robert. 1950. "The Schuman Declaration." Speech presented at Quai d'Orsay, Paris, May 9, 1950. https://european-union.europa.eu/principles-countries-history/history-eu/1945-59/schuman-declaration-may-1950_en.

Scott, James C. 2017. *Against the Grain: A Deep History of the Earliest States*. Yale Agrarian Studies. New Haven, CT: Yale University Press.

Sengupta, Somini. 2022. "Feeding a Hotter Planet: Hunger Is Rising Again Even as We Produce Enough Food." *New York Times*, October 10, 2022. www.nytimes.com/2022/06/10/climate/food-farming-climate-change.html.

Seremetakis, Constantina Nadia, ed. 1996. *The Senses Still: Perception and Memory as Material Culture in Modernity*. Chicago: University of Chicago Press.

Severson, Kim. 2000. "When Put to the Test, Here's How Butter Brands Stack Up." *San Francisco Chronicle*, December 13, 2000.

Shukin, Nicole. 2009. *Animal Capital: Rendering Life in Biopolitical Times*. Posthumanities 6. Minneapolis: University of Minnesota Press.

Sifferlin, Alexandra. 2015. "30% of Foodborne Illness Deaths Happen in Children under Age Five." *Time*, December 3, 2015. https://time.com/4133193/foodborne-illness-children-food-safety/.

Silvasti, Tiina, and Jouko Karjalainen. 2014. "Hunger in a Nordic Welfare State." In *First World Hunger Revisited*, edited by Tiina Silvasti and Graham Riches, 72–86. London: Palgrave Macmillan.

Simmel, Georg. 1964. "The Metropolis and Mental Life." In *The Sociology of Georg Simmel*, edited by Kurt H. Wolff, 409–24. A Free Press Paperback. New York: Free Press.

Simon, Ben. 2018. "Let's Talk about Food Waste and Hunger." *Imperfect Foods: The Imperfect Food Blog* (blog), October 12, 2018. http://blog.imperfectfoods.com/blog-1/2018/10/12.

Solomon, Harris. 2015. "'The Taste No Chef Can Give': Processing Street Food in Mumbai." *Cultural Anthropology* 30, no. 1 (February 16): 65–90. https://doi.org/10.14506/ca30.1.05.

———. 2016. *Metabolic Living: Food, Fat and the Absorption of Illness in India*. Critical Global Health: Evidence, Efficacy, Ethnography. Durham, NC: Duke University Press.

Starn, Orin, ed. 2015. *Writing Culture and the Life of Anthropology*. Durham, NC: Duke University Press.

Stengers, Jean. 1980. *Léopold III et Le Gouvernement: Les Deux Politiques Belges de 1940*. 2nd ed., Augm. Bruxelles: Racine.

Stewart, Kathleen. 2007. *Ordinary Affects*. Durham, NC: Duke University Press.

Sumner, David. 2022. "Which Languages Are Spoken in Belgium?" *Babbel*, August 9, 2022. www.babbel.com/en/magazine/languages-spoken-in-belgium.

Sutton, David. 2001. *Remembrance of Repasts: An Anthropology of Food and Memory*. Oxford: Berg.

———. 2014. *Secrets from the Greek Kitchen: Cooking, Skill, and Everyday Life on an Aegean Island*. Berkeley: University of California Press.

———. 2021. "Revivifying Commensality: Eating, Politics, and the Sensory Production of the Social." In *Gardens of Memory: Itineraries and Sanctuaries*, edited by Virginia Nazarea and Terese Gagnon, 133–60. Tucson: University of Arizona Press.

Sutton, David, and Peter Wogan. 2010. "Seinfeld, Potluck Dinners, and Problematic Gifts." *Popular Anthropology* 1, no. 1: 8–10.

Taylor, Janelle S. 2003. "The Story Catches You and You Fall Down: Tragedy, Ethnography, and 'Cultural Competence.'" *Medical Anthropology Quarterly* 17, no. 2: 159–81.

———. 2008. "On Recognition, Caring, and Dementia." *Medical Anthropology Quarterly* 22, no. 4: 313–35.

Taylor, Joe Gray. 1982. *Eating, Drinking, and Visiting in the South*. Baton Rouge: Louisiana State University Press.

Taylor-Gooby, Peter. 2004. *New Risks, New Welfare: The Transformation of the European Welfare State*. Oxford: Oxford University Press.

Ticktin, Miriam. 2011. *Casualties of Care: Immigration and the Politics of Humanitarianism in France*. Berkeley: University of California Press.

Trankell, Ing-Britt. 1995. *Cooking, Care and Domestication: A Culinary Ethnography of the Tai Yong, Northern Thailand*. Uppsala Studies in Cultural Anthropology 21. London: Coronet Books.

Treffers-Daller, Jeanine. 2002. "Language Use and Language Contact in Brussels." *Journal of Multilingual and Multicultural Development* 23, no. 1–2: 50–64. https://doi.org/10.1080/01434630208666454.

Tsing, Anna Lowenhaupt. 2015. *The Mushroom at the End of the World: On the Possibility of Life in Capitalist Ruins*. Princeton, NJ: Princeton University Press.

Tuchman, Gaye, and Harry Gene Levine. 1993. "New York Jews and Chinese Food: The Social Construction of an Ethnic Pattern." *Journal of Contemporary Ethnography* 22, no. 3: 382–407.

Turner, Victor W. 1974. *Dramas, Fields, and Metaphors: Symbolic Action in Human Society*. Ithaca, NY: Cornell University Press.

Twilley, Nicola. 2021. "Annals of Design: The Garden of Forking Paths." *New Yorker*, November 29, 2021. www.newyorker.com/magazine/2021/11/29/how-the-worlds-foremost-maze-maker-leads-people-astray.

U.N. Framework Convention on Climate Change annual submission of Belgium, January 12, 2010. U.N. Doc. FCCC/ARR/2009/BE, GE.10-60005. 2009. https://unfccc.int/sites/default/files/resource/docs/2010/arr/bel.pdf.

UN World Food Program USA. 2021. "8 Facts to Know about Food Waste and Hunger." *World Food Program USA* (blog), October 1, 2021. www.wfpusa.org/articles/8-facts-to-know-about-food-waste-and-hunger/.

———. 2024. "Food Waste & Food Loss." *World Food Program USA* (blog), 2024. https://www.wfpusa.org/drivers-of-hunger/food-waste/.

"United Nations, Department of Economic and Social Affairs, Population Division, World Population Prospects 2022: Summary of Results." 2022. World Population Prospectus. UN DESA. https://population.un.org/wpp/.

United Nations Global Humanities Network. 2019. "Can We Feed the World and Ensure No One Goes Hungry?" UN Global perspective human stories, October 3, 2019. https://news.un.org/en/story/2019/10/1048452.

"U.S. EPA. Report on the 2013 U.S. Environmental Protection Agency (EPA) International Decontamination Research and Development Conference." 2013. Research Triangle Park, NC: US Environmental Protection Agency, Washington, D.C., November 5, 2013. https://cfpub.epa.gov/si/si_public_record_report.cfm?dirEntryId=284802&Lab=NHSRC&fed_org_id=1253&subject=Homeland%20Security%20Research&view=desc&sortBy=pubDateYear&showCriteria=1&count=25&searchall=decontamination%20AND%20conference.

Vanderstappen, Tom. 2017. "Leopold III: The Belgian King Who Was Forced to Abdicate after the Second World War." *Brussels Times*, November 21, 2017. www.brusselstimes.com/45058/leopold-iii-the-belgian-king-who-was-forced-to-abdicate-after-the-second-world-war.

Van Parijs, Philippe. 2014. "Why Did Brussels Become the Capital of the Europe?" *Brussels Times*, September 7, 2014. www.brusselstimes.com/29273/why-did-brussels-become-the-capital-of-europe-because-belgium-starts-with-letter-b.

Velaers, Jan, and Herman Van Goethem. 1994. *Leopold III: De Konig, Het Land, De Oorlog*. Tielt, Belgium: Lannoo.

Walsh, Dylan. 2011. "A War Against Food Waste." *New York Times*, September 15, 2011. https://archive.nytimes.com/green.blogs.nytimes.com/2011/09/15/a-war-against-food-waste/.

Weinstein, Deena, and Michael A. Weinstein. 1989. "Simmel and the Dialectic of the Double Boundary: The Case of the Metropolis and Mental Life." *Sociological Inquiry* 59, no. 1 (January): 48–59. https://doi.org/10.1111/j.1475-682X.1989.tb01079.x.

Weiss, Brad. 2016. *Real Pigs: Shifting Values in the Field of Local Pork*. Durham, NC: Duke University Press.

Wike, Richard, Janell Fetterolf, and Moira Fagan. 2019. "Europeans Credit EU with Promoting Peace and Prosperity, but Say Brussels Is Out of Touch with Its Citizens." Pew Research Center, March 2019. www.pewresearch.org/global/wp-content/uploads/sites/2/2019/03/Pew-Research-Center_Views-of-EU-Report_2019-03-19.pdf.

Wilk, Richard. 1999. "'Real Belizean Food': Building Local Identity in the Transnational Caribbean." *American Anthropologist* 101, no. 2: 244–55.

Wilk, Richard, and Shingo Hamada. 2018. *Seafood: Ocean to the Plate*. London: Routledge.

Wilkerson, Isabel. 2020. *Caste: The Origins of Our Discontents*. New York: Random House.

Williams-Forson, Psyche. 2006. *Building Houses out of Chicken Legs: Black Women, Food and Power*. Chapel Hill: University of North Carolina Press.

———. 2022. *Eating while Black: Food Shaming and Race in America*. Chapel Hill: University of North Carolina Press.

Williams-Forson, Pysche, and C. Counihan, eds. 2013. *Taking Food Public: Redefining Foodways in a Changing World*. London: Routledge.

Wolfert, Paula. 1973. *Couscous and Other Good Food from Morocco*. New York: Harper & Row.

"Women of Wealth Fight Food Waste: Fifty Social Leaders in New York Will Serve Only Three Course Dinners." 1917. *New York Times*, May 16, 1917: 5. https://www.nytimes

.com/1917/05/16/archives/women-of-wealth-fight-food-waste-fifty-social-leaders-in-new-york.html.

Wynsberghe, Caroline Van, Johanne Poirier, Dave Sinardet, and Françoise Tulkens. 2009. "The Political and Institutional Development of the Brussels Metropolitan Zone: Observations and Prospects." https://api.semanticscholar.org/CorpusID:127557825.

Zamfira, Razvan. 2015. "Blood and Guts in Brussels: The Abattoir Master Plan." *Uncube Magazine*, February 10, 2015. www.uncubemagazine.com/blog/15285535.

Zimmermann, Antonia. 2021. "Poland's Waste Blame Game." *Politco*, July 30, 2021. https://www.politico.eu/article/poland-waste-management-environment/.

Zweynert, Astrid. 2017. "Food Waste in the European Union." *Thomson Reuters Foundation*, January 24, 2017. https://news.trust.org/item/20170123184255-31rrx/.

Index

Note: Page numbers in *italics* refer to illustrative matter.

Abrassart, Gia, 113
Ad Council of America, 25–26
Adzersen, Ana, 155
African Americans, 51, 115–16, 175. *See also* United States
Ahmad, 143
Albert I (king), 61
Allison, Anne, 195n4
Alonto, Christina, 105, 126
Amira, 152, 153
Anderlecht Abattoir, Brussels. *See* Cultureghem
Anderlecht commune, Brussels, 89–90, 94, 148–49. *See also* Brussels, Belgium; Cultureghem
Andres, Jose, 177
Andriukaitis, Vytenis, 37, 38
Annan, Kofi, 138–39
Anthropocene, 15
Appadurai, Arjun, 193n7
Article 60 programme, 134, 142, 145, 168
Atelier Groot Eiland, 133–34, 139–141, *140*
Atomium, 97
Austrian invasion, 60–61
author's positionality, 1, 2, 3, 5–12, 13

Babbel, 66
Barattoir, Cultureghem, 159–62. *See also* Cultureghem
Battle of Nancy, 59
Battle of the Bulge, 62
Becoming Salmon (Lien), 22, 176
Belgian Congo, 63–64
Belgian Revolution (1830), 57
Belgium: Catholicism in, 4, 52–53, 60, 68, 114, 121, 123, 168; colonial history of, 54, 55–56, 63–64, 112–13; economic status of, 62, 80–83, 132; historical overview of, 58–65; industrial history of, 89–90; language communities of, 65–67, 69–70, 92, 137–38; map of, 57; modern political and governmental conditions in, 69–72, 78–83, 194n1; size of, 84–85. *See also* Brussels, Belgium
Bel Mundo, *130*; about, 4, 129, 168; funding of, 129–31; initiatives of, 131–35, 173; leadership of, 134–35, 137–42; as research site, 86; staff of, *141*, 142–46; steak night at, 135–37, *142*
Bennett, Jane, 173–74
Bernard, Abel, 8, 9
Bilal, 156
biosemiotic, 23
Birnbaum, Michael, 69, 78–79, 195n3
Black Americans, 51, 115–16, 175
Black Food Geographies (Reese), 172
Black Lives Matter movement, 112
Blainey, Marc, 67
Bloom, Paul, 32, 51
Boas, Franz, 22
Bourdieu, Pierre, 11, 191n2
Brazil, 192n4, 194n1
brewery, 45–46
British East India Company, 41
Brock, Carol, 180
Brouwerij De Halve Maan, 45–46
Bruno, 109–10
Brussels, Belgium: commune structure of, 79, 148–49; economic conditions in, 83–86; as EU capital, 75, 83, 129; as foodie place, 51–52; historical overview of, 56, 60–61, 65, 66–78, 112–13;

Brussels, Belgium (*continued*)
Parc Maximilien, 155–58, 196n1 (ch. 5); as research site, 50–51, 53–54; social welfare services in, 129; stereotypes of, 49–50, 51. *See also* Anderlecht commune, Brussels; Belgium; Molenbeek commune, Brussels
Brussels Food Bank. *See* Food Bank of Brussels
Brussels Gare Maritime, 17
Buch, Elana, 145
Burgundian invasion, 59–60
Burundi, 16

Caldwell, Melissa, 40, 124, 196n2 (ch. 4)
Calvinism, 68, 119
Campos, Paul, 42–43
capitalism, 44–46, 129, 146. *See also* economics of food
carcinogenics, 15, 95–96
care, 145–46
catadores, 192n4
Catholicism, 4, 52–53, 60, 68, 114, 121, 123, 168. *See also* faith-based food distribution
Catholic Party, 73
Catholic Worker Movement, 127
Centre Public d'Action Sociale (CPAS), 104–5
Chan, Margaret, 21
charity and political activism, 123–26. *See also* faith-based food distribution
Charles V (king), 60
Chinese food, 174
Christianity, 58–59, 101–3, 120. *See also* faith-based food distribution
Churchill, Winston, 72
Ciciriello, Luigi, 8–9, 39
Cistercians, 59
citizenship, 134, 142–43, 144–45, 146. *See also* social belonging
citrus, 18
Claudine (king), 58
Clovis (king), 58–59
Coclanis, Peter, 42

coffee receptions, 131
Cohen, Stanley, 30–31, 32
Collectmet, Cultureghem, 151–55. *See also* Cultureghem
colonial history, 54, 55–56, 63–64, 112–13
commune structure of Brussels, 79, 148–49. *See also* Anderlecht commune, Brussels; Molenbeek commune, Brussels; Watermael-Boitsfort commune, Brussels
community gardening, 170–71
Congo, 54, 63–64, 90, 113–15
consumer-focused solutions to food waste, 36–39. *See also* moral panics
Contested Tastes (Desoucey), 194n7
Cornellis, Nena, 132, 135–37, 139, 143–44
Council on Foreign Relations, 34
COVID-19 pandemic, 8, 20, 31, 52, 177
La Cravache d'Or, 8
crowdsourcing campaign, 46
Cultureghem, 4–5; Barattoir, 159–62; Collectmet, 151–55; program goals of, 147, 162–66, 168, 173; soup serving in the park, 155–58. *See also* Anderlecht commune, Brussels
Cyprus, 77

Les Dames d'Escoffier International, 180
Davisfonds, 133
Day, Dorothy, 127
De Baerdemaeker, Eva, 147, 151–54, 159–60
De Boeck, Filip, 67
debt crisis, 56, 80–81
deciphering a meal, as concept, 23–24. *See also* Douglas, Mary
deciphering a meal, as method, 23–24
Dedeurwaerder, Tom, 134–35, 137–42, 145
De Gaulle, Charles, 75
Democratic Republic of Congo (DRC), 63–64, 112, 113–15
dental care, 143, 146
Deschouwer, Kris, 68, 69
Desoucey, Michaela, 194n7
De Souza, Rebecca, 119
De Winter, Lieven, 68, 69
dietary restrictions, 100, 101, 102, 103–4

dioxins, 95–96
discourse, Foucault on, 26
distinction, as concept, 12, 19, 20, 191n2
dollar stores, 164–65, 171
Douglas, Mary, 23–24, 25, 192n3
Dunaway, Finis, 26
Dutch East India Company, 41
Dutch invasion, 61
Dutch language, 67, 115, 142, 143
Dutch revolt (16th c.), 60
Dylan, 160–61

Earth Day, 26, 27
Eating While Black (Williams-Forson), 115–16, 165
economic security, 49
economics of food, 16, 28, 39–44, 46–47, 77–78. *See also under* food
economic status of Belgium, 62, 80–83, 132
education, 114, 134–35
Engie, 156–57
environmental argument for food waste reduction, 15, 84, 170, 182
environmental pollution, 26–27
Environmental Protection Agency (EPA), 37
Estonia, 77
European Commission for Health and Food Safety, 38
European Community for Atomic Energy, 74
European "crisis," 75–76
European Economic Community, 74
European Regional Development Fund (ERDF), 150
European Union: Brussels as capital of, 75, 83; economic conditions of, 80–81, 83–84; establishment of, 74–75; FEAD program, 90
"Excess Food Opportunities Map" (EPA), 37–39

faith-based food distribution, 4, 101–3, 120–22, 123. *See also* Catholicism; Christianity

The Fate of Food (Little), 17
Fatma, 99–100, 102
FEAD Program (EU), 90
Feeding the Other (De Souza), 119
First World Hunger, Revisited (Riches & Silvasti), 120
Fisher, Andrew, 119–20
Flemings, 60, 62
Flemish Community Commission, 133
Flemish culture, 133, 148
Flemish language, 62, 65–66, 103, 137, 138
food, as agent of social change, 53, 121, 191n1 (ch. 1). *See also* spectrum of edibility
food, defined, 22–24. *See also* economics of food
Food and Water Watch, 46
Food Bank of Brussels: building of, 88–90; *Le Magasin* at, 107–12; as research site, 3–4, 52, 88–89; sermon attendance and, 101–3; Site One, 97–103, 105, 118, 126; Site Two, 103–7, 118, 124; sorting room of, 93; staff and volunteers of, 92–94
food banks, 52, 78, 86, 87–88, 96–97, 119–20, 123. *See also* Food Bank of Brussels; food waste recirculation
food-borne diseases and deaths, 20–21
food categories, 192n3
food journalism, 5–7
Food Not Bombs movement, 17, 18
food (in)security, 77, 182
food sovereignty, 167, 168
food stamp program, 96
food waste: consumer awareness campaigns on, 36–39; defined, 24–26, 172; economic conditions and, 16; moral panics and, 29–31, 36–39; statistics on, 13, 27, 34, 77; toxic release from, 15; from La Truffe Noir, 11–12; urbanism and, 17–19, 48–49
food waste recirculation, 1–3; *vs.* capitalism, 48–49; from faith-based projects, 4, 101–3, 120–22, 123; Giles on, 18; supermarket mandate on, 34–35, 77, 91, 94. *See also* Bel Mundo; Cultureghem; Food Bank of Brussels; food banks; ugly food

food waste reduction: environmental argument for, 15, 84, 170, 182; hunger argument for, 15, 18, 36–37, 53, 77, 84, 123, 170, 182; media attention on, 19, 35–36; medical argument for, 20–2; methods for, 167–84; research and discourse on, 13–15, 22
Foucault, Michel, 26
Fox, Renée C., 67
France, 34, 61, 71–74, 76, 85, 122, 194n7
Francis (pope), 76
Franciscan Sisters of Africa, 123
Francken, Theo, 196n1 (ch. 5)
Franken, Leni, 114
Frankish German invasion, 58–59
French invasion, 61
French language, 62, 65–66
French Revolution, 61

garbage dump collectors, 192n4
García, María Elena, 49
gardening, 32, 134, 170–71
gastronationalism, 194n7
gastropolitics, 49, 164–65, 167, 193n7
General Federation of Belgian Labor (FGTB), 109
The German Ideology (Marx and Engels), 45
German invasions, 61–62, 72, 147
German language, 62, 65
Ghana, 90, 138, 159
Ghanaian immigrants, 109, 113, 159–60
Ghent, Belgium, 51, 68
Giles, David Boarder, 17, 18, 47
Glick-Schiler, Nina, 163–64
Good Food Brussels campaign, 32, 33, 35
Gould, Mrs. George J., 35
La Grande Halle de la Villette, Paris, 147
grapefruit, 18
Greece, 80, 81
Green Party, 125
Gross, Neil, 126
Gschwindt, Harry, 38, 92, 93, 94–95, 108–9, 125

Guthman, Julie, 40
Guyer, Jane, 22

Hall, Stuart, 31, 32, 36
Hapsburg Netherlands, 59–60
Haraway, Donna, 116, 174–75
Harriman, Mrs. Oliver, 35
Haspel, Tamar, 43
Henrion, Josephine, 85–86
Hien, 103, 104, 106
high-income countries, defined, 16
Hitler, Adolf, 72
Hoffman, Moshe, 32
L'Hoste Chateau, 18
hot dogs, 193n7
hunger: as argument for food waste reduction, 15, 18, 36–37, 53, 77, 84, 123, 170, 182; food stamps for, 96; systemic issues of, 28, 119–20. *See also* poverty statistics
hunger-industrial complex, 120

immigrant communities, 76, 90–91, 132, 146–47, 149. See also *names of specific individuals*; social belonging
industrial history, 89–90
"In Flanders Fields" (McCrae), 61–62
In the Belgian Château (Fox), 67
Ireland, 16, 58, 80, 81
Iron Eyes Cody, 26–27
Italy, 76, 80, 81

Japan, 195n4
Jewish people, 53, 114, 151, 174
Jordan, Jillian, 32
Joseph, Franz, 70
Judaism, 120. *See also* faith-based food distribution

Kasavubu, Joseph, 64
"Keep America Beautiful" campaign, 26–27
King, Tim, 195n3
knowledge production, 26
Kompany, Pierre, 54

Laeken, Brussels, 97
language communities, 65–67, 69–70, 92, 137–38. *See also* Flemish language; French language; German language
Laurent, 143
League of Human Rights, 196n1 (ch. 5)
Leopold (king), 54, 61, 62, 63, 71–73, 112–13
Leopold II (king), 63
Leopold III (king), 62
Levine, Harry Gene, 174
Lien, Marianne, 176, 183, 192n2
Life of Cheese (Paxson), 176
Lina, 152, 153
Lipton tea factory, 89. *See also* Food Bank of Brussels
Little, Amanda, 17
Livingston, Julie, 145
Loobuyck, Patrick, 114
low-income countries, defined, 16
Lumumba, Patrice, 64
Lutheran Christianity, 120
Luxembourg, 16, 57, 58, 72, 74, 109

Le Magasin, Food Bank of Brussels, 107–12
making oddkin, 174–75
Malawi, 16
Marcus, David, 182
Marie-Thérèse, 152, 153
Martens, Wilfried, 70
Martinez, Cristina, 177, *178*
Martin Luther, 60
Marx, Karl, 41, 44–45
Marxist Revolution, 5, 44–45
A Mass Conspiracy to Feed People (Giles), 17
matsutake mushrooms, 166, 196n2 (ch. 5)
matter out of place, as concept, 23. *See also* Douglas, Mary
Maximilian (king), 59–60
McGreger, April, 177–78, *179*, 180–81
meat industry, 149–50. *See also* Cultureghem
medical argument for food waste reduction, 20–21
Mensah, Kofi, 159–62

Mercy House, 123
#MeToo movement, 31
"The Metropolis and Mental Life" (Simmel), 48
Michel (Bel Mundo worker), 142–43
Michel, Charles, 79–80
Michiels, Tony, *38*, 97, 109, 110, 117–18, 126–127
migration, 75–76
Millar, Kathleen, 24, 192n4
Miller, Ben, 177, *178*
Mintz, Sidney, 20, 22, 39–40, 165, 174
mobile kitchens, 5
Molenbeek commune, Brussels, 129, 133. *See also* Brussels, Belgium
monopolies, 46–47
moral economy of care, 145–46
The Moral Neoliberal (Muehlebach), 145
moral outrage, 31–36
moral panics, 29–31, 36–39
Moroccan immigrants, 146, 153
Morocco, 146
Mozambique, 16
Muehlebach, Andrea, 145–46
Musée de Égots/Riolenmuseum, 95
The Mushroom at the End of the World (Tsing), 166
mushrooms, 166, 196n2 (ch. 5)
Muslims, 100, 102, 103–7, 133, 151

Napoleon Bonaparte, 61, 71
National Congress of Belgium, 71
National League of Housewives, 36
NATO (North Atlantic Treaty Organization), 129
Nazi Germany, 62, 72. *See also* German invasions
Netherlands, 59–60, 77
Nikolai, Metropolitan, 76
Norway, 22, 120, 176, 192n2
Numbeo, 49
N-VA Party, 80

obesity, 42–43, 174
The Obesity Myth (Campos), 42
"Open Ticket" (Tsing), 196n2 (ch. 5)

Ordinary Affects (Stewart), 194n2
Où va La Belgique (Deschouwer), 68

packaging waste, 195n1
Paddleford, Clementine, 6
Parc Maximilien, Brussels, 155–58, 196n1 (ch. 5)
Pascal, 112–15, 116
Paxson, Heather, 176, 183, 194n8
Peace of Utrecht (1713), 61
Peeters, Anna, 97–99, 101, 126
Peeters, Hugo, 97, 98–99
The People's Kitchen (TPK), Philadelphia, 177–82
Peru, 5, 49
Philadelphia, PA, 177–82
Philip II (king), 60
Philip III (king), 59
Philip the Bold, 59
Phoenix, Arizona, 96
Poland, 78
Policing the Crisis (Hall), 31
Pollan, Michael, 170–71
Popkin, Barry, 42–43
Poppendieck, Janet, 119, 121, 122
population statistics, 65
pork, 40, 100, 103–4, 106
Portugal, 80, 81, 164
la poubelle, 11
poverty statistics, 88, 182. See also hunger
precarite, 83–84
progressive food policy, 123–24. See also supermarket mandate
Protestantism, 60

Qatar, 16

racism, 54, 55, 175–76
Rand, David G., 32
Raskin, Hanna, 193n7
Real Pigs (Weiss), 191n2
Reese, Ashanté, 172
regional American food, as term, 6
Reichl, Ruth, 6
Renaerts, Rob, 123

Reno, Joshua, 195n1
Reparons L'Histoire, 112
research methods, 3–5, 13–14, 16–17, 18–19, 53–54, 167
research sites. See Bel Mundo; Food Bank of Brussels; La Truffe Noir
Rio de Janeiro, Brazil, 192n4
Roels, Yannick, 147, 157–58
Roman invasion, 58
Royal Meteorological Institute of Belgium, 151
Russia, 196n2 (ch. 4)
Russian Orthodox Church, 76

Sabena, 69
Salad Stéphanie, 9–11
salvage capitalism, 196n2 (ch. 5)
salvage hospitality, 5
Santo Daime, 194n1
Satanic Panic (Janisse), 29–30
Scherz, China, 123–24, 127–28
Scholliers, Peter, 52
schools, 114
Schuman, Jean-Baptiste Nicolas Robert, 73–74
Scotland, 58
Scott, James, 44
scrappiness, 50, 147, 162–63, 165, 174, 175, 184. See also worth, determining
Seinfeld (tv show), 24–25
Senegal, 90, 142, 143
Sengupta, Somini, 37
Simmel, George, 48
Singapore, 14, 16
Single European Sky initiative, 132
Site One, Food Bank of Brussels, 97–103, 105, 118, 126. See also Food Bank of Brussels
Site Two, Food Bank of Brussels, 103–7, 118, 124. See also Food Bank of Brussels
social assistance, 82
social belonging, 1, 67, 69, 74, 76, 144–45, 163, 172–74, 183, 195n4
Socialist Party, 80

sociality, 174–75
social restaurants, 131–32, 134, 167. *See also* Bel Mundo
Société Anonyme des Abattoirs et Marchés d'Anderlecht-Cureghem/Slachthuizen en Markten van Anderlecht, 151. *See also* Cultureghem
Somalia, 16
Sophie, 139
soup kitchens, 133. *See also* Bel Mundo
soup serving in the park, 155–58
South Sudan, 16
Spain, 80
Spanish invasion, 60
spectrum of edibility, 1, 3, 54, 126, 172–73. *See also* food, as agent of social change; worth, determining
spinach, 9–10
Stanley, Henry Morton, 63
Starn, Orin, 5–6
Stéphanie Clotilde Louise Herminie Marie Charlotte of Belgium (princess), 9–11
stereotypes, 49–51
"Stereotypes of Flemish and Walloon Ethnic Groups in Belgium" (Nuttin), 50
stigma, 119–20, 132
St. Mary's Food Bank Alliance, 96
#stopthewaste campaign, 37
supermarket mandate, 34–35, 77, 91, 94. *See also* progressive food policy
surplus shadow economies, 18, 28
Sutton, David, 22, 163–164
Sweden, 132
Sweetness and Power (Mintz), 20, 39, 42, 165

Tamil Brahmins, 193n7
taste, 11, 191n2. *See also* worth, determining
Taylor, Janelle S., 145
textile production, 76
Thielemans, Paul, 151
Thirty Years War (1618–48), 60
Tight Knit (Krause), 76
toxic release from food waste, 15

Trappists, 59
Treaty of Paris (1951), 74
Treaty of Rome (1957), 74
La Truffe Noir, 5, 7–12, 171, 193n6
truffles, 5, 9, 10, 39, 167
Trump, Donald, 182
Tsing, Anna, 166, 196n2 (ch. 5)
Tuchman, Gaye, 174

ugly food, 21, 32, 177. *See also* food waste recirculation; spectrum of edibility
UN Food and Agriculture Organization, 34, 56
United States, 16, 51, 96, 115–16, 175, 195n1
United States of Belgium, 61
universalism ethics, 120
UN World Food Programme, 13, 27, 37
urbanism and food waste, 17–19, 48–49
utopianism, 17

vada pav, 194n8
Valletta, Marco, 37
Van Hangel, John, 96
Van Parijs, Philippe, 115
vibrant matter, 173
"Vibrant Matter" (Bennett), 24
Victoria (queen of England), 61, 71
violence against women, 31–32, 155
Vleeshuis, 51

Walloons, 50, 62, 66, 70, 114
waste. *See* food waste
Watermael-Boitsfort commune, Brussels, 18. *See also* commune structure of Brussels
Weinstein, Harvey, 31
Weiss, Brad, 40
white flight, 133, 148
Wilk, Richard, 191n2
Wilkerson, Isabel, 175
William I (king), 71
Williams-Forson, Psyche, 51, 115–16, 171

World Bank, 16, 193n5
World Central Kitchen NGO, 177
World Health Organization (WHO), 20
World War II, 62, 70–72
worth, determining, 21, 39–40, 164–66, 174–75. *See also* economics of food; scrappiness; taste

Ximena, 156, 160

Yellow Vest movement, 76, 126
Young, Aziza, 178

zero food-waste, as concept, 129, 159, 166

Printed in the USA
CPSIA information can be obtained
at www.ICGtesting.com
CBHW021548291124
18226CB00002BA/235

9 781469 678597